LIVES

LIVES

Chinese
Working
Women

EDITED BY

Mary Sheridan and
Janet W. Salaff

Published in Association with
University of Toronto/York University
Joint Centre on Modern East Asia

INDIANA UNIVERSITY PRESS
BLOOMINGTON

This book is published in cooperation with the
University of Toronto/York University Joint
Centre on Modern East Asia.

This book has been published with the help of a grant from the
Social Science Federation of Canada, using funds provided by
the Social Sciences and Humanities Research Council of Canada.

Library of Congress Cataloging in Publication Data
Main entry under title:

Lives, Chinese working women.

"Published in association with University of Toronto/
York University Joint Centre on Modern East Asia."

  Includes bibliographical references.
   1. Working class women—China—Case studies.
  2. Working class women—Taiwan—Case studies.
  3. Working class women—Hongkong—Case studies.
  I. Sheridan, Mary, 1938–   . II. Salaff, Janet W.
III. Joint Centre on Modern East Asia.
HQ1767.L59 1984   305.4′2′0951   83-48401
ISBN 0-253-33604-X
ISBN 0-253-20319-8 (pbk.)
I   2   3   4   5   88   87   86   85   84

To Our Mothers

CONTENTS

Acknowledgments ix

- Explanatory Notes and Conversion Tables xi

Introduction / *Mary Sheridan and Janet W. Salaff* 1

1. The Life History Method / *Mary Sheridan* 11

PART I. THE OLDER GENERATION

2. Historical Background on Chinese Women /
   Andrea McElderry 25
3. Spinster Sisterhoods / *Andrea Sankar* 51
   Jing Yih Sifu: Spinster-Domestic-Nun
4. Village Wives / *Deborah Davis-Friedmann* 71
   Granny Cheung: Peasant
5. Hakka Women / *Elizabeth L. Johnson* 76
   Great-Aunt Yeung: A Hakka Wage Laborer

PART II. TAIWAN AND HONG KONG

6. Doing Fieldwork / *Lydia Kung,*
   Linda Gail Arrigo, and Janet W. Salaff 95
7. Taiwan Garment Workers / *Lydia Kung* 109
   Wang Su-lan: Filial Daughter
   Teng Hsiu-ling: Middle Sister
8. Taiwan Electronics Workers / *Linda Gail Arrigo* 123
   Lim Li-suat: Adopted Daughter
   Tsai Chen-hwei: Divorcée

9. Wage Earners in Hong Kong / *Janet W. Salaff*   146
   "Rainbow": The Café Culture
   Wai-gun: The Garment District

                    PART III.   CHINA

10. The Chinese Biographical Method: A Moral and
    Didactic Tradition / *Jerome Ch'en*   175
11. Yenan Women In Revolution / *Mary Sheridan*
    (translator and editor)   180
    Ch'en Min: In the Army and the Shoe Factory
    Old Lady Liu: Heroine of Spinning and Weaving
    Li Feng-lien: A Comrade in the Tunic Factory
12. "On the Eve of Her Departure" / *Jerome Ch'en*
    (translator and editor)   197
    Ting Chih-hui: Model Cadre
13. Contemporary Generations / *Mary Sheridan*   204
    Zhao Xiuyin: Lady of the Sties
Conclusion / *Mary Sheridan and Janet W. Salaff*   236

    Notes   243
    Biographical Sketches   257

ACKNOWLEDGMENTS

This manuscript has greatly benefited from very careful and caring comments by several anonymous readers, to whom we owe a great debt. We appreciate the continuous assistance and support of Jerome Ch'en. Norma Diamond also gave us considerable help, for which we are grateful. All of us as contributors, moreover, want to acknowledge our gratitude to the women whose lives are portrayed here. All of us feel that we learned about scholarship and personal relationships from our subjects. The process of collecting lives results in close ties with many people, and this volume is in large part a tribute to the women who were willing to share their life experiences with us so generously. Any errors of fact or interpretation remain our own responsibility.

The Editors

Toronto and Beijing, March 1983

EXPLANATORY NOTES AND CONVERSION TABLES

Spelling

Standard Chinese (Mandarin) is written in the Wade-Giles romanized system throughout this book, except in chapter 13. Chapter 13 uses the *pinyin* romanized system, for reasons given in that chapter.

Cantonese, Hakka, and Taiwanese are romanized by the authors according to conventional practice.

Festivals

The Chinese New Year holiday of the traditional lunar calendar is referred to in different chapters as Chinese New Year, Lunar New Year, and Spring Festival.

Units of Measure★

Term			
Wade-Giles	Pinyin	U.S. Equivalent	Metric Equivalent
liang (tael)	*liang*	1.77 ounces	50 grams
chin (catty)	*jin*	1.10 pounds	0.5 kilograms
kungchin	*gungjin*	2.20 pounds	1 kilogram
tan (picul)	*dan*	110.0 pounds	50 kilograms
ch'ih	*chi*	1.09 feet	0.33 meters
chang	*jang*	10.94 feet	3.33 meters
li	*li*	0.31 miles	0.5 kilometers
kungli	*gungli*	0.62 miles	1 kilometer
mou	*mou*	0.16 acres	0.07 hectares
hsiang	*xiang*	In this volume, *hsiang* is the romanization of two ideographs for (1) a small administrative unit of several villages or (2) a land measure equal to from 3 to 5 *mou* in the Northwest.★★	

★Based on Foreign Languages Institute, Peking, *The Pinyin Chinese-English Dictionary* (Hong Kong: Commercial Press, 1979), p. 975.

★★*Ibid.*, p. 596, where it is read *sheng*. See also *Mathews' Chinese English Dictionary*, rev. American edition, entry 2550a, *hsiang*.

| *fen* | *fen* | One-tenth of a given unit. For example in a discussion of acreage, *fen* represents one-tenth *mou*. |

Monetary Units

		U.S. Equivalent
yuan	1 People's Republic of China dollar	50¢ (1983)
mao	1/10 *yuan*	5¢ (1983)
NT $1	1 New Taiwan dollar	2¢ (1974)
HK $1	1 Hong Kong dollar	20¢ (1973)

LIVES

Introduction

By Mary Sheridan and Janet W. Salaff

Authors and Methods

The lives in this volume not only are the rare result of fine and exceptional research but also represent the kind of material that usually goes undocumented. Here is a wealth of new information that challenges old stereotypes of women as feeble, indifferent, and unskilled and dramatizes human factors in the processes of modernization and social change. These women of several Chinese societies work in different settings and live under contrasting political regimes. The juxtaposition of their lives provides a range of reactions to social forces in societies in transition from agrarian to industrial orders. In that sense, this book on the work and family roles of women documents the contribution of women to social life and the development of the economy.

The life history method is best understood as a mode of investigation that blends history and biography in order to explore the effects of social structures on people and to portray the ways in which people themselves create culture. This method provides in-depth materials on the course of an individual's life over time and embodies three major concerns. Primary among these is our insistence that an individual's life must be investigated in its historical context. Thus people living during a period of early industrialization experience a different set of social and economic opportunities than those in later, more industrialized settings. Our second concern is with the economic, political, educational, and other social institutions that affect family and personal life. For example, the job opportunities women have alter their family and societal roles in important ways. The account of Sifu, the silk weaver, demonstrates this point. The third emphasis of our perspective is on the course of a person's life as it is influenced by her social position. The life of an adopted daughter, for example, differs from that of a natural-born daughter, and children's opportunities often vary systematically by their birth order. We also emphasize, in turn, the ways individuals can shape their social position within a range of historically specific options. In our study, the availability

1

of resources may prompt women to turn their life course in a new direction (again, as in the case of Sifu). Within recognized social limits, ties of affection or recognized talent can also alter the life course of women.

In a parallel fashion, the life course perspective also examines the lives of families through historical time. Sociologists stress the sequencing and timing of transitions between the stages of the lives of individuals. Psychologists examine the content of stages of the lives of individuals in particular settings and may dwell upon key turning points or life cycle stages.[1] All these methods emphasize the importance of historical specificity. Thus scholars are studying lives from a variety of perspectives to address major questions, and our volume can be read in this context.

Our writers gathered these materials while conducting research projects of several years' duration. Their investigations addressed specific questions for which an understanding of the particular responses of individuals was necessary. They hit upon the life history method in the course of their research. In their publications, however, our contributors abstracted from those voluminous materials in order to address their theoretical questions more parsimoniously, and the life histories were never published. We compiled this volume when we realized the great value of the original personal documents for researchers and readers in a variety of disciplines. We wanted these lives to be accessible to others.

We gathered this particular collection explicitly to portray a range of work activities and family roles of ordinary women at various life cycle stages, from several time periods, and from different regions of Chinese society. Issues of work and the family are being explored in numerous historical and social studies of women today, and we seek to make a contribution to the contemporary study of the meaning and experiences of women's work.

Since the lives were collected by scholars of Chinese society acting independently of each other, without central direction, and at different times, they represent a variety of approaches and styles. The materials in this volume may be too diverse to prove theories, but they are rich in fresh ideas that will generate new inquiries into the roles women play. These original case materials will suggest new facets of the personal face of social change as it occurs.

Two Genres of Lives

All the people in this volume are real; none of the lives is a composite. Only the names of people and places of work have been changed to preserve anonymity. Two genres of lives are presented in this volume.

Fieldworkers trained in Western social science methods have written the majority of the lives. Despite our diverse origins, the common intellectual and personal backgrounds of the authors resulted in a genre of lives that bear a certain resemblance to each other. We all received social science-grounded training, with an emphasis on reporting all perspectives of a social situation. We matured in the individual-centered humanism of Western civilization.

Our acquaintance with Western biographical literature, in which the dramatic forces of personal needs assume main stage, encourages our stress on the drama of personality. We are as concerned with the affective reactions of our respondents to their social constraints as we are with those constraints. Our post-Freudian awareness prompts our persistent inquiry into the emotions of our respondents. We wish to know how a Chinese woman really feels about her position in a tightly structured, demanding family setting. Like women everywhere, we experience the difficulties of juggling work and family roles, so we explore the topic of role conflict in our studies. Diverse in style (composition, dialogue, and phrasing) and inclusive of several disciplines (sociology, anthropology, and history), the lives present a common reading experience.

The second genre of lives consists of translations of Chinese biographies of working women in Yenan and the People's Republic of China, originally recorded by Chinese fieldworkers. These biographies personalize success stories of ordinary working women who, against great odds, improved their output and helped their co-workers as well. The lives of these women are presented as models in order to motivate others whose work settings, production tasks, and family burdens are similar but who have not yet achieved such standards or levels of political commitment.

These lives of model Chinese women obviously flow from a different tradition than that grounded in the Western social sciences. In the Chinese political context, the individual's interests are portrayed as merging with the goals of the collective, and political leaders are concerned with reorienting family goals toward those of the collective. A subjective biographical perspective dealing with emotional concerns is excluded in this political context. The Chinese model lives are not silent on the personal costs of work or the difficulties in combining work and family roles, but psychological dilemmas are played down.

At present, such model lives are the only form of biography published in the People's Republic of China; autobiography does not exist in print. However, these model lives are the result of field investigation and form a vital source of data and thematic ideas. The juxtaposition of lives collected under two different traditions will generate topics for further investigation. In the future, we hope to be able to collect a wider spectrum of lives in China itself by both Chinese and non-Chinese writers.

Three Chinese Societies

As a working collection, this volume is arranged to stimulate interdisci-
plinary and crosscultural comparisons. Therefore, we begin with a brief
historical guide to the regimes under which the women in this book
matured and labored.

The women in this volume live in the People's Republic of China; the
Republic of Taiwan, an island that formed part of Fukien Province on
China's southeastern coast; and the British Crown Colony of Hong Kong,
which was ceded from China's southeastern Kwangtung Province in the
nineteenth century. The women are part of the Chinese culture area, and
the following discussion sketches the general social environment.[2]

The older women, in their seventies, were born under the collapsing
imperial system of the last Chinese dynasty (the Ch'ing, 1644–1911). Sun
Yat Sen's republican revolution of 1911 and the full-blown emergence of
warlordism over the following decade led to regional political-military
bases, fighting, and pillage. The older generation of women spent their
girlhood and early married years in this extremely difficult time of political fragmentation. The women raised their families and concentrated on
personal survival during the civil war, the Pacific war against the Japanese,
World War II, and the last Chinese civil war, which ended with Liberation, or establishment of the People's Republic of China.

In telling their stories, Sifu, Granny Cheung, and Great-Aunt Yeung do
not refer to these events directly; we see only their personal struggles. The
interview format, by stressing family and work roles, may not have
delved into their political actions. Alternatively, these women may not
have engaged in such activities. However, women in southeastern China
were politically active in the 1920s, and McElderry reports on the women
revolutionaries who joined their energies to alter the society that oppressed them as women and as workers.[3] In direct contrast, Old Lady Liu,
Ch'en Min, and Li Feng-lien describe their work leadership activities in
Yenan, elaborated by their biographers, in order to encourage other
ordinary women to be more active in these trying times. Ting Chih-hui is
a modern successor to the Yenan lifestyle.

Until 1949, women in China, Taiwan, and Hong Kong lived in patriarchal societies, where the opportunities for women were very similar.
Moreover, people migrated between the political areas, where kinship
networks or even nuclear families frequently spanned both sides of the
Hong Kong-China border. The establishment of the new political order of
the People's Republic of China became the point of divergence for the
three political cultures.

Family and Marriage System

We can distinguish analytically between several facets of the Chinese family in order to trace the changes that occur later in the family roles of our respondents. These are the lineage (line), the *chia*⁴ (economic family), and the uterine family (family of affection). The lineage consists of the core of men linked by male descent and rights to property. In the lives in this book, we find that despite changes in property forms, the line remains socially significant, perpetuating women's lesser family status. The *chia* is the basic unit of production and consumption and includes women as well as men. This unit is based on the common household budget, to which unmarried women contribute even if they are living separately. This unit retains considerable strength today in our factory workers' lives. Third, the uterine family is based on sentiment, gains strength from the nurtural bonds between women and children, and is focused on child rearing. The lives in this book evidence the ways these affective bonds may alter the standing of women in the family from that destined for them by their inherited family role.⁵

Important points of pre-1949 similarity among women in China, Taiwan, and Hong Kong are found in the family and marriage system. Older women in all three settings matured in the patrilineal family, which traces descent through the male line. Men inherited the ancestral property of their lineage, and most of the property acquired over the lifetime of the family was passed on to male descendants. Women's social status was defined by their relation to the men in their lineage. Marriage signified the transfer of rights over a woman from her parents, who were obligated to support her until she married, to her husband, whose father's line was committed to supporting her materially in this life and ritually in the next. Women were expected to marry; unmarried daughters could not expect to receive ritual worship from their natal families after their death.

There are several important life cycle stages for women in the patrilineal family. A woman enters her natal family either at birth or through adoption; the status of adopted daughters is particularly low. A woman leaves her own family and enters her husband's family through marriage, of which there are several forms in our volume—major and minor marriage, concubinage, taking spinster roles, and remarriage. In major marriage, a family gives away in marriage a daughter shortly after puberty and takes in her place a wife for a son. Minor marriage refers to those who adopt a girl at an early age (*saam po chai*, in Hokkien) and rear her to be a son's wife; sometime after puberty, a simple ceremony marks the transition from unmarried to married couple. Another form of marriage is concubinage, when the second wife is married according to a ceremony that signifies her recognition by the husband's family. An unusual variant is entry into a religious sisterhood by means of a quasi-marriage ceremony. Finally, there is divorcée or widow remarriage, when the remarrying woman severs her ties to her offspring from her first union; henceforth these children have no obligation to support or mourn their mother.[6] The lives in this volume document all these forms of marriage.

A young wife's status in the family is low in the patrilineal system, improves at the birth of a son, and climaxes when she becomes a dowager with adult sons and heads the domestic unit (*chia*) and uterine family. Her particular life script, notably the type of marriage she enters, affects her actual domestic standing. Poverty also levels the influence of the older generation of women and men over their offspring.[7]

The People's Republic of China

The changes in life cycle patterns visible in this volume may be traced socially, politically, and historically for each of the Chinese societies. In 1949, the new government in Peking proclaimed equal rights and opportunities for women, and the women themselves began the long struggle—by no means over—to realize these rights through their own efforts and with political support. Chief among these changes was the new marriage law of the People's Republic of China, passed in 1950 and amended in 1980. The 1950 marriage law asserted the right of youths to select their own spouse and to marry without an exchange of money. This marriage law also inaugurated substantial changes in the position of women. Marriage was defined as a voluntary union of a man and woman; adopted child wives (the minor form of marriage) and concubinage were forbidden. Women's rights to property were established. The land reform of the 1950s gave substance to the marriage law, allowing women property rights to a house, furnishings, personal belongings, and small tools (lands were collectivized).

The laws governing family and marriage since 1949 have raised the marital age and legalized divorce (under conditions conforming to moral strictures). However, their general tenor has been to emphasize the economic responsibility of the nuclear family for its members. Thus there are limits to the structural changes brought about by the law, and many customary family relationships have persisted.[8]

In China, work is seen as an important liberating force. Political ideology has encouraged women's productive labor on behalf of the collective as critical to the improvement of women's position. This ideology clearly emerges in our translated biographies. These Chinese-written biographies were developed during the Yenan production drive, a movement to raise output and develop self-sufficiency (1942–1944), and during the period that promoted the "four modernizations," when cadres were urged to become technically efficient (c. 1980). Then as well as at other times, drives to increase output were aimed at stimulating innovation, solving job problems, and raising worker productivity. These movements to activate women's participation in labor have not always remained at an equally high pitch. Nevertheless, the possibility of asserting some influence over their work environment remains an important incentive for women to participate.[9]

The population of China is over 1 billion people, 80 percent of whom reside in villages. The work rhythms of China's towns and cities pulse less strongly in this volume than those of the countryside, but the lives of the women in Chapter 13 represent villagers who are beginning to feel the effects of urban influences.

Taiwan

One of China's provinces, with a population originally drawn mainly from Fukien Province, Taiwan was colonized by the Japanese at the turn of the century. Contemporary Taiwan took shape in 1949, when Chiang Kai-shek, with those who remained in his defeated army and bureaucracy, fled to the island as a refuge supported by the American military and imposed their rule on a hostile population. The governing Mandarin-speaking, refugee-based Kuomintang Party elevated patriarchal values into an expedient state ideology to pacify women, the peasantry, and the local Hokkien- and Hakka-speaking populace. The Taiwan government embarked upon land reform, introduced a Mandarin-based system of nine years of public education, and sponsored a rapid industrialization program. This program featured foreign-led investment in light consumer industries for export. Women have gained a sizable place in these industries. Average annual wages have risen to US $809 per capita (1976), and the income gap has narrowed since the early 1950s.[10]

The prevailing authoritarian political structure affects industrial management in Taiwan. Political franchise is extremely limited, unions are outlawed, and workers' strikes are illegal. Many indigenous investors are former landlords, bourgeois, or compradores (agents of foreign establishments) who fled from China, while foreign investors are committed to Taiwan because of their high profits. Consequently, management is wary of unleashing pent-up grievances, in this milieu workers are discouraged from addressing work-related or social problems, even at a rudimentary level.[11]

The civil code of Taiwan is based on the precepts of the codes in mainland China in the late 1920s and 1930s, which promulgated and established important conjugal rights for women within the family. However, field studies have found that family property remains under patrilineal control and that women are dependent upon and subordinated to their families by custom. Minor marriages and arranged betrothals are now illegal and are less frequent in any case because of economic prosperity, education, and political negotiation between parents and children who wish to choose their own spouse. Adoption of girls is frequent for families who hope for religious reasons that the new daughters will bear grandsons. Their blemished status still marks many women of poor families, such as the adopted daughter in this volume.[12]

Today, over half of the nearly 18 million Taiwanese reside in towns and cities. Because of the prevalence of small landholding and the recent advent of industrialization, however, the urban work force retains rural roots, and there is a high level of urban-rural exchange of people. Thus many factory women are recruited from the villages and return there when they are laid off or work conditions become insupportable. This outlet permits management to bypass factory reforms. The flow of new workers, combined with the contemporary sex structure, clearly depresses women's wages and work opportunities. The lives of the Taiwanese factory workers in this volume can be understood only in this context.

Hong Kong

Hong Kong represents a third variant of Chinese cultural development. Since 1842, Hong Kong has been a British colony, predominantly consisting of Cantonese speakers, with a number of subdialect speech groups. The Chinese population lacks political franchise. After the 1950s, Chinese emigrés from Kwangtung Province and bourgeois from Shanghai invested in and provided the labor power for Hong Kong's industrial base. Today, Hong Kong industry is primarily export-oriented and dominated by transnational corporate investment. Women play a significant role in the manufacturing sector and a growing role in the services.[13]

Hong Kong is urbanized and industrial. Most of the over 5 million people live in the city and engage in nonagricultural pursuits. The typical family lives in a high-rise, government-constructed apartment (resettlement estate) and works for a large organization. British authorities give local capitalists, traditional interest groups, and opinion leaders considerable political and social influence. However, families are forced to solve their economic and social problems with a minimum of outside support. The government offers little assistance to the poor today; even less was offered when the women in this volume were growing up. These economic, social, and political conditions lead families to turn to their own resources for survival and advancement.[14]

The marriage law that prevails is an outgrowth of law reforms of the 1960s and 1970s; in dealing with the position of women, it supersedes the civil codes previously in force.[15] Arranged betrothals are less frequent, concubinage uncommon, and minor marriages a rarity. In rural Hong Kong, line property remains the preserve of males; however, in urban Hong Kong, acquired property is most significant. In both cases, women's rights to inheritance are considerably less than those of their brothers. In addition, a woman is still considered an economic loss to her parents when she marries, which may severely circumscribe her schooling in poor families.

In a parallel fashion to Taiwan, although for different reasons, Hong Kong political-economic conditions give rise to stability, and while labor unions are legal, they play scant part in addressing the needs of women workers. Workers are disenfranchised from industrial decision-making. The lives in this volume reflect the considerable economic insecurity and lack of political options for the female labor force. While Hong Kong women may appear "Westernized" in their dress and attitudes, they are under extreme pressure to continue a more traditional, family-centered, and male-focused life, as shown in the lives of "Rainbow" and Waigun.

A Word of Caution

The reader must bear in mind that China (the People's Republic of China, governed from Peking by the Chinese Communist Party), Taiwan (the island republic governed by the Kuomintang), and Hong Kong (the British island colony with its small bits of territory on the continent) are three separate and distinct political and social systems. Despite all the similarities stemming from common cultural roots, their differences are profound, and one cannot generalize from a Taiwanese woman worker's attitudes and experiences to that of a woman in China without extreme caution.

It is also important to remember that many subcultures, ethnic, and language groups make up Chinese society as a whole. Standard Mandarin Chinese, the most common language in the north, is unintelligible to the Cantonese speakers of the south, and subdialect speech groups proliferate in the mountainous southeast region, where many of the women portrayed in this book live. We therefore expect considerable variations around common structural themes in the lives of the Chinese working women in this volume.

Structure of This Book

This volume is divided into three parts, arranged by cultural area and temporal order. A methods chapter introduces the book as a whole, and each part begins with a methods chapter introducing the lives which follow it.

Methods chapters facilitate comparisons: chapter 1 presents the life history method used in this book; chapter 2 provides a review of Western literature on Chinese women and some historical background on women's roles, and chapter 6 discusses fieldwork methods used by three of the authors. Finally, chapter 10 addresses differences between Western life history methods and the biographical methods used by Chinese authors in China.

Lives chapters in the three parts also invite comparisons. Part I introduces older women whose lives were rooted in China before 1949. Part II contains lives of younger women in Taiwan and Hong Kong. Part III returns to China, this time focusing on lives of women in revolution and reconstruction, thus providing a continuity of experience which brings us to the contemporary generations of 1983.

1

The Life History Method

By Mary Sheridan

The Uses of Life Histories

The life histories in this volume are autobiographical or biographical in nature, reported through oral and written documentation. This chapter addresses the process of their unfolding through the acts of recording and writing.

Life histories have several uses in the social sciences. They are a source of factual data—a base for generating hypotheses, testing theories, and opening new inquiries along thematic lines, our major concern in this volume.[1] Our purpose is to bring together a number of lives to fill in some gaps in our information on working-class women and by juxtaposition to stimulate fresh inquiries. In our conclusion, we indicate themes that the lives have suggested. We hope that these may stimulate some of our readers to enter into the realm of life history collection for themselves.

Participant observation and in-depth interviews, strongly supported by historical and documentary research, are the most important methods used here. Interviews conducted for publication by social scientists and journalists not only translate oral material into written records, but also reveal for scientific analysis what may otherwise be hidden. Life histories can incorporate the sensitivity that is an established tradition in good biography, fiction, and reporting.

Our authors from the social sciences worked with both interviews and autobiographical accounts. Supporting sources include government census and annual reports, the researcher's own census of a community, the financial and historical accounts of organizations, genealogical study, questionnaires, and newspapers and other secondary reports. Life histories add something distinctive to these other forms of data, and the presentation of material in terms of lives contributes a unique format for understanding social process. In contrast to the life history method, many social scientists present short quotes, separated from the life context, as substantiation for hypotheses. Short quotations, accompanied by tables, are a useful format for condensing large amounts of material. Such a

11

format, however, disconnects events from their organic relationship to the experience of individuals.

As a form of data, life histories supplement other analytic procedures and sources of data. Few social scientists would deny the role of social forces in shaping the character of the individual; consequently, biographies and life histories, significant as they are, must be read in conjunction with materials that provide a firm grasp of the institutional and cultural changes in the background of the subjects. Only in such combination can the illuminating significance of the biographies and life histories be fully appreciated.

We must underscore the differences, and complementarity, between the biographical method used with eminent people and the life history method used with ordinary people. Biographers of eminent people usually have a wide variety of documentary sources to draw from that provide background on their subject, such as legal documents and writings by the individual. These may be accompanied by material drawn from direct interviews with the subject and those with personal knowledge of the subject. In contrast, the published record for an ordinary individual may be negligible; thus the importance of oral material comes to the fore in life histories.

Missing until very recently from the mainstream of social science was a sufficient sociology or anthropology of the individual. These disciplines had largely abandoned the individual to the fields of psychology and psychoanalysis, which have different starting points and their own proper aims. We could draw on only the work of the Chicago school of sociology in the 1930s, the powerful lives recorded by the late anthropologist Oscar Lewis, the studies of Eric Erikson, and the pleas of L. L. Langness in the 1960s for the resuscitation of the life history method.[2] Apart from these contributions, our attention was stimulated mainly by publications based on feminist studies, where a body of literature on women's lives is growing increasingly healthy. Crosscultural documentation of women's life histories is providing germane material for understanding the individual in society.

Life histories can illustrate the operation of the social order because through them we are able to observe how people adapt to the goals of society. They give us access to "the subjective springs of action."[3] The relationship between the individual and her environment is well brought out by her life history, which depicts organically, or all in one place, each subject's biography. In this volume we learn about behavior that each subject considers meaningful and issues that each interviewer, with her own concerns, considers important. In the classic phrase of C. Wright Mills, life histories investigate the ways that social structure and social problems appear to individuals as their private dilemma or as public issues to be resolved by the wider community.[4] The public issue/private dilemma perspective permeates all the lives in this book.

Our entry into the flow of social action by means of life histories allows insight into the ways our respondents handle social problems known to be common to several people or cultures. We also learn about particular dilemmas which we may not have perceived beforehand. Our accounts describe the structure of an individual's environment as she perceives it and the quality of relationships she enters. These lives may suggest groupings or associations of phenomena which could be investigated in the future. The insights into and ideas about society stimulated by the lives are what we consider possible thematic uses of life histories.

The Collection of Life Histories through Participant Observation

Lives can serve as documentation of the interaction of individuals with social structure as long as they provide an accurate accounting of the situations that affect people. This accounting is well accomplished by fieldwork but is also possible through interviews or requesting the respondent to record her own life. In crafting these lives, our authors found that the physical setting was an important factor. Most of our authors followed their subjects into several different environments and among many different people, either physically or verbally. The authors noted the social interaction of the women and the roles they assumed in different contexts. The authors also became aware of themselves as a factor in the environment; if the setting of the interactions changed, the interviewer herself sometimes assumed a different role. This method is fluid, many-faceted, and distinct from the single "neutral" or controlled environment interview paradigm adapted from laboratory science. If a "neutral" interview setting had been used for collecting these lives (an office with tape recorders, questionnaires, closed interview format, etc.), it would likely have elicited much narrower responses and less depth of field in personal landscapes.

Our fieldworkers found natural settings the most conducive for eliciting a full account of each subject's biography. Trial and error was apparently responsible for their preference for participant observation combined with informal, flexible interviews. Direct interaction with the respondent in a variety of environments circumvented the likelihood of the respondents' providing self-censored and conventionally acceptable answers. Movement between environments triggered unpremeditated responses which revealed character and situations beyond the immediately observable context.

Lydia Kung, Linda Gail Arrigo, and Janet W. Salaff discuss below the different ways in which they used environment and physical settings (see chapter 6). Kung records the problems encountered when the respondent is interviewed in the factory, a convenient and time-saving device but one that may raise a problem of frankness for the researcher. She must be careful to address this issue in her relationship with the respondent. Arrigo notes the difficulties raised by interviewing in the factory dormitory—the women fear that their revelations may be used against them by their rivals for the scarce opportunities of employment, education, and status in marriage. Salaff describes visits to the respondents' homes and participation in their peer group outings as a means of obtaining information in a natural manner and without having to question the respondent directly about it. Sheridan (see chapter 13) worked in the field entirely as a participant observer. Friendship formed the basis for all biographical notes, and no formal interviews took place.

Interviewers have long noticed that Chinese families make great efforts to hide secrets and to protect the reputation of their family. This concern frequently leads people to gloss over incidents that the student of culture would find very illuminating of human nature, especially in their range of variation. Chinese culture contains a well-drawn demarcation between information accessible to "insiders" and "outsiders." Insiders have access to private information that will not be permitted in the public arena.

All cultures make a distinction between insider and outsider views; participant observation helps to remove those distinctions.[5] The life history approach is an excellent means for learning the covert nuances and ideas of a culture. Outsiders by nationality, race, family origin, social class, and education or training, the authors in this volume sought to enter as much as possible the milieu of the women about whom they were writing. As newcomers, we had to be open to unfamiliar cultural cues. As Langness points out, every culture makes assumptions that are unstated but tacitly understood and shared by most people. These assumptions influence behavior.[6] Such assumptions are part of the insider's view of culture that our authors attempted to understand. After accepting a fieldworker as an "insider" through participation, it was difficult for people to maintain clear distinctions between inside and outside information. Indeed, several of our authors discuss how they were taught the meaning of implicit cultural assumptions and how this experience transformed them. Arrigo describes her struggle to break through but not violate, to incorporate but not be bound by, her subjects' definition of private information. Sheridan notes her emotional bonding with the women of whom she writes and the personal quest which her work with them represents.

In our view, the life history method requires a good understanding of the nuances of the respondent's language. All the authors of our lives have lived and worked in Chinese society for many years and are fluent in the Chinese dialects they encountered. The immediacy of cultural cues is sometimes lost through the process of translation. Since we attempt to use these life histories as a means of generating ideas, or what Glaser and Strauss call "grounded theory," we cannot risk losing the valuable chance comments, jokes, and gestures that might provide important hidden cues to a culture.[7] The process of cultural translation, which includes overcoming various structural barriers, is difficult enough without linguistic translation via an intermediary, who, moreover, may censor or omit considerable material.

All our authors were academically trained for research in the field. Nevertheless, the collection of life histories brought us into contact with learning experiences that few of us had anticipated. The many hours we spent with our respondents inevitably developed into friendship. The process of collecting lives results in the development of close ties with many people, and by reflecting upon their lives we become more aware of our own. This occurs in at least two ways. As social psychologists describe it, we come to take the role of the "other," and we view ourselves as others see us. In addition, Kung and Arrigo point out in chapter 6 that involvement in the lives of others brings us to a deeper awareness of levels of reality, meaning, and relationships—"deep structures."[8] Indeed, Arrigo found herself faced with an identity crisis when compelled by the research situation to reevaluate her self-image as an outsider and dispassionate observer. This crisis of meaning is fairly common to anthropologists and is described in moving accounts by many.[9]

We wish to stress the learning that occurs when a fieldworker must reassess her own assumptions and values as a result of her participant role. Over and above the training she receives in preparation, she almost invariably continues learning in the field. We believe in the importance of the self-discovery that occurs as the researcher is transformed by her work and in turn transforms her subject matter into meaningful communication. We thus encourage our contributors to keep themselves in each account.

The recording of a life is clearly enhanced by good rapport between the researcher and respondent. Chapter 6, "Doing Fieldwork," describes several ways that three of our contributors enhanced rapport but is by no means exhaustive of the possibilities. Arrigo successfully established rapport when she gave permission to her respondents to feel "OK" about themselves (to use the terms of interactionist psychology), with regard to behavior that their society defines as "not OK." Indeed, this may have been the first time her informants had experienced such nonjudgmental openness.

Arrigo, Salaff, and Sheridan deepened rapport by returning to the field. Return of the fieldworker from far away evidences good faith and often brings a deeper level of rapport than that of previous visits. Salaff further describes the rapport she unwittingly gained by allowing herself to be vulnerable, in this instance by bringing her young child to the homes of her respondents and accepting their assistance and advice.

Reciprocity is essential to rapport. Reciprocity is an exchange of equal value but does not necessitate that the two parties be equal in status (as Kung points out, they are most likely not equal) or that the exchange involve items of the same kind, such as information. Arrigo and Salaff occasionally exchanged information with their respondents, but Kung and other interviewers emphasize that their respondents enjoyed finding a good listener. Researchers in many contexts have reported that interested and sympathetic listening is often a welcome exchange between the social scientist and respondent.[10]

Reciprocity may also take active forms. Sheridan found that she had entertainment value in village situations which people found otherwise mundane. When learning to use unfamiliar tools for scything grain or threshing, or to do unfamiliar tasks like chopping and mixing pig fodder, she was at first in the way but soon provided a source of good humor which developed into exchanges of gossip and then deepened into heartfelt confidences. Salaff and Sheridan engaged in intellectual discussions which ranged beyond the focus of the research, and Sheridan instigated musical evenings, playing violin and teaching the children folk dances to enliven family gatherings.

Direct and indirect exchanges all contribute to reciprocal giving. Arrigo, Salaff, and Sheridan found the people to whom they became closest were those who were reciprocally curious about them. For example, Arrigo found that her respondents asked many questions of her as a representative of American womanhood. Wai-gun drew out Salaff at great length on intimate details of her American family, her career, and her travels, commenting freely and interjecting social analysis. Sheridan was perceived by her village family as atypical of foreigners in general. They began commenting, "Mali—that's the way *you* do it—but what about other foreigners?" as their way of establishing a view of normative behavior for North Americans.

Problems of Judgment and Assessment of Material

It has been commented that the degree of accuracy or validity for a body of data is inversely related to the distance of the observer from the phenomenon under study.[11] The further away we are from our subject matter, the less confidence we may have in its accuracy. Participant observation as the strategy closest to the action provides relatively accurate data, because we share the scene with our subjects and empathetically experience their feelings.[12] Arrigo advocates lengthy field participation for that purpose. Another method is to visit the locality, factory, temple, or home of the informant to obtain several perspectives on the data and to improve the quality of the probes into the subject's response.

One step further removed from the present action is a person's recollection of past events. How does one know that a subject's remembered perceptions, feelings, and attributed motivations are accurate? In order to crosscheck this kind of information, we may talk formally or informally with other people of the same or similar social group.[13] Remaining alert to internal consistencies, the fieldworker benefits greatly by following up initial interviews with new questions of respondents. However, we do not believe that contradictory statements and actions are necessarily false fronts or that they should be eliminated. On the contrary, sensitive recording of inconsistencies in what people say or do may show how perceptions of objective reality actually reflect different levels of a more complex reality. We could edit out contradictory materials, but we advocate including them and attempting to explain them.

Arrigo calls our attention to the importance of role conflict in understanding levels of social reality. As people adopt different social roles, they may behave differently. It behooves the biographer to report these variations not only to increase our understanding of the subject but also to introduce data that may indicate significant social change in the offing. We also begin to glimpse the potential for deviance in a society by documenting how ostensibly contradictory roles are adopted by the same person. This revelation of contradictions allows us to see things from more than one perspective, from both inside and outside the veil.

The accuracy of life histories may also be improved by checking the personal recitation against other sources. This technique may determine if events actually happened that were reported by the subject. We should emphasize that we are using the life history method in this book partly as a source of ideas that would be otherwise inaccessible and partly because the subjective interpretations of the respondent, which are part of her entire social context, are of central importance to us. We therefore do not wish to edit out our informants' "errors" of historical perception and replace them with a text of our own construction.[14] We have preferred to quote as given and make editorial comments in footnotes.

All our social scientist biographers collected life histories of several individuals and selected among them for inclusion here. However, by its very nature, the life history method is time-consuming and emotionally demanding, and its contribution can never be judged in terms of quantity. Thus we face the necessity of relating our cases to the number of people in the society who were not interviewed. We make an effort to describe our sampling procedure and to discuss how our cases represent the field of study.

We approach the problem of representativeness from several directions. First, we examine the social category represented by each case, and we try to interview individuals who are similar in a number of sociologically significant and interesting variables. These might include age, place of birth, marital status, and job. Sociologists refer to the procedure of sampling with an eye to representing important categories as "quota sampling," and some of our researchers use that method.[15] Other field investigators feel that an individual will invariably represent the language, norms, and values of the group of which she is a member and that attention to the group setting is thus most important.[16]

Another problem is the imperative to report each life fully and our concern to document as many roles or aspects of the subject as possible. We try to present relatively complex portraits, whether or not they fit our preconceptions of typicalness, without making prejudgments. Through these multi-faceted perceptions and recordings of an individual's behavior, we may better understand what part she plays in the broader society. We found, indeed, that many of our respondents deviated from our view of the norm. In recording this, we approach a better understanding of how the society operates and what the possibilities are of social variation and change. The life history method enables us to perceive a range of social structures; ultimately, each life in this volume represents a separate response to prevailing social issues. The lives are more a spectrum than an average. Each life history is a starting point, a document to stimulate further inquiry.

Writing and Interpreting a Life

After gathering a life history in the field, we turn to the equally sensitive issue of writing it up for circulation. Writing a life history for publication requires balancing several considerations in order for it to be both believable and readable. In the field, the informant's articulation of her life may be more or less expressive, detailed, and self-aware. Lives are rarely recounted in chronological order, and information necessary for understanding each life may be taken for granted and omitted by the informant.

In writing the life histories for this volume, the authors chose a variety of means to portray their subjects. They all rewrote the data collected over days and weeks and had to make certain decisions: (1) whether to write in the first person using the informant's own words, the third person, or both; (2) whether to organize the information around major themes, such as work and family life, or chronologically; (3) which material is necessary for an understanding of the person and which should be deleted to enhance the flow; and (4) what information should be added to aid comprehension by others.[17]

There is no single correct way to portray a life. The life history method is an evolving, creative mode that gains strength and significance because of its variety in form and expression. The range of styles in this volume reflects the writers' need to convey nuance and particularity for each subject and their own responses to her, at the same time tracing major issues and questions. Successful portrayal of lives must resolve the tension between depicting an individual in a dynamic, interesting, dramatic, but particular fashion *and* addressing larger issues of social significance and scope.

Our authors tell the readers the editorial choices they have made. Stylistic decisions were made for accuracy and clarity and to develop the richness and value of the material. One of our most difficult problems was to enhance dramatic interest in our subjects in order to convey the inherent human qualities of our work. This difficulty arises from both an understandable focus on precision of detail and a reluctance to weight events according to our own criteria.

The problem of dramatization is addressed by anthropologist David Mandelbaum, who suggests that biographies emphasize the dramatic qualities of a life and convey its significant points, or crises, which he refers to as "turnings":

> The principal periods of a life are marked by the main turnings, the major transitions, that the person had made. Such a turning is accomplished when the person takes on a new set of roles, enters into fresh relations with a new set of people, and acquires a new self-conception. . . . A life does not proceed in a projectable, unilinear curve like a cannon shot. Rather, it involves ongoing development in various spheres of behavior; it includes continuous adjustment and periodic adaptation. Personal adaptations are both the source of social adaptation and also responses to it.[18]

Eric Erikson's views on the psychology of life stages and the concept of transitions, or passages, have also been fruitfully pursued by other scholars as a framework for collection and portrayal of data.[19]

The lives recorded in the field constitute unpolished data; the reorganized, published lives presented here can be called semi-polished. An important reason for our presenting these semi-polished versions, which have been kept as close as possible to field recordings, is to retain them as primary documents. Years from now, after further change takes place in the societies studied, the lives of these women will be useful historical documents. They can be compared with lives of women from later generations. These comparisons will help us understand how societies change.

The Collection of Life Histories from Documentation

In contrast to the lives collected through participant observation (chapters 3–9 and 13), the translations of highly stylized lives of emulation models (chapters 11 and 12) were written for a purpose which exceeds simple documentation. They were intended to bring about social change. Their different function means that they are relatively highly polished; all material irrelevant to a didactic point has been edited out. We include these translations not only as further data on the behavior of Chinese women but also as illustrations of another use of the biographical method—to direct social change.

Chinese "heroic" life histories differ in content and methodology from the life histories collected by Western social scientists, primarily because they aim to inspire and mobilize. These are the lives of real people who have been in the vanguard of the sort of change that the leadership considers necessary to alter the larger society. In fact, these crafted and polished lives are intended to deal with one of the issues identified in our Western fieldwork biographies—the rendering of private dilemmas as public issues. These documents from China clearly define women's problems as structural rather than personal or psychological attributes.

Chinese readers of the model biographies are supposed to learn that their own problems are rarely purely personal and instead result from social structures. Such problems can be overcome only by means of social transformation. The model lives illustrate the heroic heights to which ordinary women may rise if they dedicate their energies toward the resolution of dilemmas on behalf of the collective. Women in these lives may suffer and falter, but they eventually succeed in finding the true forward path. They become heroic by overcoming considerable odds, but the odds are the same as those facing most people in their social group. The Chinese biographers of heroic women direct us to this conclusion by attempting to remove all ambiguity from their characters' motivations and actions. The Chinese model lives are thus in contrast to those written by Western authors, which deliberately record ambiguities, failures, weaknesses, and contradictions.

There are several rules of thumb in the use of heroic lives. We must first keep in mind the period during which the materials were transcribed, because the political goals of the time determine who is chosen as a model and the kind of problems she is portrayed as facing. These represent commonly felt problems of the social environment of the time.[20] Second, the lives presented here are of real people; they are not composites.[21] Thus the reader can glean from them socially significant variables—the social class of the activist, the composition of her family, her method of handling role conflicts, how she arranges for care of her children while she works. One does glimpse personality but only as a feature of praiseworthy character traits. One may also note her significant relationships to others, the relative wealth of her area, how people regard the status of her occupation, and attitudes toward her work. Our analysis of such variables helps us place each heroic life in context and enables us to use the biographies to gain a deeper comprehension of Chinese society. In sum, the analytic tools of the sociology of knowledge, often used by those who study literature, can also be brought to bear when we study model women.[22]

The Place of Our Volume in Women's Studies

Our volume as a whole presents women as active participants in and creators of their culture. Few consider themselves victims, and their biographers see the women not as victims but as self-motivated persons. In the past, women may have appeared as secondary and passive because they were so often faceless, but feminist studies have now brought to publication some materials to fill the void created by the rejection of inappropriate male psychological and social models.[23] Our volume can thus be read as a contribution to feminist literature and historiography, because it portrays women as active creators of social forms. We are also inheritors of the Chinese studies tradition, which gave us Ida Pruitt's life history of a domestic servant in the 1940s and Margery Wolf's sensitive account of a Taiwanese family with whom she lived for a year in the 1960s.[24]

In non-Sinological contexts, important studies of nineteenth-century women draw upon diaries and letters to document women as feeling individuals who are full participants in family and community affairs. Indeed, such studies find that the family work of women gave rise to the nuclear family and child-centered socialization practices. Among these recent classics are Carol Smith-Rosenberg, "The Female World of Love and Ritual," Nancy Cott, *The Bonds of Womanhood*, and Ann Douglas, *The Feminization of American Culture*.[25]

Short interviews and participant observation techniques are used in several contemporary social science works. Carol Stack's *All Our Kin* ably portrayed black families on welfare and revolutionized social science perspectives on the so-called culture of poverty that had long pilloried the black family. Other studies that convincingly portray women in their work roles include Barbara Garson, *All the Livelong Day*; Kathy Kahn,

Hillbilly Women; Louise Kapp Howe, *Pink Collar Workers*; and Mimi Conway, *Rise, Gonna Rise*. In addition, there are Akemi Kikimura, *Through Harsh Winters: The Life of a Japanese Immigrant Woman*; Ann Cornelisen, *Women of the Shadows*, on Italian women; Jean McCrindle and Sheila Rowbotham, *Dutiful Daughters*, on British women; and Jane Holden Kelley, *Yaqui Women*, on Mexican women.[26]

These and other works use intensive interviews and life histories to document the contribution women have made to culture and society. We hope that the lives in this volume will also be read in this context. Some of the contributions of our women to their society have not been documented elsewhere, and many activities described are no longer common. Thus, our volume's lives enter the historical record not only on the role of women in Chinese social structure and change but also as broader documentation on the contributions of women internationally.

PART I

The Older Generation

Part I introduces lives of the older generation, focusing mainly on their experiences before 1949. To begin with, a methods chapter surveys the Western literature on Chinese women and provides historical background on women's work and family roles. Three lives follow. All the women are from rural backgrounds. One's economic independence allows her to depart from the patrilineal family pattern; one remains an ordinary peasant all her life; and one is a stevedore Hakka woman. All three lives were collected by Western women fluent in Chinese and closely associated with Chinese culture.

2

Historical Background
on Chinese Women

By Andrea McElderry

Life history literature before 1949 contains themes similar to those in the contemporary lives in this volume. The lives of the women discussed here were directed toward specific goals of self-determination and meaningful work. Attainment of these goals involved struggle with both their families and forces in the outside world. In this review of lives before 1949, we find active women beginning to take advantage of new options for them opened by historical circumstance and in the process deliberately broadening these options for themselves and others. We find that like their sisters who succeeded them in post-Liberation China, Hong Kong, and Taiwan, these women did not reject the family. Rather, they sought a new role within a changed family structure. They also sought support from significant others, especially radical organizations outside the family. The theme that clearly permeates the lives discussed in this chapter is their desire and willingness to use their talent, intelligence, and education productively for collective and individual goals. Underlying the accounts is the desire to remove through change the stumbling blocks to the application of their talents and training.

Women as Workers

The women who left autobiographies before 1949 were part of a small elite of educated women. Accounts of the lives of working-class and peasant women are very sparse.

We have only one full-length autobiographical record in English of a Chinese working woman from the pre-Liberation period—Ida Pruitt's outstanding oral history of Lao Ning recorded in Peking in 1936–1938, *A Daughter of Han.*[1] Lao Ning had been married off by her parents to a man who became an "opium sot." She supported herself and her children by working as a servant for both Chinese and Western families, thereby obtaining a rare view of China's old elite. Lao Ning's willingness to express strong opinions on any subject and her sense of humor make the book eminently readable and human. Moreover, the friendship between Ida Pruitt and Lao Ning allowed the slow unfolding of the story over a long time, a relationship also rare in recording life histories.

With this exception, most of the accounts we have in English on Chinese working women are limited to casual observations by foreign visitors beginning in the mid-nineteenth century.[2] Alicia Little wrote many such travel documents, including *The Land of the Blue Gown*.[3] In the summer of 1898, Little and her businessman husband went to Chungking, then a city with few foreigners, to set up a trading company and a steam navigation service. During the summer, they moved to a farm to escape the heat of the city, and Little recorded the work of the peasant women in her diary.

In early July, she records, the women were busy spinning yarn on the concrete threshing floor; in late July, the married daughter was helping her mother remove nettles from the fiber used for making cloth. The daughter "worked at this pretty well all day, when not suckling her child." At night Little notes that the "threshing floor was again spread with peas . . . and beautiful cobs of Indian corn . . . raked about preparatory to unhusking them." In mid-August, "everyone was requisitioned to strip the Indian corn off the cobs." In late August, Little writes, "The farm family seem at last to have finished unhusking their Indian corn, the business of so many evenings past." In addition to farm work, the women brought cash into the household by doing needlework and making shoes. "One of the married daughters has been making sandals for A. [Archibald, her husband] and me, soles and all, they are quite a success! She came to discuss a nightdress bag, which I want worked in cross stitch as elaborately as her little boy's pinafore. She says it will take her a month, and asks a thousand cash (three shillings)."[4]

Grace Thompson Seton was a world traveler who introduced her readers to women in all walks of life—suffragettes, day laborers, factory workers, writers, and bankers. In her book *Chinese Lanterns*, she introduces Mrs. Nelson H. Y. Chen, who ran the Women's Department in her husband's Peking bank.[5] To increase savings accounts, Mrs. Chen had a staff of canvassers who called upon wealthy women in their homes to educate them about banks and to solicit their business. Mrs. C. Z. Wang founded the Chinese Women's Commercial Savings Bank of Peking in 1922, the first of its kind.

Interested in industrial workers and laborers, Seton notes that women in south China did more manual labor than women in the north. "Everywhere in Hong Kong . . . women were carrying the yoke and doing hard physical labor. A great variety of loads, heavy trunks, bags of food, cement and coal are carried by these slim, erect, muscular Amazons. . . .

They are stone-breakers, road-builders and road-menders." She watched a group of women coaling a hospital and writes, "While I stood aghast watching them, I was finally forced to admit that conditions in China being what they are, these women are quite as well off as the man. I am told that they do not allow themselves to be over-worked and that they make enough for bean-curd and to satisfy their simple needs."

One of the most delightful stories in *Chinese Lanterns* concerns a young American gentleman of generous proportions who hired a sedan chair only to find that it was being carried by four women. "He protested at this violation of his traditional upbringing. As they would not stop, and were literally carrying him off, he finally jumped out of the chair. The leader in great distress inquired wherein they had failed to give satisfaction, and told him that his refusal to employ them meant deprivation and disgrace. His gallantry thus doubly appealed to, he kept the chair but spared the Amazons . . . by walking most of the way."[6]

When we catch glimpses of women traders, transport workers, construction workers, and women traveling on business of their own, we realize that the fabric of women's work stretched the breadth of the land and has by no means been fairly measured by accounts of only their family role. Observer accounts continue, of course, to the present, and we will return to them at the end of this chapter. However, they are an auxiliary source and lead us back to our focus on close-up portraiture.

Women's Place in the Home

Upper-class women in traditional China were supposed to remain inside the family compound, emerging only when well concealed in curtained sedan chairs. In prosperous families, where the Confucian ideal of five generations under one roof and the seclusion of women could be achieved, the women's quarters constituted a world of its own, as first portrayed in the classic Ch'ing dynasty novel, *The Dream of the Red Chamber*.

Nora Waln, a Philadelphia Quaker, lived with the wealthy Lin family in their house on the Grand Canal in the early 1920s. The first part of her book, *The House of Exile*, recounts her life as a "maiden of marriageable age" in a six-generation household of 83 men, women, and children.[7] A Waln ancestor and a Lin ancestor had had business connections in Canton in the early nineteenth century. A hundred years later, Lin Yang-peng and his wife Shun-ko called on Waln when they were touring the United States and invited her to live with them in China. When she arrived in 1920, they met her with a family party to accompany her up the Grand Canal to the Lin family home. Along the way, she describes her glimpses of women at work. At an ice-cutting site, "women wheeled hamper barrows down to the opened water and exchanged banter with the ice-cutter, while they let their ducks and geese out to swim." When they disembarked from the boat, "young girls, carrying kettles of steaming water, soap, soft towels, and blue basins, sold 'Wash your face for a penny!'" An incident on the boat, however, made it clear that young women of the Lin family led quite a different life from the young working women. Some oranges were accidentally knocked off the boat onto the frozen river. A male ice skater picked up the oranges and returned them, speaking briefly to the men of the party. Shun-ko reprimanded Waln, saying, "Girls of a marriageable age are as dangerous to the peace of a family as smuggled salt. Don't ever again, while under my chaperonage, look *at* a man. Direct your gaze modestly to the ground when one is in front of you."[8]

Once Waln was established in the Lin home, she was as carefully sheltered as the unmarried Lin daughters. At Spring Festival, the married women and female children were allowed to join the men and boys in the "welcome to spring procession" while the unmarried young women stayed behind to prepare the spring clothes and finish the preparation of the spring feast. Waln writes of the control of the "first lady in authority": "Maids under her protection do not join in any festival procession which includes men—except the procession which goes directly to the bridegroom's door."[9]

In the household routine, unmarried women helped cut the sprouted seed potatoes and had other gardening duties. All women in the household had cooking, cleaning, and sewing duties. One of the wives had the duty of keeping the "chart of the lessening of the cold." This was an annual record for agricultural and horticultural purposes. It consisted of a painting of a plum tree with 81 twigs. Beginning with the winter solstice, a blossom was painted on one of the twigs each day to depict the weather on that day.[10]

Waln's book contains a great deal of information on weddings and marriage. Three weddings took place in the Lin household while Waln lived there, and she described the ceremonies attendant upon a woman coming to live in the house of her husband's family. The new bride's duty was to serve her husband and her in-laws and to bear sons to continue the family. She had to be monogamous, and she could not divorce her husband. The man, on the other hand, could take a concubine and also had rights over the slaves (girls and young women who had been bought from poor families who could not support them). Two incidents illustrate the double standard. Chien-lu, one of the Lin sons, went to work in Shanghai and took a concubine there who had a child by him. One day, she appeared at the main gate of the House of Exile. Waln explains the situation: "Although Lin Chien-lu had not communicated with his homestead since the day, nine years previously, when he departed . . . [and] although the woman had not known his whereabouts for seven years, she was entitled to shelter, food, and [clothing] in accord with the family fortune. . . , to a funeral with banners and music; to have her spirit tablet set in the Circle of Ancestors. She [had to] do her share of the cooking, cleaning, and sewing. But she [could not] be forced to earn for the common fund, and she [had to] be nursed in sickness. His first wife . . . had to give the newcomer living space. . . . The children he sired at Shanghai [had] inheritance in their father's house equal to the rights of his children born [in the house]. In the event of the death of the first wife, the newcomer would speak with the authority of Lin Chien-lu in his absence, in matters concerning the property and concerning *all* his children."[11]

The other incident concerned the first wife of one of the Lin sons. Her husband had been away working in Canton, and there he had taken a concubine who bore him three sons. His first wife became pregnant, and it was clearly not her husband's child. The punishment for a woman's adultery was death by strangulation. Since in this case her infidelity was considered to be the husband's fault, it was his duty to inflict the punishment. The husband was called home and astonished his family when he agreed to accept the child as his own. The family refused to permit him to do so, but the wife could not be punished while she carried the child. After the birth, she killed both herself and the child. The young man suspected of being the father was disinherited and sent from the homestead.

Women's Place outside the Home

At the turn of the twentieth century, young upper-class Chinese women began to challenge tradition-bound ideas regarding their place in society. Confrontations were unavoidable if they were to achieve modern goals, and several autobiographies document these early stages of female rebellion. Chao Yang Bu-wei was one of the few fortunate women who had a supportive family. Her *Autobiography of a Chinese Woman* was translated from Chinese into English by her husband, Chao Yuenren, a well-known linguist.[12] Bu-wei was born in Nanking in 1889, and even though her father and grandfather had both been influenced by progressive ideas, she was betrothed at birth. Her family sent her to school in Shanghai; there she took the radical action of breaking her engagement, which received her grandfather's blessing.

Shortly after the Revolution of 1911, Bu-wei, a high school graduate, became principal of a special girls' school for members of the Women's Expeditionary Corps organized by General Po Wen-wei, military governor of Anhwei. Bu-wei took the job because she had been promised an Anhwei government scholarship to study medicine in England. When the

Second Revolution of 1913 failed, however, General Po lost his job, and Bu-wei had to study in Japan instead.

The presence of Bu-wei and her Chinese women classmates in Tokyo attested to the progress that these daughters of well-to-do families had made by the 1910s. Still, they had a long way to go. Although Bu-wei wanted to study general medicine, the Chinese government ordered all women holders of government medical scholarships to specialize in gynecology and obstetrics.

When Bu-wei returned to China, she learned that her father's recent death had left the family in financial straits. She took the responsibility of supporting her mother, her brother, and his young bride. She and three other women doctors opened a hospital in Peking, the first non-missionary women doctors to set up practice on their own. She gave up her practice in 1921, when she married and accompanied her husband to the United States. Two of their four daughters were born there.

In 1925, the Chao family returned to China, and Yuenren took a position at Tsinghua University, which was changing from American sponsorship to Chinese administration. Bu-wei worked for cultural reorientation of the university by championing language reform and the use of standard Chinese rather than English among faculty wives. She also organized a company to stimulate local women's handicraft industries and set up a birth control clinic in Peking. The war years took her family to Kunming in western China and then to the United States, where Bu-wei wrote her autobiography in 1947.

Another affluent rebel, Chow Chung-cheng, was born in Tientsin a generation after Bu-wei and was influenced by the ideas of the May Fourth Movement of 1919. This broad-based assault on traditional social structure included the feminist concerns of eliminating foot-binding and arranged marriages and establishing wider education for women. Chung-cheng's autobiography, *The Lotus Pool*, covers her teenage years in the period around 1919.[13] Unlike Bu-wei, Chung-cheng did not have a supportive family and had to run away from home in order to attend high school and university. She recalls many oppressive incidents from girlhood, including one in T'ao Park in her hometown.

Chung-cheng writes that among the flower beds, goldfish ponds, and fine old trees of T'ao Park, modern plays and full-length films were shown, while visitors improvised at the "poets' tables" for the occasional poetry prize. Chung-cheng's parents sometimes attended plays in the park, allowing their children to amuse themselves. Chung-cheng reminisces, "We had complete freedom for two hours . . . I enjoyed myself tremendously and laughed especially loudly when a handsome young man passed by. Possibly we exchanged glances, even smiles. But we never spoke to each other. . . . But one day Ho [her brother] said: 'One of our cousins told me he had noticed you in the T'ao Park and heard you laughing. You must not let that happen again. You're a respectable girl of a good family. You mustn't laugh like that in the T'ao Park again. . . .' " Chung-cheng knew that if her conservative mother heard such a comment, she would not be allowed to go to the park again. She concludes, "It was better not to laugh any more. I had to learn not to laugh; probably I ought to learn not to love."[14]

Chung-cheng was tutored at home, but she was determined to attend a regular school like her brothers and plotted an escape from the family fortress. Her grandfather's death provided the first opportunity to escape by requiring her parents' presence at the funeral in another city for several days. Through correspondence, Chung-cheng had obtained a promise of aid from Li Ssu-shan, a woman contributor to the progressive *New People's Opinion*. Chung-cheng's first step was to obtain money. Her father occasionally had a servant telephone the bank to request delivery of $200 or so for household expenses, and sometimes Chung-cheng signed the receipt. On the day of her escape, she requested delivery of $500 paid in small change appropriate to household expenses. The total was unexpectedly too heavy to carry, however, and she had to leave $200 hidden with her sister. She then walked out of her family home. "For the first time in my life I was alone in the street! . . . but my legs felt weak, I could hardly walk. I needed a rickshaw, but did not know how to call one. Luckily one came past at that moment, and I remembered that people I had watched idly from my window simply climbed into rickshaws without asking the price." She climbed aboard and gave the name of the cinema where she was to meet Ssu-shan. Many years later, she learned that Ssu-shan had had someone follow her in case something went wrong.

Ssu-shan arranged for Chung-cheng to go to Peking, where she was introduced to progressive students. She negotiated with her parents for several months through representatives of *New People's Opinion*, and eventually she and her sister were allowed to attend school. Her parents also accepted her demand that she and her sister be allowed to choose their own husbands. When Chung-cheng returned home, her parents pretended that nothing had happened, but their servants said, "It could only happen in a rich family living in town . . . on the land a girl who behaved in so shameless a fashion would not have come back alive."[15]

These comments by the Chow family servants reflected the unevenness of the changes taking place in Chinese society. In the countryside, new ideas were even more dangerous than in the city, as the case of Wang Su Chun illustrates. Her peasant father, a Christian, sent her to a mission school. On her return, Su Chun announced her engagement, which amounted to licentious behavior in the eyes of the community. She also wore the "immodest" dresses seen mainly in Shanghai or Hankow, not in rural Hunan. During the Revolution of 1926–1927, Su Chun participated in the Women's Association. Women members paraded in the streets, went to mass meetings with men, and advocated divorce rights for women. When the soldiers of the counterrevolution came to her town, the neighbors reported her and then watched the soldiers' mutilation of her. "The soldiers shouted many bad words at her till they stirred their rage up. Then they cut her to pieces with knives and bayonets. . . . Then they cut off her arms; they cut off many pieces. By and by they [fired] seventeen shots into what was left," records Anna Louise Strong of the incident.[16]

Bu-wei, Chung-cheng, and Su Chun were among many women influenced by the revolutionary ideas that had begun to take root in China in the early twentieth century. Women's rights were among the most important, but historical circumstance made it impossible for the feminist movement to exist outside the larger revolutionary movement. In the West, the American Declaration of Independence and the French Declaration on the Rights of Man had provided a moral framework within which women sought equality. The development of stable governments meant that women could attempt to gain their rights by influencing the government in power. American and Canadian women also gained political experience by joining existing political campaigns, such as the anti-slavery and prohibition movements. In China, on the other hand, there was no stable Chinese authority sympathetic to ideals of equality; nor was there an appropriate ideology that was already widespread. Thus women's demands for equality could be made only within a larger revolutionary movement that attacked the traditional social and political hierarchy.

Women and the Revolution of 1911

The most famous woman revolutionary of this period is Ch'iu Chin, who is considered a heroine in China, Taiwan, and Hong Kong. The best English source on her life is Mary Backus Rankin's article in *Women in Chinese Society*.[17]

Ch'iu Chin, born around 1879, was educated along with her two brothers. Her arranged marriage took place in 1896, and in 1900 she and her husband moved to Peking, where she came into contact with women of avant-garde circles. Like many in her generation, she was alarmed when Japan defeated China in 1895 and Peking was occupied by foreign troops after the Boxer War in 1900. Chin became a revolutionary nationalist and argued that women needed equal rights and education so that they could contribute to national reconstruction. Frustrated by her own limited options and with the support of her mother and her women friends in Peking, she left her husband—an extremely radical action at the time. In 1904, she went to study in rapidly industrializing Japan, a popular place for

Chinese students to seek Western learning. Many of these students sought the overthrow of the Manchu dynasty, which they perceived as a block to national progress, and thus Ch'iu Chin joined the Revolutionary Alliance (the T'ung Meng Hui, which later became the Nationalist Party). She returned to China in 1905. While working as a schoolteacher in Shaohsing, Chekiang, Chin plotted with her cousin, Hsü Hsi-lin, to overthrow the government. Hsü launched a premature insurrection from which Ch'iu Chin could have escaped, but instead she and her students resisted government troops and were arrested. Chin was beheaded on July 15, 1907.

Another woman activist of this period was Wei Yu-hsiu (later Madam Wei Tao-ming) whose autobiography, *My Revolutionary Years*, begins with her childhood in Canton.[18] She was born in 1896. Her father worked in Peking, but she and her siblings lived with their mother in her father's family home in Canton, where they were subject to the authority of her paternal grandmother. Her mother was often depressed, suspecting that her husband maintained a concubine in Peking. Yu-hsiu sympathized with her mother, but no one else in the family, including the grandmother, considered the concubine any grounds for "tearful behavior."

Yu-hsiu was a rebel from her earliest years but was often forced to compromise to prevent her grandmother from scolding her mother. She describes her experience with footbinding thus: "When the bandages were first put on my feet, I submitted not only because it was being done to all little girls of the house, but because I knew if I rebelled it would bring fresh humiliation on my mother. But I simply could not stand it. . . . My final rebellion was supported by the fact that I felt that Mother did not want my feet to be bound. She deeply regretted that her own had been so crippled. . . . [One morning] I suddenly started screaming, without tears, but in great volume. I lay on my back, kicking and yelling. I kept up this bedlam for the greater part of the morning, disturbing the entire household. [In the end, Grandmother]—whose final word was necessary to make any decision . . . looked down at me with great distaste and said: 'Very well, then. Take the bandages off. Her feet will grow the size of an elephant's. No one will ever marry her, but so be it. I wash my hands of the whole business.'"[19]

In fact, someone was willing to marry Yu-hsiu, and her family arranged an engagement. Although she did not want to marry yet, Yu-hsiu ignored the engagement until she heard that her fiancé was eager to set a date. "I was panic stricken. The idea of marrying someone who was a total stranger frightened me. Moreover, reports of the young man from my brothers and various friends had not painted him as a prepossessing character." Her brother reported that the fellow "was not particularly industrious, but was, in fact, such a playboy that he had to have a servant especially designated to follow him around to give him assistance whenever needed." In addition, her future father-in-law disapproved of women with a modern education. Yu-hsiu's own father sought a face-saving way to break the engagement, but he did not act quickly enough, and she broke the engagement herself. "The hubbub which ensued was unbelieveable. . . . My father was shocked beyond words, and, needless to say, my grandmother took to her bed and gave every appearance of dying of shock. My only support was Mother, who though miserable at the disgrace which had been brought on the family, was still secretly happy that I had not been forced into marriage."[20]

Soon after, influenced by her brother, Yu-hsiu joined the Nationalist Party at age 15. During the Revolution of 1911, she smuggled dynamite between Tientsin and Peking, where she lived with her mother and father. After the warlord Yüan Shih-k'ai came to power in 1912, Yu-hsiu participated in the struggle against him and attempted to assassinate one of his ministers. For this purpose, she once again had to carry explosives to Peking. There she was nearly apprehended by government agents, but she put her pursuers on a false trail. She describes her narrow escape: "Out in the street I ambled along, stopping now and then to look in shop windows as if I had nothing to do. But as soon as I had turned the corner and saw the railroad station some two or three hundred yards ahead, I picked up my skirts and tore lickety-split up to the platform. I had timed myself to arrive at the moment when the 9:45 a.m. train would be pulling out, and it was already in motion when I jumped for the steps and scrambled up into the vestibule of the car. Two hours after my arrival in Tientsin, I sailed on an English ship for Shanghai."[21]

From Shanghai, Yu-hsiu returned to her family home in Canton with plans to study in France. The family approved, anxious to get her out of the country before she caused more trouble. After her studies abroad, she set up a law practice in Shanghai, becoming the first Chinese and the first woman president of the District Court. Her partner was Wei Tao-ming, whom she eventually married. In 1928, Yu-hsiu was sent to France to seek diplomatic recognition for the Nanking government and later served in the Legislative Council, where she and Soong Mei-ling (Madame Chiang Kai-shek) were the only women representatives. Tao-ming became Minister of Justice, and when the Japanese attacked in 1937, he and Yu-hsiu followed the Nationalist government to its wartime capital in Chungking. When Tao-ming was appointed Minister to France, she accompanied him.

As a supporter of the Nationalist government, Yu-hsiu omits all comment on the May Fourth Movement of 1919. Save for brief mention of her participation in the Chinese student protests against the Treaty of Versailles while studying in Paris, she is silent on her feelings about the May Fourth Movement, which grew out of this protest.

Women in the Revolution of 1926–1927

The politics of the 1920s took a definite turn to the left. The Chinese Communist Party was founded in 1921, and Sun Yat-sen, leader of the Nationalist Party, approached the Soviet Union for aid. After Sun's death in 1925, his successor, Chiang Kai-shek, led an alliance of Nationalists and Communists in a military expedition against the warlords who controlled North China. Known as the Revolution of 1926–1927, this was a period of great social upheaval. Peasant associations, labor unions, and women's organizations supported the revolutionary army, while fear of social revolution brought a reaction from China's elite—the military commanders, rural landlords, urban businessmen, and foreign residents. In 1927, Chiang Kai-shek betrayed the revolution with a bloody coup in Shanghai, and the counterrevolution spread rapidly to other cities. Many patriotic Chinese, both Communist and non–Communist, lost their lives.

Women had participated in all aspects of the Revolution of 1926–1927, and they were executed along with men in the counterrevolution. Some women were murdered simply for having bobbed hair, the feminine symbol of liberation which suddenly marked them for suspicion of leftist leanings.[22]

Hsieh Ping-ying, one of China's well-known writers, was a soldier during this period. Her popular autobiography has been translated into English as *Autobiography of a Chinese Girl*.[23] Born in rural Hunan Province, Ping-ying was raised by a domineering mother of strictly old-fashioned attitudes toward woman's place, but Ping-ying describes herself as a young rebel. Her older sister's unhappy marriage served as a warning to Ping-ying. "When she came home she pretended she was well treated. She knew that if she acted otherwise she would get no sympathy from our mother, who would naturally upbraid her for being undutiful as a wife. When we met privately in the lavatory she would shed tears before me and tell me all her sufferings."[24]

Ping-ying lived in a tea-growing area in Hunan, and her family's attitude toward the women tea pickers illustrates the gulf between working people and landowners. Many tea pickers were grateful to work and to have an income, but Ping-ying's mother sent her to pick tea leaves as a punishment. Ping-ying writes of the tea pickers: "Their life was full of misery. Every day they had to pick at least forty or fifty *catties* of tea-leaves, and their wages would be only ten or twenty coppers a day, which they had to give to their mothers-in-law. If they were found to be keeping any of the money for their private use they would be severely punished. Rarely did they have a good meal. . . . They were as thin as skeletons."[25]

With the support of her brothers, Ping-ying overcame her mother's objections and attended school. Once she left home, she unbound her feet. One of her brothers introduced her to socialist and communist writings, and her own writing began to reflect these new ideas. Political awareness and determination to avoid an arranged marriage led to her decision to join the army mobilized for the Revolution of 1926–1927. She was not alone. She writes, "I believe that all the girl students who wanted to join the Army had as their motive, in nine cases out of ten, to get away from their families, by whom they were suppressed. They all wanted to find their own way out. But the moment they put on their uniforms and shouldered their guns, their ideas became less selfish." Speaking of their first day in camp, she writes, "From that day onwards, we considered ourselves soldiers and began to discard our former silly habits." With the counter-revolution, the women's corps was demobilized, and the women put on dresses to go home. "When we looked at the new dresses . . . we were very much like mourners who were present at a funeral. . . . We loved our uniform, and especially the leather belt . . . and our rifle. . . . Our rifle, of course, was more dear to us than our lives. The destruction of the old system and the creation of a new society depended upon it."[26]

Around the same time, Agnes Smedley, an American journalist, talked to many Chinese women and recorded their stories. Her publications are a record of the Chinese revolution from the late 1920s to the late 1930s.[27] Through Smedley, we meet Ch'ang Hsiao-hung, daughter of a wealthy family, who had become a Communist and survived the terror of the counterrevolution;[28] Hsü Mei-ling, "an old-fashioned girl, with all the faults and virtues of an old-fashioned girl," whose pseudo-modern husband was seeking to put her away;[29] and Teng Hua-ch'uan, a widow who betrayed her revolutionary husband.[30]

Anna Louise Strong was another woman journalist writing during the 1920s. Her accounts introduce us to women trade unionists at the All China Labor Congress of 1927, to women propagandists who followed in the wake of the revolutionary army, to urban women attempting to provide shelter houses for abused wives and slave girls, and to women martyred for their independence, such as Wang Su Chun.[31] Without these accounts, many of these women would have remained nameless and faceless.

Other foreign visitors described the hardships of workers in the factories. Chang Sui-ying told her story to Dymphna Cusack in the 1950s. At the age of 12, Sui-ying was smuggled into a textile factory by her older sister so that she could learn the skills to get a job. She began at 18 cents a day and was beaten by the foreman for poor work. Accidents were common, and if a worker lost a finger or was otherwise maimed, she was dismissed. Pans on the floor served as factory toilets; there was no ventilation. "In the summer temperatures in the workshops would often rise to a hundred and ten degrees Fahrenheit. We perpetually had headaches and often fainted. We were left lying where we fell . . . the stench and the flies were everywhere. . . . Women were so terrified of losing their job if it was known that they were pregnant they would bind their bellies tightly and hope their conditions would not be noticed. It wasn't uncommon for a woman to be taken with labour-pains in the mill and have to sneak off to the toilet and have her baby there."[32] A foreign observer in the 1920s notes that "often, two or three babies roll about on a dirty quilt. They are there by sufferance because the mothers have no place to leave their children."[33] Sui-ying pointed proudly to the changes since Liberation—good ventilation, proper toilets, a nursery for children, and a canteen with cheap meals.

Women textile workers were in the forefront of the labor movement. In 1922, Shanghai workers from seventy filatures organized the Society for Promoting the Welfare of Working Women. Sixty thousand employees went on strike, demanding a 10-hour day, a higher hourly wage, one day of rest every two weeks, and no interference by mill owners in the organization of the society. Lack of a strike fund forced the women back to work, but the union movement grew. In 1924, strikes in the Shanghai silk filatures and the Nanyang tobacco plant found Hsiang Ching-yü among the leadership. The unions also played an important role in the abortive Revolution of 1926–1927.

Hsiang Ching-yü was born in 1894 to a well-to-do merchant family in a small Hunan town. Her family supported her middle school education, and after she graduated from Chou-nan Girls' School in 1915, she returned to her hometown. There she established a co-ed primary school and encouraged progressive education and egalitarian relationships between teachers and students. Her brother influenced her toward radical political thought, and Ching-yü became active in the movement against the warlord Yüan Shih-k'ai in 1915. Later, she organized protests during the May Fourth Movement of 1919. In the same year, Ching-yü embarked for France as a student in the work-study program, came into contact with revolutionary ideas and the Soviet revolution. She married Ts'ai Ho-sen, and both became Communists. When they returned to Shanghai in 1922, both were elected to the Central Committee of the Communist Party. Ching-yü then served as head of the party's Woman Department. She also studied at the Toilers of the East University in Moscow. On her return to China, Ching-yü worked in Wuhan and during the counterrevolution was arrested and executed on May 1, 1928, at the age of 33. As a revolutionary martyr, Ching-yü is a role model in contemporary China. Several writings and reminiscences about her have been published, and information about her can also be found in English-language publications.[34]

The bloody counterrevolution of 1927–1928 forced the surviving Communists underground but at the same time caused many intellectuals to make a deeper political commitment. One of these was the writer Ting Ling.[35] Like the revolutionary martyr Hsiang Ching-yü, Ting Ling came from Hunan where their mothers had been classmates. Both young women were feminists and joined the Communist Party. Ting Ling went alone to Shanghai as a young woman to escape the constraints of her large patriarchal family. After some involvement with anarchists in her school days in Shanghai, Ting Ling joined the Left-Wing Writers League in 1930 and the Communist Party in 1931. Her decision to become a Communist was influenced by Japan's invasion of Manchuria and the execution of her Communist husband, Hu Yeh-p'ing. In 1933, she herself was arrested but eventually escaped to the Communist base in the Northwest. There she worked with women's groups and organized the Front Service Group, "a kind of flying squadron of propagandists."[36] She also edited a literary journal. In 1942, she published "Thoughts on March Eighth," describing the plight of women in Yenan caught between traditional and revolutionary expectations. She conceded that women's position in Yenan was better than in other parts of China but complained that the Party did not sufficiently push in practice their theories about women's emancipation. Her criticisms of the Party led to her self-study and reeducation under Party guidance.

Ting Ling touches upon questions of sexuality in her early writings, and she unself-consciously refers to her various affairs. Hsiang Ching-yü is reported to have said of Ting Ling, "She is a bourgeois individualist, a romanticist, and an anarchist. Her ideas are far removed from Communism. It's not that I don't want to work with her, but she oppresses us. Let her worry about her own life."[37]

During the early 1950s, Ting Ling and her associates came into conflict with the powerful Party leader Chou Yang. Ting Ling sought greater artistic freedom within the socialist state, whereas Chou Yang worked to bring writers strictly under the control of the Party. By the mid-1950s, Chou Yang had gained control over the cultural apparatus of the new government and in 1957 publicly attacked Ting Ling and her associates. Ting Ling was expelled from the party, deprived of her rights as a writer and citizen, and sent to Northern Manchuria for labor reform.[38] After two decades of obscurity, she was recently brought back into the public limelight and rehabilitated.

Women on Their Own

Like that of her contemporaries among Chinese women writers, much of Ting Ling's fiction was autobiographical. Yi-tsi Feuerwerker points out that frequent themes in this genre of autobiographical fiction, set mainly in cities, concern individual struggles of middle-class women against family for the choice of a marriage partner and an education.[39] Using fiction allowed women writers to discuss sexual desires and frustrations; autobiographies could touch only obliquely on such themes. For women seeking self-affirmation, one way to escape social restrictions was to live apart from the family. The promises and pitfalls for a woman living on her own become clear in two life histories: *Daughter of the Khans* by Margaret Yang Briggs (Liang Yen, pseudonym) and *Comrade Chiang Ch'ing* by Roxanne Witke.[40]

Liang Yen, as she called herself in her book, was born to a wealthy Mongolian family in Peking. Although her family was thoroughly Chinese in its culture, Yen held that she was Mongolian throughout her life. Her strict and old-fashioned father hired a tutor for Yen and her sister, but he himself quizzed them: "Sometimes, unnerved by his cold face and sharp tongue, I couldn't remember which emperor belonged to which dynasty, what capital belonged to what part of the country. Father would pinch my eyelids with his long sharp nails. 'What are your eyes for—just to look for food?' He would slap my face with his long, heavy sleeves. I would hide my face in my arms, and he would kick me, kick me to the floor, kick me again and again as I rolled and twisted, trying to get away. 'Now get out of my sight!' " Yen's mother did not protest but comforted the girls later.

Yen was determined to attend a university, preferably in the United States. To achieve her goal, she began tutoring the young sons of a Manchu prince in the Chinese classics, but was stopped by her father. In protest, she retreated to her quarters: "As I sat mournfully in my courtyard, I found myself gazing at a middle-aged servant woman as she passed by. She carried her head high, shoulders back. Why so proudly? Well, for one thing, she supported two children and a mother-in-law on the pittance that was her salary. Though illiterate, she did that." Yen reflects on her situation, "Here I sit idly, grieving over myself, though I'm a healthy young woman; I can read and write and am certainly as capable as she. And I don't even have anyone to support. That very hour, with nothing but four *yüan* and a parcel containing toothbrush, soap and pajamas, I made for the gate of the compound."[41]

Upon leaving her family home, Yen convinced a close woman friend of the family to take her to Shanghai. Once they arrived, however, Yen was expected to wait on the woman and her family like a servant. It turned out that the woman had expected the rich Yen to be helpless at self-support and her father to pay handsomely to get her back. Yen proved this wrong by finding a secretarial job a day later. (Yen adopted her pseudonym at this point.) Yen's employer, Mr. Ch'en, was a businessman with interests in central and southern China and southeast Asia, and she traveled with him to many cities doing market research and secretarial work. Mr. Ch'en decided that he was very smart to have hired a woman and explained to Yen, "On other trips I've taken male secretaries, and they were always so tied up with their own interests—little deals on the side, you know—that they were slipshod with mine."[42] Yen accepted the invitation to live with Mr. Ch'en and his wife, but after several months he made romantic advances, so she left.

Through a cousin, Yen found a job teaching the Chinese classics and Mandarin at an overseas Chinese school in Rangoon, Burma. After 18 months, exhaustion and the tropical climate drove her back to Shanghai, where she held a series of different jobs. She ran an information booth at the New Asia Hotel, where prostitutes took clients, and warded off propositions while working 15-hour shifts daily. She was secretary to an association of overseas Chinese businessmen until the president made advances to her. She tutored a wealthy industrialist's children. She taught knitting at a Chinese women's club but left over a salary dispute. She got a job sewing shirts with a rented machine on precut material farmed out by a factory, but the pay was barely adequate, so she began knitting dresses for the White Russian couturiers on Avenue Joffre, a job she liked because she invented the pattern. However, she quit when she saw 300-*yüan* price tags on dresses for which she had received 30 *yüan* to design and make. Finally she began teaching Mandarin to foreigners; this was lucrative work which put her in touch with Shanghai's cosmopolitan foreign community. She also did some interpreting for the Nationalist government. When war scattered her clientele, she accepted an intelligence job with the Nationalist government.

Yen's spying and smuggling activities across Japanese lines and a number of narrow escapes make this part of her autobiography pure adventure story. Eventually she settled in Kunming, Yunnan, where she was employed by the American Office of Strategic Services as a Chinese language teacher. After the war, she met and married an American correspondent. The newlyweds spent a few weeks with her reconciled family in Peking, then left for the United States. When her husband asked her first impressions of America, she replied that she was happy but privately thought, "There was, despite this dream fulfilled, a reservation—a prick at my pride. I would manage to reach America on my own, I had always boasted to myself, and now I was here with the help of another. I wasn't the self-sufficient woman I had always prided myself on being."[43]

One of Liang Yen's contemporaries in Shanghai during the 1930s was Chiang Ch'ing, who later in Yenan became Mao Tse-tung's third wife, rose to power in the Cultural Revolution of the 1960s, and was purged in 1976. Her biography (as told to Roxanne Witke), *Comrade Chiang Ch'ing,* remains controversial today, but the early years of her life are representative of many aspects of ordinary Chinese women's lives. Unlike Liang Yen, Chiang Ch'ing came from a poor family. She lacked the friends that Yen had in Shanghai and a family to support her if she wanted to return.

Born in Shantung in 1914, Chiang Ch'ing was the youngest of several children in a family unable to provide sufficient food and clothing. Her father, a carpenter, beat her mother, causing some permanent damage, and he "beat the children whenever he felt the urge."[44] After her mother had received a particularly cruel thrashing one day, she took Ch'ing and fled. She found work as a servant and managed to send Ch'ing to school.

At 15, Ch'ing went to Tsinan, the capital of Shantung, and entered a drama school. At that time, it was still unusual for women to enter the theater, so Ch'ing was accepted without her high school diploma because the school wanted more women students. Subsequently she traveled to Peking and to Tsingtao. Like many poor students unable to afford tuition, she audited classes at Tsingtao University. In 1931, the Japanese seized Manchuria. This invasion elicited a strong anti-imperialist response from patriotic Chinese, and Chiang Ch'ing became part of the anti-Japanese movement. Disgusted with the Nationalist government's retreat before the Japanese, she turned to the Communist Party, which advocated complete resistance. In 1933, she finally made contact with the underground organization. We are told that "at least for her there was a price tag on party membership," and she had to subsist on two *shao-ping* (wheat flour pancakes) a day in order to pay off the Tsingtao party secretary.[45]

The year she joined the party, Ch'ing went to Shanghai, a logical destination for a left-wing actress. She achieved a reputation in modern stage plays and films. As a leftist, she participated in numerous demonstrations, and in the mid-1930s she became a teacher and organizer among factory women.

Because Ch'ing lacked the protection of a family and influential connections, she was particularly vulnerable to sexual harrassment. On the boat trip from Tsingtao to Shanghai, she was propositioned by the young man who was supposed to be her protector. In Shanghai, she sought help from the League of Left-Wing Dramatists, hoping that they would put her in touch with the Shanghai Communist Party. T'ien Han, one of the well-known playwrights in the League's leadership, assigned his brother, T'ien Hung, to follow her. Hung interfered with her work and made amorous advances. She was unable to make contact with the party and was thus politically vulnerable. Witke writes, "T'ien Hung was using devious tactics to prevent her from making contact with other [Communist Party] members who, in the future, could possibly shield her against government reprisal. Without those vital links, but already known in some circles to be involved in leftist operations, she was left to 'drift in dangerous waters.'

Inexorably, it became known that she was floundering without the protective environment of the Communist underground organization. Some people she once counted as friends now refused to open their doors to her. They realized that a person in her position was destined for arrest, in which event they also would suffer."[46]

Chiang Ch'ing's efforts to make contact with the party organization led to arrest and imprisonment. She managed to conceal her identity, but, like other women prisoners, she was subject to the whims of her jailers. She finally obtained her release through the auspices of the YMCA, with which she had been connected during her work with factory women. From 1935 until sometime after the Japanese invasion of North China, she remained in Shanghai. Then she made the trip to the Communist base area in Yenan, where she met and married Mao Tse-tung.

Women in the War Years

Following the 1927 counterrevolution, Mao Tse-tung and remnants of the Communist Party and the revolutionary army established a base area in the hinterlands of Kiangsi Province in central China. The rival Nationalists and Communists were finally brought together under the pressure of the imminent Japanese invasion, a development which hastened the outbreak of the war of resistance in 1937. By 1938, the Nationalists had retreated to Chungking, and the Communists made their base in Yenan. Chungking and Yenan drew thousands of patriotic educated youths. Liang Yen and Chiang Ch'ing were only two of many who retreated to western China with the Nationalist government or made the dangerous journey north to Yenan to join the Communists.

In the early 1940s, Tang Sheng, a college student, left her well-to-do Shanghai family to travel across Japanese lines to Chungking. *The Long Journey Home* is her account of that trip.[47] Written in England, where she went to continue her education, it recalls her awakening to a life previously unknown to her as a sheltered daughter in Shanghai.

Tang Sheng's political ideas were liberal democratic, reflecting her generation's middle-class concerns with women's rights. During her two-month journey to Chungking, she came into contact with the masses for the first time and developed a sincere respect for them. After living close to some boatmen while traveling by junk, Sheng wrote, "What actually impressed me was the good sense shown by the sailors, these men whom I had believed to be illiterate, dumb workers, but whom I found to be illiterate but not dumb. In fact they were very clever people."[48]

On one occasion, a hotel maid hid Sheng from a Japanese patrol. The maid fixed Sheng's hair so that she would look less like a college student and asked her if it was true that she could speak and write foreign languages. When the illiterate maid learned that Sheng knew both the Confucian classics and foreign science, she regarded Sheng with awe and astonishment. Sheng describes her feelings: "Her simple admiration made me very ashamed that I, who had never done anything to deserve it, had had so many years of schooling, while this good woman, who even in her late thirties yearned for some sort of education, had had none at all. I discovered that she did not think much of her goodness to me, 'I'm a woman and you are a young maiden. I have to save you from the evil hands of the Japs. Heaven forbid that a sweet innocent like you should suffer in their wicked hands.'"[49]

Sheng also describes people at work. One morning at an inn, she watched a family do their chores. "They started very early so as to get everything ready before they opened the shop after daybreak." The husband was grinding beans in the back room with a huge hand mill. In the front room, the wife built a fire. "I observed how expertly she washed the rice and put it to boil, and how quickly she swept the room and had it spick and span." Sheng was so impressed with simple household chores because she herself had never learned to do such things. The men in the group were shocked to learn that a woman could read foreign languages and knew Western science but knew nothing of the things that made a good wife. When they were traveling by junk, the men divided up the necessary tasks among themselves; Sheng felt left out until she found various miscellaneous tasks to do. "I got out some soap and washed handkerchiefs and vests in a corner on deck, then I opened my sewing-box and turned my berth into a mending ground where I stitched up torn sleeves and darned dirty socks for my companions, who most impolitely told me the truth when they saw my work and in one voice said: 'You need more practice . . . .'"[50]

Sheng also learned a great deal about how things worked in China at that time. In Tunchi, the party was able to get a telegram sent because one of them had an influential friend there. He quoted the popular saying: "One depends on the family while at home, but on friends when out in the world." Sheng's feelings were confused: "In a way I felt troubled over the way our telegram was sent[;] having condemned favouritism so heatedly I was ashamed that we too were profiting from special favours. I could no longer feel righteous against the bad habit, yet it would be silly if I had insisted that we should refuse the help."[51] Earlier on the trip, a stranger had traveled with and protected the party. After he left the group, Sheng learned that he was an important figure in Shanghai's underworld and had aided the group because of her father's underworld connections. Tu Yueh-sheng, godfather of the Green Gang, and Sheng's father had been elementary school classmates, and he had given the group leader some of Tu's calling cards to use if the party met robbers on their journey.

In normal times, as the daughter of a wealthy Shanghai family, Sheng would probably not have been allowed to make such a trip without a female chaperone. The unusual circumstance of the war caused many changes in Chinese habits and influenced Sheng's life in a liberal direction. In 1940, relations between young men and women still required propriety, but Japanese enemy aircraft occasioned "air raid romances," as Sheng observed. Although her journey afforded her a less circumscribed life, she was expected at her destination to resume the role of a protected wealthy Shanghai daughter. She described her indignation at a welcome banquet, where female decorum required her to sit passively and let her host select all her food, whether or not she liked the dishes.[52]

One cannot help wonder what Tang Sheng thought of Chungking society, since others who traveled there to resist the Japanese often found more self-aggrandizement than patriotic concern. Han Su-yin has described her life in Chungking in *Birdless Summer*, the third volume of her autobiographical history of China.[53] Su-yin met and married Pao, a Nationalist officer, and they returned to China in 1938. Like Tang Sheng, Su-yin was looking forward to doing her part in the war of resistance against Japan. Instead, she found corruption and totally unreformed attitudes toward women among her husband and his fellow officers.

The young men lived in an intensely competitive atmosphere. "Much gossip about higher ranking officers occupied Pao's time. . . . There was restlessness among the pushy young officers because 'the old ones glue their backsides to their chairs.' The competition for advancement was intense, covert, and perfidious." Their frustration was taken out on the women. Since many women who made the journey to Chungking were not the officers' first wives but were "temporary" wives or concubines, they were especially vulnerable. One woman suspected of infidelity was wrapped with barbed wire and left naked in a cage made of bamboo. Her family tried to save her, but they were not wealthy or influential enough. The officer wrote her off, saying, "She is only a borrowed wife . . . and she has thrown my face away."[54]

Su-yin was beaten by her husband, who lectured her on morality. She describes one such lesson: "The country could only be saved by the practice of ancient virtues. Chiang Kai-shek had said it. I must also learn these Ancient Virtues, and one of them was obedience. 'A woman of talent is not a virtuous woman.' I must be a 'virtuous wife and an exemplary mother.' And therefore I must never contradict anything he said. 'To contradict your husband is a sign of immorality.'" When Su-yin disagreed, he slapped her. She writes, "For the next three years I was to endure the growing terror, the increasing physical duress, which came in whirlwind fits. I learnt to wait out the hours of beastliness, counting, taking deep breaths, counting."[55] She found some happiness through contact with her father's family in Szechuan. She also found purpose by working as a midwife. When her husband was appointed a military attaché to the Chinese mission in England, she enrolled in medical school in London. He returned to China and was killed in the civil war; she remained in London and continued her studies.

Su-yin's work as a midwife brought her face to face with poor women. One day, a rickshaw coolie took her to a shack against the city wall, where his wife was giving birth. The husband sheltered the midwives from pouring rain and held his wife when the pain became strong. Because there was nothing for swaddling, the husband took off his trousers to wrap the infant. But the midwives knew he would need his trousers the next day for work. "We left a towel [although towels were precious] for them to wrap the baby in. They would have to sell the baby as soon as the cord dropped off; perhaps the mother would hire herself out as a wet nurse."[56]

A child thus sold might become a slave girl in a rich family, a prostitute, or a concubine. One of Su-yin's colleagues, Miss Ma, had been sold as a slave girl by her starving parents. Her mistress beat her with split bamboo and married her off to a widower. When she did not bear sons, he threatened to sell her to a brothel. She ran away and participated in the revolutionary movement between 1919 and 1927 but nearly starved to death under the counterrevolution. Eventually she became the companion to an old lady who was half-blind and paralyzed. Miss Ma carried the invalid about on her back, and the lady repaid her dutiful service by engaging a servant to teach her to read and write. She studied further to become a midwife, which took her 10 years because she had so little money.

In one sense, Miss Ma was lucky, because she was not directly subject to male authority. All women in old China, rich or poor, were subject to men, and even in childbirth, a woman was not safe from the whims of her master. Su-yin details some of the horror stories. In one case, a warlord "only two hours after his concubine had given birth insisted on intercourse with her. . . . We were called in haste, but she died bleeding to death."[57]

The women subject to such abuse, sold as slave girls, or relinquishing their baby daughters for sale were those who had escaped murder at birth. Female infanticide was common, because daughters were considered an economic liability in poor families since their labor was lost at marriage. Su-yin tells one story about a woman who had borne nine female children: "The first was alive, and also the third; but the second had been strangled at birth by the husband and so had the fifth and the sixth; the seventh had been born in a bad year, a year of famine when her belly skin stuck to her spine, and the husband had smashed her skull in with his axe; at the eighth female child the husband had been so angry that he had hurled it against a

wall; the ninth was a year old and had been given away to a neighbor."
Pregnant again, superstition had brought the wife to the hospital to give
birth. A neighbor had had a son at the hospital; perhaps she would too. She
didn't; her tenth child was also a girl.

In contrast to the corruption and deteriorating social conditions in
Nationalist China, a new society was evolving in the areas under Communist control. While women like Tang Sheng were slowly awakening to
the potential of ordinary people, the Communist Party was mobilizing the
masses against the Japanese and in the process politicizing China's peasantry. Many young intellectuals gravitated to Yenan because they were
impressed with the Communist record in resisting Japan; Kuo Tsin-yüan
was one of them.

In the early 1950s, Kuo Tsin-yüan was director of a flax mill in Harbin,
her hometown in Manchuria. There she was interviewed by Dymphna
Cusack, who published Tsin-yüan's story in *Chinese Women Speak*.[58]
Tsin-yüan's political odyssey began in 1935, while she was studying at
Peking University. Students from several universities staged a mass dem-
onstration and demanded that the Nationalist government resist Japanese
aggression. Known as the December Ninth Movement, it became a
nationwide protest. Tsin-yüan was marked as a student activist and expelled from the university. This ended her plans to become an engineer or
a doctor. She joined the Communist underground resistance in occupied
China. The work was very dangerous; "many women underground
workers were tortured and murdered." Tsin-yüan worked specifically to
mobilize village women. Women cared for the wounded and made uniforms and shoes for the troops. Older women tended the children, releas-
ing younger women for traditionally male jobs. Men were then able to
join the Red Army. Many younger women became transportation workers and scouts. Women also began to do field labor, which had previously
been almost exclusively a male job in north China. All villagers were on
the lookout for spies, "and usually the first to discover their presence were
the women and children who then arrested them and kept them till [the]
army units came." Tsin-yüan points out that these wartime activities
taught village women how "to organize themselves democratically."[59]

Eventually Tsin-yüan made her way to Yenan, where she became the
General Secretary for the Women's University. The curriculum included
weaving, spinning, infant care, and politics as well as regular academic
subjects. The object was to teach students how to provide for their daily
needs and contribute to the war effort while studying. Since the Communist base area was blockaded on all sides, its economy had to be
self-sufficient. Everyone in the base area was expected to do manual labor.
If students and teachers wanted buildings for the university, they had to
construct these themselves. Food production was an item of top priority.

"Each government worker and student had to reclaim a quarter of land and harvest a hundredweight of grain a year. Life came down to its simplest."[60]

Two years after the Japanese surrender in 1945, civil war broke out between the Communists and the Nationalists. Women continued their revolutionary work; among the most remarkable was Teng Ying-ch'ao (Madame Chou En-lai), about whom we know regrettably little. Helen Snow interviewed Ying-Ch'ao in Yenan and published her autobiography in *Women in Modern China*. Cusack's *Chinese Women Speak* contains a more detailed life history and brings Ying-ch'ao's life up to the early 1950s.[61]

Ying-ch'ao was born in 1903 in Nanning, Kuangsi. Her father died while she was young, and her mother had to provide for herself and her young child by nursing and teaching. Ying-ch'ao decided early that women should be trained to support themselves. As a university student in Tientsin, she participated in the May Fourth demonstrations and met Chou En-lai. They were married on his return from France in 1925. They had no marriage ceremony but in the presence of friends promised "to love, respect, help, encourage, console, be considerate of, have confidence in and understand each other" (these "Eight Mutuals" subsequently became the basis of marriages among all young revolutionaries). When Chiang Kai-shek turned on his Communist allies in 1927, the young couple began five years of work in the underground resistance. During this time, Ying-ch'ao lost at least one child; she never bore any surviving children.

Ying-ch'ao and Chou En-lai eventually made their way to the Kiangsi Soviet, and Ying-ch'ao became one of the 30 women to make the Long March with the First Front Army. She points out that "women acted as nurses and collected provisions from the peasants, explaining to them what we were, what we stood for."[62] During the Anti-Japanese War, she spent time in Yenan, the Soviet Union, and Chungking, where Chou En-lai was the liaison with the Nationalist government. When the civil war broke out, the Communists resumed the land reform movement. Ying-ch'ao helped organize the peasants' struggle against their landlords and the redistribution of confiscated land.

Ying-ch'ao speaks of the peasant women with respect: "I learnt how full of wisdom and understanding our peasant women are. . . . Our job wasn't easy: giving them a sense of *their* importance, and awareness of what we wanted *our* country to be. At first their role was underestimated by the peasants. 'The women know nothing but household affairs,' the men would say, explaining their absence from meetings to discuss land-distribution. Then the next day they would come back with a long face and say, 'I've changed my mind.' 'My mother says . . .' or, 'My wife says. . . .' So women were brought into the meetings and surprised

everybody by their knowledge of the land, and their practical wisdom."[63]
During the civil war period, women began to organize their struggle
against bad marriages. One of the best accounts of this movement is
"Goldflower's Story" in Jack Belden's *China Shakes the World*.[64]

In 1950, shortly after the People's Republic was established, the new
marriage law incorporated many demands of the women's movement.
Marriage was to be based on free choice and monogamous for both
partners. Women were also given the right of divorce, and they literally
flocked to the courts. Claude Roy recounts the story of a divorce trial in an
Anhwei village in his book *Into China*; the woman filing for divorce had
been married at 17 to a boy of nine. Another problem faced by the village
Women's Federation was that of a mother who wanted her son to sell the
six *mou* of land received during land reform so she could buy him a wife.[65]

The Swedish writer Jan Myrdal stayed for several months in the Shensi
village of Liulin in 1962, and his *Report from a Chinese Village* contains
some brief life histories of peasant women.[66] One was Chia Ying-lan, who
was 53 in 1962. At 16, her poor family had married her to a tinker-peddler
who smoked opium. When she was 22, her husband sold her and her
daughter to a slave dealer to pay for his opium. The dealer sold them to an
old farmer to whom Ying-lan bore a son. When the farmer died, she lied
about her age and said that she was 41. Believing she was too old to bear
children, the landlord did not force her to marry again.

In contrast, the story of a Liulin housewife of 25 reflects more recent
changes. She told Myrdal, "My husband does most of the work [on our
private plot] on his free days, but I help him. Every year we discuss what
we are going to grow there. In the older families, it is the husband alone
who decides, but my husband and I discuss everything together, because
we are a young couple."[67]

Dymphna Cusack provides a wider variety of life stories, including
those of a former lady-in-waiting to the empress-dowager, a capitalist's
wife, a former concubine, a lady with "lily feet," a woman mechanic, a
woman living in a former Nanking slum, and a prostitute. Before Liberation, Cusack tells us, brothels appeared to be well run and well regulated,
but in fact 90 percent of the licensed prostitutes suffered from venereal
disease. She continues, " 'Precious Pure One,' 'Flying Cloud,' and 'White
Jade' *were* always smiling. They knew what awaited them if they were
not, because 'public women' whether famous courtesans or worn-out
drudges, were virtually slaves who had no hope of escape except by death
or purchase as a concubine."[68]

One of these smiling women was Huang Wu-yu, who was working for
a knitting factory when Dymphna interviewed her. Wu-yu's mother had
died during a famine year, and her father had remarried. She continues her

story, "He didn't want two daughters around the place with his new wife, and a distant relative came to the village and she said she would look after me. I was then fourteen. She said she would take me to a town nearby where I could get work. Instead, she brought me straight to Peking, and when we got here she told me: 'I've got no more money and I've sold you to a brothel. . . .' Ours was a poor-class brothel and therefore it was harder to earn enough money to satisfy the brothel-keeper. We had to receive so many men that most of us were in bad health. Sometimes I was so sick that I simply couldn't receive men and then the brothel-keeper would rage and beat me with a bamboo cane and give me very little food. There were a dozen of us there and we lived in a state of constant terror, fearing that what happened to one of the girls when she was sick would happen to us, for we'd heard the lid of the coffin being nailed down while she was still alive."[69]

After Liberation, the police closed the brothel, and Wu-yu assumed that they would kill her since she was too sick to be put in prison. Instead, she received medical treatment and was sent to a literacy class. Later she got a job at the knitting factory, where she was a model worker. She explains, "More than half of the women who came from the brothels to this factory are model workers. They feel that this is such a small return for the new life given them."[70]

Wu-yu's life represents one of the more dramatic transformations of the twentieth century. A strength and determination emerge which belie the passive stereotype of lily-footed Chinese women. Some took drastic steps by breaking with their families, and many struggled to gain better working conditions and a more equitable society. In the process, they changed history.

Conclusion

Pre-1949 women struggled to enlarge their options for self-determination and meaningful work, a struggle that began with changing their role in the family. A crucial first step in their self-determination was the right to choose their own mate. Some were allowed more freedom than others within the patriarchal family of their childhood, but even those who ran away from home, like Chow Chung-cheng and Liang Yen, were eventually reconciled with their families.

These women also sought assistance outside the family. Political parties were one outstanding source of support for women's claims for independence. Hsiang Ching-yü, Chiang Ch'ing, and Teng Ying-ch'ao became members of the Chinese Communist Party, and all married fellow Communists. Thus the family and significant others merged to broaden the women's options more effectively. Wei Yu-hsiu supported the Nationalist party; Hsieh Ping-ying found support in the women's detachment of a northern expedition army.

The theme which runs clearly through all of these women's lives is a desire and willingness to use their talent, intelligence, and education in a productive way for either personal or collective goals. Perhaps the most poignant example of the personal rationale is Han Su-yin, whose work as a midwife helped her survive a brutal and unhappy marriage. For most of the women, their work and their efforts to achieve options for themselves merged into political and social goals. Chao Yang Bu-wei directed a school for the Women's Expeditionary Corps in order to gain a medical scholarship. Ting Ling used her writing skills to further the Communist struggle against the Japanese and to advance the cause of women. Underlying all the accounts is a desire for change—revolutionary or reformist, individual or societal. Only structural changes would address the problems that most Chinese women of the era faced. For them, private dilemmas were quickly transformed into public issues.

3

Spinster Sisterhoods
Jing Yih Sifu: Spinster-Domestic-Nun

By Andrea Sankar

Introduction

During the last half of the nineteenth century, the Canton delta of southern Kwangtung witnessed the formation of an unusual population of marriage-resisting spinsters, who chose life in a communal sisterhood over the formation of their own nuclear family.[1] "Sister" was the term used for all women who chose to take vows of spinsterhood rather than marry. Sisters and the sisterhood organizations they formed were of vital importance in the lives of the spinsters.

The sisterhoods and popular spinsterhood emerged from a unique combination of cultural, social, and economic factors. This life history traces the evolution of these sisterhoods from their early form as a culturally sanctioned, affective bond among adolescent girls which assisted the girls in resisting marriage, through several transformations created by changing economic and social demands, to its final adaptation in which the sisterhood takes on the guise of a family through the adoption of the religious kinship system of Buddhism, or Hsien-t'ien Ta Tao, a Taoist sect.

The emergence of popular spinsterhood and of the strong sisterhood associations was closely linked to, but not attributable to, the prosperous silk industry in the Canton delta. Women's labor was essential in silk filature. Their contribution became even more valuable after the mechanization of the silk industry in the latter half of the nineteenth century and the advent of wage labor for women.[2] When material and social conditions changed with the collapse of the silk industry in the late 1920s and the Japanese invasion in the 1930s, however, the spinsters were able to maintain their autonomous and singular life-style through the mutual support and assistance of the sisterhoods. The spinsters migrated from the delta to the cities of Canton, Hong Kong, Singapore, and Kuala Lumpur, where they found work as domestic servants. The sisterhoods helped their

51

members to make the transition more smoothly from industrial laborer to domestic servant by transforming themselves into part-guild, part-family associations. In this new form, the sisterhoods provided networks for migration, helped to train members in domestic skills, and assisted members in finding work. The sisterhoods freed the spinsters from the traditional servant's dependence on the paternalism of the master and allowed their members to choose employment which best suited their needs.

Separated from their cultural roots, the sisterhoods needed legitimation for their life-style. Many in Hong Kong and Singapore chose to join Buddhist or Taoist vegetarian halls (*jaii tohng*). Vegetarian halls offered stability, financial security, safety, companionship, and a religious justification for their way of life. Many larger sisterhoods (five or more members) preferred to join Buddhist vegetarian halls because their egalitarian organization harmonizes well with the sisterhood structure. Buddhist vegetarian halls are organized around the religious family system, which fortifies the bond of sisterhood by combining it with that of religious brotherhood. Membership in the religious family of a vegetarian hall gives a spinster a socially legitimate status within the religious community. It also helps to secure her financial future and old age care as well as her right to ancestor worship.

The bond of sisterhood endures. Organization and meaning have varied from place to place and changed over time, but the basic structure of the sisterhood survived when it was transplanted outside the original culture area that had nurtured it. Having taken a vow of celibacy eschewing marriage in their spinster ceremony, the women relied on the sisterhood, a highly committed yet flexible support system. The sisterhood provided the cultural, social, and economic support which had helped the women to resist marriage as adolescent girls. This bond continued to be strong and reliable in assisting the women as they moved into different contexts and led new lives.

Jing Yih Sifu: Spinster-Domestic-Nun

The bits and pieces which have come together to make up the biography of Jing Yih Sifu were told to me during several long stays between 1975 and 1976 at the vegetarian hall in Hong Kong belonging to her and her sisters.[3] The anecdotes were not told in the order in which they appear here. She related the different fragments and thoughts as we sat smoking together on the hall's roof during hot summer evenings or bundled in quilts on our platform beds on winter nights. She is 79 years old, a spinster and a Buddhist nun. In her youth, she participated in what I have called the practice of popular spinsterhood. This singular phenomenon of tens of thousands of women refusing to marry occurred in southern Kwangtung, primarily in the county of Shunte and the neighboring alluvial lands of the Nanhai and Panyü counties. She matured during this movement and participated in its most developed and articulated formulations. With the collapse of the silk industry, which had provided the financial basis for the movement, she and her sisters experienced a variety of transformations in their life-styles. She and many other spinsters finally came to live in the vegetarian halls of Hong Kong and Singapore.

I have arranged her story into chronological sequence. Footnotes and some commentary have been added to explain unfamiliar and important terms as well as to provide background on significant people in her life. She very much enjoyed telling me about herself and felt that she had lived a good, happy, and successful life. She was flattered that I took such an interest in her life. She felt that since neither of us had married and since we were both working women, I could understand her. She was only one of many spinsters whom I came to know, but I felt that she taught me more than any other single person. I hope I have done her justice. I call her Sifu because this is the term everyone used in the vegetarian hall.[4]

Early Life (1899–1922)

Sifu was born in 1899 in the village of Lungsan in Shunte county of Kwangtung. She had an older brother and a younger brother. Her father was a peasant who grew mulberry for silk production and fish farming. Some of his kinsmen were of the gentry class. Their village was prosperous. Few people migrated overseas, because there was enough work and enough money available at home. By the time Sifu was five years old, she too was involved in silk production.

"We were neither rich nor poor. My father had several *mou* of land. On these he raised mulberry bushes, whose leaves were fed to the silkworms. We also had a fish pond on our land. We fed the fish with the refuse from our silk production, such things as worms' excrement and dead pupae. Once a year my father drained the pond and caught all the fish. He sold these in the market. Then he dug out the rich silt at the bottom of the pond and spread it on the mulberry fields. We had six to eight mulberry harvests a year, and sometimes for the last harvest he would scoop out some mud from the pond to help feed the plants.

"My mother did not go out of the home to work. She helped my father pick the mulberry leaves and took care of the silkworms. This was a lot of work. She and my brothers and I would pick the mulberry leaves (later, when the worms got bigger and demanded more food, my father often had to purchase additional leaves in the leaf market). When the worms were very small, we had to cut up the leaves into little pieces and feed the worms several times a day. As they grew, we had to transfer them to different trays so there would be enough room for them. They made so much noise when they ate that you could hardly sleep, but the noise made us happy. When the worms got to be about 20 days old, the work became terribly hard. We fed them every two hours. We did not have to cut up the leaves into such small pieces, but the work was still hard. Everyone in the family worked to feed those hungry worms; we were all exhausted by the time they began to spin their cocoons.

"I began working in the production of silk when I was five years old. I was taught to identify the dead worms and to pick them out. Boys and girls did this work. When I was nine or ten, I began to help pick the mulberry leaves and to chop them up. Often I did this work with my sisters. It was easier to do the work with my sisters because we talked and laughed together. When there was no work to do in making silk, we gathered sticks and grass for fuel. This was for our families, but we could sell anything that was left over and keep the money.

"About this time I entered a girls' house association. All girls aged 10 to 40 in my area belonged to a girls' house association of their *seh* [particular surname group]. Unlike other areas of Shunte county, we did not have a residential girls' house. In our village, we met nightly at the house of a member (often it was my home) and talked and chatted. Sometimes we played cards. We would wait until all the members came before we would disband and return home for the night, even if it was late at night and we had to leave as soon as the tardiest member had arrived.[5]

"As I grew older, I learned more about the different processes of reeling silk. One was called *cho gaan*, which means pulling the threads from the cocoon, unwinding them, and hanging them in the breeze to dry. The other skill was *wuh si*, which involves spinning the strands of the cocoon into silk thread. Oh, the work was hard, but we young girls did not mind. Often we unwound the cocoons while sitting in our doorways so we could chat with one another. Not only the young girls (aged 12 to 18) but married women, old people, even fathers and brothers, helped.

"When my mother and I had finished spinning our cocoons into silk thread, my father took them to the market to sell. We lived near a silk market. Later, when I was working in the factory, men from the factory would go out to more distant villages and purchase their cocoons for the factory to spin. Sometimes farmers took their cocoons right to the factory to sell.

"When my labors at home were finished, I would often work for the neighbors. Since the silkworms and mulberry leaves matured at different rates, I was able to work for other families when my own family did not need much labor or when our family's crop was already mature. I was a very good worker, quiet and industrious. They paid me by the amount I spun each day. Sometimes people could not pay me right away. They had to wait until all their silk or fish had been sold. But this was all right with me. My neighbors were good, honest people, and I knew they would pay me when they had the money. There was so much work to do for my family and my neighbors that I did not need to work in the factories. I even made more money working for my neighbors than the factory paid because the factory paid a flat daily wage whereas my neighbors paid by weight.

"In my village, Lungsan, there were three silk filatures. The factory whistle blew at six-thirty in the morning to call people to work and again at six in the evening to send them home. Because my village was in a rich silk-growing area and the girls from families with land were busy helping at home or working for their neighbors, many of the girls who worked in the factories came from far away. Quite a few even came from Nanhai county. They lived in dormitories built by the factory owner. The girls who lived in the factory dormitories were much bolder than we village girls. They joked and flirted with the male overseers.

"One of my friends in the factory told me a funny story. She said that she and her sisters came to Shunte to work in the factories because they had heard there was a labor shortage and wages were high. On the road to our village, they met a group of girls from another area in Shunte who were headed to Nanhai in search of work!

"After my father died and there was less work to do for my family, I sometimes worked in the factories. I worked as a substitute for women who had returned home or were on leave. I moved about and did all sorts of work. There I learned a very skilled new job called *nau-si* [plaiting the silk threads]. Most of the silk from our area was sold to the United States. The silk threads had to be twisted and bundled in a very special way to fetch a high price. The thread came off the spinning machine in a long loop. The women had to twist the loop together into a plait as it came from the wheel. Then they had to fold it in half again and put one end through the other and make an "L." The neater the shape of the silk rolls, the higher the price they fetched, so this was considered skilled work.

"Factory work was hard. The lighting was bad, and many women had to quit because they were going blind. The water where the cocoons were soaked to loosen the threads was boiling hot, and reaching into the pots time after time, day after day, caused many women to get crippled hands. Some married women whose families owned little land worked in these factories. They brought their children with them, and these children were always getting in the way. Slightly older children, girls of eight and nine, worked as apprentices. They were paid nothing. If you agreed to let them stand by your machine and watch you work (and sometimes, of course, you taught them), they would help you and run errands, like getting your tea or lunch. I never had an apprentice because I worked in the factory only three or four weeks at a time.

"Even though I did not particularly enjoy working in the factories, many of my sisters did, especially those I met after I left the village. They liked the life among the girls living in the dormitories. Eight girls lived in one room, and usually these girls were all sisters, often from the same girls' house. After work they would go out together and stroll around the streets of the town. Sometimes they went to plays or operas; they were bold and free."

Marriage Resistance (1916–1922)

"Because I was such a hard, quiet worker, many men sought my hand in marriage. But in our area it was the custom for the women to resist marriage. The custom is very old. It was practiced by my grandmother and as many generations back as I know. However, there was a big difference between girls in my grandmother's time and girls in my time. In my grandmother's day, girls went through with the marriage ceremony but refused to reside with their husband's family after the marriage; this is called *mh lohk ga*. Instead they returned to live with their parents or in the girls' house. They visited their husbands on special feast days and for celebrations in his family. Then they returned home. They did not go to live with their husbands until they were pregnant. Usually this took five to six years because they saw their husbands at most a dozen days a year. Girls when I was young were much 'naughtier.' We refused to marry at all! Instead we took a *sou hei* [literally, self-comber] vow and became spinsters. We held a hair-combing ceremony and a dinner banquet that resembled the wedding ceremony, where an unmarried girl changes her hair from that of a maiden, with two long braids, to that of a woman, with hair knotted in a bun. In our ceremony, the spinster's hair is plaited in a single braid. This braid tells everyone that the woman has taken a vow of spinsterhood and celibacy.

"When I was 16, I did not yet understand that I must resist marriage. My parents tried to arrange a marriage for me then. They did not tell me about it because they were afraid I might run off like other girls I knew. Actually, I was too ignorant to do so at that time. Fortunately, the wedding was called off because we had a dispute over the size of the ceremony. The groom's family, which had to pay for the banquet, sought to limit the number of dinner tables and guests, while my family wanted to invite more people. Then my paternal aunt, who was a spinster, and my elder sisters in the girls' house told me I must resist marriage. If a girl is forced to marry before she is old enough to understand these things, then her sisters will not abandon her but will instead help and comfort her if her marriage is difficult. But if a girl willingly marries, then her sisters will despise her and she can never again turn to them for help.

"Sometimes girls understand at a very young age that they will resist marriage. To indicate this to their parents, they go out and get a job in the factories. Sister Yan Cheung did this when she was only 13 [Yan Cheung is discussed further, below].

"When I was 19, I had a dream that my mother was again trying to arrange a marriage for me. Fortunately I understood what I had to do and was prepared. I went before my parents and told them I knew of their plans. They were shocked because a young girl is not supposed to know these things, and they did not understand how I found out [it is likely that Sifu heard news of her impending marriage from the talk among the factory girls]. I told my parents that I refused to marry and that if they proceeded, they would have to repay the price of the wedding because I would never go to a husband. Then I said that to make me marry was like cutting off their arm, because I was such a valuable worker. They were silent for a long time, then my mother said, 'Very well, but you must promise to behave yourself.' I planned to hold my hair-combing ceremony as soon as I could save enough money, but my father died four months later and we all went into mourning for three years.

"During those three years, I was able to save a lot of money. I would save 100 *yüan* and put them in a coin roll. I bought gold jewelry, bracelets, and earrings. I also loaned my money to the neighbors for 20 *fen* interest a month. In our area, we had to pay all the rent in cash at the end of each year. Often the neighbors were short, so I helped them until the silk harvests came in. Sometimes people just needed money to buy furniture or rebuild their house. The silk industry was growing more and more prosperous, and wages continued to rise. When I first started working for neighbors in 1914, I earned 20 to 30 *fen* a day for *cho gaan*, which increased by 1922 to 50 or 60 *fen* a day. I could then earn 90 *fen* to a *yüan* a day for spinning, 80 *fen* for picking mulberry leaves, or 40 *fen* for gathering firewood and cutting grass. Labor was so much in demand that the factories had to give bonuses to keep people working. These bonuses were called *kahn gung*. For every 14 consecutive days you worked, you got two and a half days' extra pay. It probably sounds like a lot of people would have wanted to work in the factories because of this extra money. But this wasn't so. The work was very hard; you only got a half-hour break for lunch. Besides, a good spinner could earn as much or more working for her neighbors.

"After three years, the mourning period was over, and I had enough money to pay for my celibacy ceremony. My aunt (my father's sister) who was also a spinster told me that the hair-combing ceremony should be a very important occasion. 'If you have money,' she said, 'you should spend most of it on the ceremony because it is very important and only happens once in a girl's life.'

"The *sou hei* ceremony is similar to a marriage ceremony. Your friends and your relatives came. All the guests bring gifts. Mine was very grand; many people came. Many older spinster women came. People gave me gold rings and bracelets and household things like bedding and wash-basins. The banquet was held at my mother's home. There were nine dinner tables and nearly 100 guests. Two of the tables were occupied with guards and guns, because my relatives and the people in the village were rich. They worked hard and had their savings in gold, so the village needed many guards.

"I paid for the whole celebration except for the rice, which my mother gave. The banquet cost me 100 *yüan*. I bought a lot of long buns to distribute to the guests informing them of the celebrations. Women who are about to marry also distribute cakes to relatives and friends. After giving out the long buns, I went to the temple of Kuan Yin, the Goddess of Mercy, to worship. Every spinster must worship Kuan Yin because she is a woman and remained unwed. I went to the temple alone to worship for the hair-combing ceremony and brought a lot of food as offering to the goddess; mainly I gave her chicken backs. I also offered chicken backs and tea to my ancestors in the ancestor hall. After I returned home, I paid my respects to my mother and offered her a cup of tea. I would have done this for both my parents if my father had been alive. Then my *kai ma* [god-mother] dressed my hair as a married woman's.

"On the second night there was a banquet. My sisters stayed at home to play mah-jongg. Some sisters and cousins came from other villages; a few of these were sisters who had married. In the village where my cousins lived, they did not have to work. They were able to read; they had leisure time and could be educated. My cousins were rich because their father was in business. Their village was far away, and they had to come by boat and sedan chair. Some of my friends who had been married off to other villages returned for my ceremony. I gave each aunt, uncle, and sister 50 long buns.

"During the banquet, I had to eat chicken and duck eggs preserved in vinegar. The eggs were symbols of the need to control one's behavior. This is because the written character for yolk is also the word for king; he controls other people just as we spinsters have to control ourselves."

Life as a Spinster

"A father cannot allow his spinster daughter to live in her natal home, because after the celibacy ceremony she is considered 'married' and married women are forbidden to die at home. If she dies within her own kin group, then all the bad things that happen to her family will be blamed on her spirit. Instead, she can live only in a spinster house, and that house is the only place for her to die. A spinster must also build her spinster house in a different surname section from that of her family. In my village there were several surname sections.

"I built my spinster house together with several sisters. One was my godmother, one was her younger sister, and the other was my *kai neui* [goddaughter]. It took us a long time to get the spinster house built; it cost us 180 *yüan*. We bought bricks from a rich man who kept having to sell the bricks from his house to pay his gambling debts. We also got some building materials from another man who needed money and sold us an old building which we had to pull down ourselves. After we collected enough materials to build a house, we hired a group of builders and paid for a shed so they could rest and eat in the shade. Of course, they paid us rent for the shed. But they were too slow and could not finish the house. We hired another man, but he just ran off with our money. Finally we hired a third group. This time *we* paid the rent for the shed; it cost us 10 *yüan* a month. We ran out of money, and I had to borrow many *yüan* from my mother so we could finish. When we moved in, we had a joyful *yahp fo* [entering] ceremony. All our friends came to help us move our possessions in.

"We did not all live together for long. One of my sisters left for South Vietnam to work and only returned to the spinster house later to die. I was either out working in the silk filature or in Canton and rarely lived in the spinster house. When I became a nun in 1972, I decided that I was no longer the owner of the spinster house or of any home. Now one of my sisters is still living there. She is the younger sibling of my godmother, who died a few years ago. This sister lives in the spinster house with her nephew and his family. I brought the spirit of my godmother to this vegetarian hall and settled it here. I had to chant for a week to bring the spirit here."

Leaving the Village (1925–1926)

"By 1925, I was making almost one *yüan* a day working outside the family. I made only 20 *fen* a day, although when I started working in the factory, this increased fast—first to 30, then to 40, then 50 and then 60. There were three filatures in our town; each one employed 250 to 300 people. About two-thirds of the workers in every factory were women. The men were checkers, buyers, managers, and bosses.

"When I left in 1925, it seemed like the wealth of the silk industry would never cease to grow. I did not know it at the time, but I was fortunate that I left the village when I did. A few years later, the man who owned the three factories, who had always boasted that the river would run dry before his pockets would be empty, added a chemical to make his silk whiter and more desirable for the Americans. But this chemical made the material so coarse that no one would buy it. His factories shut down, and all the people were thrown out of work. The women streamed into Canton looking for work as servants, but jobs were difficult to find and wages were very low. Since I had left earlier, my wage was high and my job secure.

"It is easy to say this all now, but when I left I did not feel fortunate. I left in anger and with many bad feelings. I had quarreled with my mother about my brother, who handled the family business. He was her oldest son, and she spoiled him terribly. One day I found out that he pocketed 10 *yüan* each time he sold the silk I had spun. I would not have minded if he had been working too, but all he did was gamble and sit around the house while my younger brother and I had to work hard. Our silkworm house had become old and dilapidated, so we were building a new one which would be better to raise worms in. We had to borrow a lot of money to build this house, and I was working to pay off these debts. My mother refused to see my older brother's faults, so she and I quarreled and I left. I did not contact her for a year, and she was very worried. Eventually she saw that I was right and said that I was a very good person, especially because I continued to make so much money and to send some to her. But even before I quarreled with my mother, I had been thinking of leaving the village. I wanted to see other places, and the silk work was too demanding.

"In my village there were three or four women traders, called *seui haaks* [sailors], who came to sell notions. They traded between Canton and the nearby towns and villages. They sold different goods, depending on what was in demand. The traders also acted as guides. For money they would lead you from the countryside to the city and often help you find employment. There used to be many such people, but they disappeared in 1949 after the Liberation.

"In my village, I was friendly with one trader who sold buttons and thread. She knew of amah vacancies in Canton; she also knew that I was unhappy at home and willing to leave the village. She left me the name and address of a master in Canton who needed another servant. She knew about the opening because her son worked in the house as a messenger. After my fight with my mother, I found another trader to lead me to this house. When I arrived there, the master asked me how I knew of this opening and who recommended me. I told him about the trader, and he said this was good and let me have the job.

"I left my village at 26. At that time, only a few of my sisters had left because the work of silk production was very profitable and there was no need to leave. People migrate when they are attracted by foreign places, like nowadays many people want to go to Canada and Hong Kong. But very few from my village did this. There must be a link before people will migrate, like Guh Ma brought you here and you brought Yuk Sim. People do not migrate without first knowing someone in the place where they go."

Life as a Domestic Servant (1926–1942)

"In my first master's house, there were different sorts of servants—a cook, a houseboy, a messenger, and many maids. I applied to be a cook. The trader asked me if I could cook, but I was quite ignorant; I could only work in silk production. The family's cook and another servant taught me how to cook the different dishes and how to shop in the market. There were only three kinds of dishes—fish, meat, and vegetables. I could spend only 40 *fen* for each meal, and from this I had to prepare two sets of meals—one for the father and son and one for the rest of the household. For example, a dish of pork might cost 10 *fen*, with five *fen* for a vegetable dish and another five *fen* for condiments. That came to 40 *fen*. The father and son could not eat all their food and gave the remainder to the two male messengers. The ladies gave their leftovers to the maids.

"Usually I just cooked three dishes for each meal, but on special days I made 10. I was very lucky that the head servant who managed the house taught me how to shop well. That way I could make very tasty dishes for little money. I also had to iron the school uniforms of the son of the family.

"It was difficult to know whether you would get along well with a master. Even if a master was mean, you might be lucky and get along well with him. This is *yun faan* [good fate]. The master's mother was very mean and severe with the servants. The old woman would often try to check on the servants in the kitchen, but they would fool her and pour water on the floor, saying they were washing it and that she could not come in. I had *yun faan* with her. She always treated me well. She taught me the manners of being a servant. At first I did not know things like a servant must not sit in the master's presence. Whether one has a good master depends on one's destiny. I have had good luck and have always had kind masters as long as I have worked.

"I worked in Canton for five or six years, then we fled to Macao when the Japanese invaded Canton. In Macao, my master rented part of a vegetarian hall for us to live in. This was my first contact with such halls. I was a weak baby, so my mother had made me a goddaughter of Kuan Yin, the Goddess of Mercy. I went with my mother to the temples to worship Kuan Yin and the other gods when I was very young, but I had no great religious inclination. When I was working in Hong Kong, I visited the temples on Lantao Island but only for outings. I never thought of joining a vegetarian hall. My membership in the Macao hall at that time and my becoming a nun later were pure coincidence.

"When I lived in the Macao vegetarian hall of the Hsien-t'ien Ta Tao sect, there were Buddhist dieties worshipped there. I still did not feel religious, even though I saw the Buddha every day. But in that hall I met an important wealthy woman who had started her own hall in Hong Kong. She wore a huge belt with the deeds to all her property in it. But she was very weak and sweated a lot. When I had free time, I helped wipe off her sweat.

"Once this woman wanted to invite many of her friends and supporters to eat Chinese vegetarian cooking. My master's third wife recommended me as a good cook. I had to make 10 dishes. Everyone liked my cooking very much. The news spread that I was a very good vegetarian cook, and the rich lady asked me to join her hall in Hong Kong as the cook. I feared the Japanese who occupied Hong Kong then and thought living in a vegetarian hall would be safe. The woman told me to take the boat to Hong Kong and then to take a train, and after going through the [Shatin] tunnel I would find the hall. She said I could join without paying any money because I was such a good cook. The woman said that I would have to show the customs officers that I had enough Hong Kong money to support myself. My master was very kind and gave me enough money to make the trip and to satisfy the officers. But so many people were trying to get on the ships and escape the Japanese that I could not get on board. Although I was very young at the time and most people who joined such halls were old, I had really wanted to join. But I could not get to Hong Kong and so gave up the idea of joining. I did not think about it again for years.

"I returned to my master, but the situation was not good. The family was trying to take care of all the servants who had accompanied them, but prices were high and their money was running out. I heard that there were many servant jobs in Kwangsi. I told the master I wished to leave and he gave me money for the trip.

"I found a woman trader who traveled between Canton and Kwangsi, and she led me there. This trader had led many of my sisters and many other amahs from Macao to Kwangsi. My sisterhood in Macao did not decide to go to Kwangsi together. Everything was very confused then, so I just found my own trader to lead me there. On the way, I met many new sisters and even met one of my sisters from Macao. Many people had heard that there was a demand for amahs in Kwangsi. I found work immediately after arriving there.

"There was a demand for amahs in Kwangsi, because so many refugees from Kwangtung had fled there and because few of the local women could work as amahs. In Kwangtung there were many free, single women who could go other places seeking work. But in Kwangsi most of the women were married. They preferred to work in the markets so that they could return to their families at night. Moreover, women from Shunte district were famed for their skill as cooks and were much in demand. Most of the amahs I met in Kwangsi were from our area. The Kwangsi women were mainly engaged in selling fruit.

"My first job in Kwangsi was for a Kwangtung man who had moved there to escape the Japanese. He was a businessman. I worked for them for several years. It was a good job. But as the Japanese moved closer, he decided to move his family to Nanking. Of course, he wanted me to accompany the family, because good servants were hard to find, but I would not. I wanted first to return to Kwangtung and to see my family. However, at this time I was without savings. I had loaned all my savings to a friend who was a trader working between Kwangtung and Kwangsi. She had used the money to buy articles in Kwangtung and was selling them as she returned to Kwangsi. I knew it would take several months for her to return and repay me, so I began to look for another job. The temporary job I next found ended up lasting many years."

Working for the Barbers (1942–1946)

"I soon found a job working as a washerwoman in a shop of female barbers. There were 11 women barbers; the shop was owned by a man from Canton who had come there to avoid the Japanese. All the barbers had come with him from his shop in Canton. This was a barbershop for men. When I first began my job, there was a Kwangsi man working there as cook and water carrier, but he was a bad cook. The barbers hated his cooking. Once he was very late in coming to work, so I took the opportunity to show them how I could cook. I went out and bought some food and prepared it. For this dinner I made very elaborate dishes of peanuts and chopped pork. The barbers liked it so much that they asked me to be their cook. They could not fire the Kwangsi man, so the barbers collected extra money to pay me to be cook. From then on, I was cook as well as washerwoman. All the Kwangsi man had to do was to carry water, but he still got the same pay.

"I worked there for 10 years and really enjoyed it.[6] We all slept above the shop. There were 12 of us altogether, young and playful. At night we would sing songs and act out the parts of the Cantonese operas. If the barbers were very friendly with a certain customer, they would sometimes ask him to buy them all *dim sum* [small Chinese pastries], and I was always included in the treat. We were like one big family. I liked this life a lot. The female barbers were my friends, but they were not sisters. None of them had taken the *sou hei* vows. Even though most of them were over 30, they eventually planned to marry.

"When the war was over, the master sold his shop and returned to Canton. At this time I decided to return to Shunte. By then I was knowledgeable about traveling and was able to make the journey alone. My mother was very glad to see me when I returned home. I accompanied her on a journey to visit some of her relatives whom she had not seen in many years. Then I returned with her to our village. Back in the village, I met some of my old sisters from the girls' house. They were working in Hong Kong at the time. They said that there was a great need for servants in Hong Kong and that I should accompany them there. I decided to return with them and said goodbye to my mother. This was the last time I saw her. By then we had settled our differences. She realized how she had spoiled my older brother and that he had turned out to be a 'no-good.' She was very proud of me. I continued to send her money until she died. After I became a nun, I brought her soul to this vegetarian hall by chanting."

Hong Kong (1946–1966)

"When I first arrived in Hong Kong, I stayed with some of my sisters from Shunte who lived in Happy Valley and worked for famous movie stars. In this way I was able to meet people. Soon my sisters found me a job working for a family named Yuh. In Canton, the Yuhs had lived very close to the family for whom I once worked. Two of my sisters also once worked for the Yuh family. I visited there often, and I soon came to know everyone in the household. In Hong Kong, no members of the old Canton sisterhood were working for the family, but their former servants still visited them. They recommended me as a cook, and the family was delighted to have me.

"The head of the household had two wives. There were four daughters of the first wife, and each one had her separate servant. The second wife had a son. The second wife was Japanese, and when her husband brought her to his home in Canton, she was very upset to learn that he was already married. She insisted that she have special quarters. These rooms were called the Japanese rooms. She was very kind to me. While I was working for this family, one of the daughters married. A Chinese man came from the United States looking for a bride. The master knew the man and arranged a match with his second daughter. The wedding was very grand. By then I was considered part of the family, and I appeared in many of the wedding pictures. Several of the other children moved to the United States, and eventually the master and mistress moved there too. The old grandmother is still living in Hong Kong. Often the grandchildren send the grandmother packages of cigarettes or deertail medicine. When this happens, the grandmother contacts me and asks me to share these with her.

"When the family left Hong Kong, the Japanese wife helped me to find my next job. Her son was a member of the Kuomintang. Several of his Kuomintang friends were working in Hong Kong, and they needed a cook. The Japanese wife introduced me to these men. All five of them took me out to a restaurant to discuss the job and the pay. I worked for them for several years, cooking and washing. They were not there much, so I had little work to do and spent a lot of time listening to the radio. It turned out that these men were spies for the Kuomintang. Late one night, I awoke to find them burning all the papers in the house. After they did this, they left and I never saw them again. The next morning the police came and searched the house. They did not bother me. I was left all alone, so I decided to leave.

"During the time I was visiting my mother in Shunte, I had gotten back in contact with some of my sisters with whom I had built the spinster house. One of these sisters, my goddaughter, also had a job in Hong Kong. She and I and my niece, who was also a spinster working in Hong Kong, decided to establish a spinster house there. Life in China was very unsettled then, and I was not sure that I wanted to retire there. Together the three of us purchased a small stone house in Wong Tai Sin [Hong Kong]. After the Kuomintang men disappeared, I decided it was time to retire, so I moved to this house and bought some pigs to raise.

"Soon after I moved there, I discovered the treachery of my goddaughter! When we had bought the house, she had offered to register the deed because she knew more about Hong Kong and said it was a difficult thing to do. I discovered she had put only her name on the deed. There was nothing I could do. I had lost all my savings except my gold jewelry. She informed me of what she had done and that she was the sole owner of the house soon after I moved in. I was very upset. I refused to move out until the pigs I had purchased were fully grown and I had sold them.

"I often visited the market in Wong Tai Sin, and there I sometimes met sisters and friends. One day I met an old friend, King Guh.[7] We had been in a sisterhood together in Canton before the Japanese war. King Guh took me to a celebration at her Seven Sisters Club in Wong Tai Sin.[8] There I met Ah Saam. I became very friendly with Ah Saam, and she invited me often to celebrations at her house in Wong Tai Sin. On several occasions I acted as cook. Once Ah Saam said to me, 'My sifu left me a vegetarian hall. It is small, and we are trying to recruit new members so we might expand it. Would you like to be the cook?' At that time I said that I was not interested.

"Celebrations at her Wong Tai Sin house were great fun. Often we would stay up all night playing mah-jongg, talking, and eating. Once we were so noisy that the neighbors called the police! Often a member would bring pillows and blankets from her master's house if the family was away. If the servant had been with the family for a long time, the master did not mind this.

"One day in the market, I met Ah Cheung, one of the barbers from Kwangsi. She said that she had her own barbershop and that several of the old barbers from Kwangsi worked there. This shop had been owned by

the same man who owned the shop in Kwangsi. But he had run into debt
and had had to sell the shop. So the barbers got together and collectively
purchased it. She suggested that I return to work for them. I told her that I
would have to wait until my pigs were slaughtered. Within a few months,
I was back working for the barbers.

"I worked there for several years and might still be working there if it
had not been for some mysterious coincidences and an attempt on my life.
Even after my goddaughter had cheated me, I still saw her occasionally.
One day she came to visit me at the barbershop. She wanted to borrow
money from me. Can you imagine? Of course I said no. She became
furious and screamed at me. Then she left. Shortly after she left, I took a
drink from the glass of water which had been sitting in front of me. It
tasted very bitter, and I spat it out. Then I went out to do some shopping.
When I returned, a woman peddler said that during my absence my
goddaughter had returned and had told the peddler that I was dead and
that she was coming to take care of the body and get her inheritance. The
peddler said that she came running out of the house when she found no
body. After that, I kept all my jewelry in a safe-deposit box in the bank.
But I no longer felt very safe. At that time I was 59, and my goddaughter
had predicted that I would die when I was 59. Thus I was able to avoid
death. She does not know that I have become a nun. All the members of
the vegetarian hall know of this incident, and if my goddaughter comes
looking for me, they will say they do not know such a person. That is true
because now I am a nun, I am no longer the same person.

"After this incident, I began to think more seriously about Ah Saam's
offer to join her vegetarian hall. Quietly I began making plans to join the
hall. I told no one what my intentions were. One day something very
mysterious happened. A stranger came into the barbershop. After he had
his haircut, he announced that he was a fortune teller and that he would tell
everyone's fortune for free. Just as he was finishing, I was serving tea, and
he said that he would tell my fortune also. As soon as he looked at me, he
said, 'I can tell that you are making plans, and they are good.' Everyone
asked me what this meant, and then I told them that I was leaving for the
vegetarian hall. I believe that this man must have been a bodhisattva in
disguise."

Entering the Yan Gap Vegetarian Hall (1957)

"When I decided to become a member of the Yan Gap vegetarian hall,
Ah Saam and the other successor, Ah Gwong, said I could enter without
paying the membership fee of HK $6,000 because I was to be cook and
manager. But I did not feel easy with this offer, so I decided to consult the
Buddha. I did this by tossing the *bok*—two wooden objects, each with a
flat and curved side. After three throws, the combination of flat and

curved sides that fall gives the answer to the question. The answer was that I should pay, so I did.

"Ah Saam and Ah Gwong decided to expand the vegetarian hall by using the members' entrance fees plus $10,000 left by the founder. They built a new addition and the ancestor tablet room, the kitchen, the bathroom, and an additional bathroom outside. When the work was completed, we were over HK $30,000 in debt.

"I bought much of the furniture for the common rooms, Ah Saam's masters donated all the chairs, and the mistress of another member gave three white chests. Everyone supplied her own bed and dresser. We had all the furniture shipped to Tai Po, a port located a quarter of a mile away. Then we paid two men HK $400 to bring the furniture here by cart.

"To begin with, only four of us—Ah Muk, Luhk Guh, Man Man Guh, and I—lived here. The rest of the members still kept their jobs and only visited here for special occasions and vacations. Later, when we were concerned about the debt, we asked Ling Guy [a member of the Chungking sisterhood who often visited there] to become a member.

"Once the new building was completed, it was very beautiful and many people, especially Ling Yeung and Man Kai, coveted it.[9] Ling Yeung had introduced Ah Saam and Ah Gwong, who was her goddaughter, to the founder of the vegetarian hall. Ling Yeung did not have enough money to build her own. Knowing that neither Ah Saam nor Ah Gwong ever wanted to become a nun, she hoped to fill the role of manager of the hall after the founder was dead. She did not count on Ah Saam's recruiting me to become cook and manager. Angered at my presence, she began spreading rumors that I had not contributed any money to the hall and that I was stealing money from it. I responded by saying that no one was paying rent and that there was little income, so what could I steal? But they said I could have stolen money from the building fund. It was difficult to fight back at the time because we were so much in debt. Now, however, I am no longer afraid. Our debts have all been repaid. In fact, I now welcome the public ridicule of Ling Yeung and her group, because it allows us to bring out the story of what they tried to do, which is much better than leaving it all to rumors.

"At Yan Gap vegetarian hall, there are two groups, Ah Saam's and Ah Gwong's. Ah Saam was the original successor of the founder, so her group is the stronger. In fact, Ah Gwong agreed to become co-successor only when Ah Saam said that her responsibility was too great. Also, Ah Saam recruited all the members of her group herself, and they are all very committed to Yan Gap. But as for Ah Gwong, her group is really controlled by Ling Yeung, and all are related to Ling Yeung in some way.

"Ling Yeung had planned to take over Yan Gap by becoming manager of the hall when help was needed. When they hired me instead, Ling

Yeung began to plot with Man Man Guh to take over the hall. Man Man Guh was the natural-born sister of the founder. Man Man Guh was living at Yan Gap when the founder died and even though she was quite rich, she never paid her sister, the founder, any money to live there. Some nuns at Ling Faht Jih monastery even said that Man Man Guh stole from her sister. I was very unhappy when I first moved into Yan Gap and discovered that Man Man Guh was aligning with Ling Yeung to try to drive me out of the hall. They spread terrible rumors, saying that I was a bad cook and manager and that I had a mean face—that indicated I had a bad destiny. They also said that Yan Gap had bad *feng shui* [geomancy] and urged worshippers not to visit us. At one point, Man Man Guh even decided to shave her head and become a nun in order to strengthen her claim as successor to the founder, her sister, and get Yan Gap.[10]

"I realized that it is best to have an ordained nun as manager of a vegetarian hall, because she then can send out the red subscription books for funds for the hall, light incense, and perform other rites to earn money. The government permits ordained nuns and people who live with them to circulate the red books, and people who give money have their names written down so that it can be read to the Buddha. All the members and their friends, and even people like you, volunteer to carry these books; even people who are not believers contribute because it is a good deed. Some give only a few dollars, others give hundreds. Usually each book collects about HK $500. No one asked me to become a nun, but they were glad when I made this decision myself.

"When I joined Yan Gap, all the members had a posthumous *gwai yih* [conversion ceremony] and took the founder as their official teacher, although actually only Ah Saam and Ah Gwong had ever met her. Yan Cheung, one of the head nuns at the Ling Faht Jih monastery, acted as the replacement for the founder and presided at my head-shaving ceremony. I shaved most of my hair myself on the terrace of our hall, and then Yan Chueng shaved the last bit off in the ancestor tablet room.[11]

"I took my vows to become ordained in 1969. This ceremony, called *sau gaai*, is held every three years at a large monastery, and novices and initiates come from all over southeast Asia to the largest monastery, called Bou Maahn Jih, for ordination. In 1969, over 1,000 people came to receive the vow from Faht Ho, who was very old. The monastery was so crowded with friends, relatives, and spectators that we could not find a place to sleep. Fortunately, Ling Guh had a sister at one of the neighboring vegetarian halls, so all of us from Yan Gap could sleep there.

"You have to study for 20 days before the ordination ceremony. During this time you live at the monastery. Monks and nuns teach the classes, and you learn all the rules of being part of a Sangha [Buddhist monastic order]—how to step into a room, how to hold your bowl and chopsticks while eating, how to dress, how to talk, and how to walk. When we first arrived, we were assigned a certain place in turn, and we had to walk in order all the time.

"On the day of the ordination ceremony you have small scars burned on your head; this is called *yin heung*. The head monk paints dots on your head with black ink the night before. Many women feared the pain of the burning so much that they cried the entire night. The next morning, the burning ceremony is performed by high-ranking monks. Two monks hold your head and place some fast-burning incense on the painted spots. This is then lighted and allowed to burn down, leaving a permanent mark. Afterwards the initiates run outside to some cool place, because their heads feel very hot. Some people's heads swell up, and sometimes the burning is done sloppily and you get more than nine dots, or you get them in the wrong place.

"Altogether the 20 days at Bou Maahn Jih monastery cost me about HK $800. The initiates were divided into 12 groups, and each group was responsible for preparing a vegetarian meal and inviting others to eat it. I had to help pay for that meal, contribute to a special worship for the Buddha, and do a chanting to calm the spirits of the dead before the ordination ceremony.

"After the ordination, I invited many people from Ling Faht Jih monastery and the vegetarian hall in our area to eat a vegetarian banquet in my honor. I gave Ling Faht Jih monastery $500 to prepare tables of vegetarian food for the members, my friends, and my sisters."

A Nun (1969–present)

"When I became a nun and legitimate successor, my position as manager of Yan Gap vegetarian hall was more secure; however, Ling Yeung and her group continued to criticize me. Ah Saam suggested that if they pressed me too hard, I should reply, 'Yes, you can pay back the money that I invested in the hall, but I have shaved off my hair. Can you give me back my hair? I also invited all those people to eat a vegetarian meal; can you invite them all back, many of whom are now dead?' Of course not!

"We were still HK $30,000 in debt when I became ordained, and it was difficult for our hall to be respectable and refute the rumors of others. But after my ordination, I purchased all the religious instruments necessary to worship the Buddha and then immediately began doing services to make money. Now that an ordained nun lives at Yan Gap vegetarian hall, more visitors and worshippers come. But most important, we can now give out the red subscription books.

"I also cleared our spiritual debt. Before the founder died, she vowed to recite 10,000 sutras for the well-being and prosperity of the hall, but she died before she was able to do so. With the help of a very wise and pious nun, I was able to fulfill the founder's debt to the Buddha and within a year recite all 10,000 sutras. Now I am truly her successor.

"With my help and some additional contributions from other members, we were able to pay off our construction debt within a few years. We were low-key about this. Ah Saam had a plan to bring the plotters into the open and vindicate us. Man Man Guh and the others continued to ask Ah Saam how much money we owed, and Ah Saam kept replying that we still owed HK $30,000, even after the debt was fully paid off. This encouraged the ambition of the plotters, who tried to raise the HK $30,000. Saying that they only wanted to help, Man Man Guh offered Ah Saam the HK $30,000 if she would turn over the management to them. They even planned to change the name to Kai Gap in honor of the nun Man Kai, who is Ling Yeung's lover, which clearly revealed their base intentions to all. Shortly after this, Man Man Guh died of cancer, but Ling Yeung continued to visit here. Finally, a big fight between Ling Yeung and one of our sisters made Ling Yeung cease her visits. She no longer bothers us.

"Since I have become a nun, I spend most of my time here. During the winter, when there are few festivals or visitors, I go to town to visit my sisters who live there. Some are sisters from Shunte, some from Canton, and others from Macao. Many of them go to the big March festival for the vegetarian halls. I also see the barbers. Many of them are married now or have broken up into smaller groups and formed their own shops.

"Everything I have belongs to Yan Gap. After I die, all my savings will go to the hall. I belong to a death benefit club for the people who live in the vegetarian halls and monasteries on Lantao Island. Initially I invested HK $1,000, but within three years I have made HK $5,000, which will go to Yan Gap.

"It is good to live in a vegetarian hall. Here is a place where you can depend on your sisters and where you won't be too lonely when you are old. Mainly, old people join a hall because they wish companionship and support. Even if you have property, the walls and bricks can't serve you tea or give you what you need. Moreover, here you have meditation and training to reach the self-realization that will relieve your grief in the future life."

4

Village Wives

Granny Cheung: Peasant

By Deborah Davis-Friedmann

Introduction

Lam Mei-ying is a woman of 70. I met her in Hong Kong in 1975, the year after she and her husband left China. They came from a small village in Maoming, a mountainous county of southeastern Kwangtung. Although their village is not poor by national standards, in contrast to the rich delta area of the province, such as Shunte and Nanhai counties, Maoming is considered economically depressed. Before 1949, many of its poorest families had sent men to Southeast Asia, first to toil as laborers on Malay rubber plantations, later to join small commercial enterprises owned or managed by kinsmen. Through emigration, Mei-ying and her husband similarly sought to improve their livelihood.

Mei-ying recalled in several interviews her hard life in old age and the continuous labor she and her kinsmen performed.[1] Her accounts of her work in the mountainous village are not substantially different from those of elderly heroines of contemporary fiction or of the old model workers praised in the Chinese press of the period. I believe that her memories of some 60 years of hard physical labor speak for more than just one elderly woman from an isolated village and address the experiences of an entire generation of women working in the countryside.

Granny Cheung: Peasant

"My surname is Lam; my full name is Lam Mei-ying. Now, however, I am usually called Ah-lam or Granny Cheung. I was born around 1905 in a small hamlet about an hour's walk from the village of my present husband. I am the eldest daughter and second child. I had one older brother, Sai-kok, one younger brother, Sai-yeung, and a younger sister, Mei-lai. There was nothing special about my home village. It was small and had no roads, stores, crafts, or industries. My own family was poor and short-handed for farming.

71

"When I was about 12, a cousin helped my father leave our village. He went to Southeast Asia to work on a rubber plantation. He told us that he would return a rich man and that before I married he would build a new house. But he died a few months later. My mother was 38. The next year, my older brother Sai-kok also left. He did well—he married, had six sons, and became the owner of a fish pond. My mother couldn't write, my younger brother couldn't write, and I can't write. So it has been very difficult for us to keep contact with him. After Sai-kok left, my mother, brother, sister, and I rented small pieces of land from a fellow clansman. We grew a little rice on the lowland and sweet potatoes on the hillside. As long as my brother could work full-time, we stayed out of debt.

"When I was almost 20, my mother's sister came to visit. She said she knew a family in the next village who would pay 110 *catties* of rice if my mother would allow me to marry their son. My mother agreed, so I was married for one *picul* of unhusked grain. After I married, I was no longer able to help her. A year later, my younger sister was also married for 110 *catties* of rice. With the two *piculs* of grain, my mother got a wife for my younger brother. I didn't live very far from my mother, but after the marriage of my younger brother, I rarely saw any of my own family. Even at festivals, we were all too busy with our husbands' families.

"When I was first married, life wasn't too bad. But five years later, our poverty had become really bitter. My first husband and I had several children, but only one lived past four years of age. My sister had an even worse time. Her husband's family was very poor, and she died without leaving a single child.

"Right before the end of the Japanese war, my first husband died. I had just given birth to another girl. She survived, and the two of us continued to share a household with my husband's mother. It was truly a difficult life. Three women and no men!

"In 1952, a go-between proposed that I marry again. This marriage was to my present husband. He had been living in Malaysia, where he had a wife and sons. He returned to China in 1949 because his mother was dying. After he had arranged the funeral, he could no longer return to his family in Malaysia, so he wanted to marry again. It was a simple affair because we were not young, and our parents were not concerned. Before I moved to the village of my new husband, I arranged a marriage for my little girl. She was seven years old. The household had many sons, and she was to become the wife to one of them. Actually, I later heard that they didn't marry her to their own son but found another husband instead. I once saw her oldest child, but I've never seen her other children. After all, I am not her mother any more; her first mother-in-law is.

"Soon after my second marriage, I had a child, again a girl. She is our only child. We lived together in a single room in a terrace of three houses that had been built by my husband's father after his return from Southeast Asia in 1900. Next to us lived the families of my husband's nephews, sons of his second older brother. My husband's oldest brother never married; he died in Canton while waiting for a ship to Malaysia. The second older one, however, made it to Malaysia and stayed there eight years. He returned to marry and raise a family in the village. When I first moved to the village, he had already died, and his wife was living with her oldest son, my husband's oldest nephew. The youngest son and his family lived in the house beside ours. But we supported ourselves entirely. My daughter could work very hard. She never went to school but always stayed with us to work. She could carry heavy loads, had very strong legs, and was good with the pigs.

"In 1970, a woman go-between came from a nearby village and asked if our daughter would marry the son of a family she knew. We agreed and our daughter agreed, so it was arranged. His family gave us 50 *yüan*, the price of one pig, and sent some special wedding cakes as a present. It was quite old-fashioned, I guess. We played the game of teasing the bride, and we had a dinner for about 30 kinsmen.

"After she left, we couldn't manage to raise more than one pig. But since she was married, we didn't have as many expenses. We worked just as we did when we were middle-aged, and except for some really heavy work or sudden illness, we didn't need any help at all. Actually, even when we were sick, we cared for ourselves. Since 1970, our village has had a barefoot doctor and a cooperative health plan. Anyone can join, old or young, but we didn't bother. We could make the same herb teas and poultices as the doctor, and it didn't cost us even one *fen*!

"Our work was quite ordinary. Every morning, we would rise at dawn and go to our assigned tasks in the fields. I am still quite strong. I have lived through several difficult childbirths, famines, and hard winters. But one of my legs is shorter than the other, so I can't work as well as some people. Mostly I did weeding and cultivating. I received about the same number of work points as a school-age girl. After I worked for two hours, I would leave the fields and go home to start a fire and cook breakfast. My husband came back to eat, then we would return to work. At noon we stopped, ate lunch, and rested for an hour. After our rest, we went back to the fields. In winter, I worked only six hours, but in the busy seasons, we often went out for 10 or 12 hours every day.

"When our collective farming was finished, we cultivated our private plot, cared for the pig, and gathered mountain grass for fuel. It took a lot of time to feed that pig! First we had to gather the pig's vegetables and chop them. We needed lots of grass from the hillside to fire the stove and to cook the slop. But it wasn't a hard job, and our pig was always one of the best. Besides, every month we got work points for the manure. When the pig was small, we got only 30 work points, about what I earned for one week's work, but after two months, we got 40 points and after three months 50 points.

"My husband knows how to weave the bamboo baskets we used for storing and transporting rice. It pays quite well, and he could do it at night or in slack seasons. Many old people in our village have this skill. Now they are teaching it to young men and women. I myself don't have any special skill. I never learned to read, or sew, or do a craft. My clothes are quite simple—nothing special at all.

"We also had several chickens. They were easy to care for. My husband didn't even have to bother with them. Sometimes we sold the eggs. Often we traded them for salt. Once or twice a week, we ate an egg. Usually we ate rice boiled with dried sweet potato and salted vegetables. At festivals, we would have pork or chicken and fried vegetables. It's not like some places where they use oil every meal. In our village, we use oil only occasionally. But we need salt every day. That's why we needed the chickens. Two old people like us don't need eggs or meat, but we can't live without salt.

"Since the Cultural Revolution, life has been both different and the same. We now have our own barefoot doctor and everyone can see him for just 10 *fen*. Our house also has an electric light bulb and one of our nephews is a tractor driver. But actually there were no big changes. There are no landlords in our production team. One of the clansmen of a landlord is even a team cadre, and the head of our brigade has been the same since 1958. No outside youngsters are sent from the city to settle. So our village is rather calm, not at all like the rumpus that has been going on in some places. In fact, the two most exciting things that happened to me since the Cultural Revolution were my mother's ninety-first birthday in 1972 and her funeral in 1973.

"Until her death, my mother lived with my younger brother, his wife, their eldest son and daughter-in-law, and five great-grandchildren. My mother was the oldest person in the commune and in the entire county. So when she was 91, we held a big feast. I brought pork, chicken, and rice as presents. Even the production team contributed food. Altogether, I think my brother spent 100 *yüan*, twice what we paid for our daughter's wedding.

"Soon after her birthday, my mother died. She died after a quarrel with her daughter-in-law. My mother ate three eggs every day, but one day one of the great-grandsons ran off with one of her eggs and ate it. She was furious. She grabbed him and hit him hard in the face. His grandmother, my mother's daughter-in-law, tried to calm my mother down. She said that she would give my mother another egg and to ignore the little boy. But my mother refused. Instead she rushed out of the house and began to wash some old clothes at the edge of the river. She was really old, and for several years someone else had always done her washing for her. She slipped on a rock and hit her head. A neighbor saw her fall and brought her home. My brother tried and tried to get her to take a special medicine he had bought. But she refused. She wouldn't even open her mouth. For three days, she lay in bed. She wouldn't eat or drink. Then she died.

"The funeral was even more elaborate than her birthday. She was the oldest person in the entire commune. Nobody else was even 80, so the cadres allowed us to have a traditional funeral. After all, it might be the very last one in the county. My brother hired someone to build a coffin—a really big, heavy one. He didn't need to buy any wood because my mother had already gotten the wood herself. For many years, she had cultivated a tall pine tree. When she was about 75, she had it cut down and kept the wood. She had used some of it for her bed.

"We bought special funeral clothes and gave a big feast. I brought food but gave no money; daughters do not provide money for the funerals of their own parents. My brother and my mother paid for it. Yes, before she died, my mother had saved a lot of rice in jars under her bed, so in a way she did pay for her own funeral.

"When my husband and I first married, we applied to leave China and go to Malaysia. Nothing came of it. Occasionally his sons there sent us money, but since 1966 we had received nothing. We depended solely on ourselves. We didn't need any help. Sometimes, though, we wondered who would care for us if both of us got very sick and couldn't work. We had a good house and the team would guarantee us food and clothes, but we did worry about sickness. We finally asked a cadre to write to the sons in Malaysia and ask if we could come join them. We heard nothing, but one day a cadre came from the commune and said we could go to Hong Kong. Everyone was happy for us and helped us get to the bus. Once we left our county, other cadres helped us all the way to the train for Hong Kong. Now we must wait for my husband's sons to write and tell us when to come."

5

Hakka Women

Great-Aunt Yeung: A Hakka Wage Laborer

By Elizabeth L. Johnson

Introduction

The Hakka are one of a number of distinct Chinese speech groups; they have a long history of gradual migration from north to south China, finally settling in the provinces of Kwangtung, Kwangsi, Fukien, Kiangsi, and Szechuan.[1] Because of their relatively late arrival in these areas, they became known as the "guest families," or Hakka. Even after reaching the limits of settlement within China, it was common for individual men to work outside their home district, becoming itinerants, urban workers, or temporary migrants overseas.[2] Such migration was not limited to the Hakka but seems to have been particularly characteristic of them, perhaps because the generally poorer lands which they had settled did not offer them an adequate living.[3] The fact that able-bodied men were often away from home meant that in many cases women had to assume the full burden of farm work to provide for their families.

Hakka women are no different than most Chinese women throughout history in that their lives are passed in obscurity, with little record of how they individually live, work, and die. As a group, however, they have a certain reputation which has set them apart from others. They have unbound feet and therefore some freedom to move beyond their houses and courtyards, and they are able to work to support themselves. Other Chinese women share these characteristics to some degree,[4] but the Hakka are particularly known for their ability to engage in hard work.

The economic role of Hakka women has been studied in detail by only one other anthropologist, Myron Cohen. In the course of his research on a Taiwanese village, he examined women's economic rights and responsibilities.[5] In my research on a Hakka village in the New Territories of Hong Kong,[6] I was concerned with women's roles in household and outside work and with defining women's economic rights with respect to their household budgets and property management. As part of this re-

76

search, I recorded the life histories of several older village women. One of them, Great-Aunt Yeung, is typical of many village women. The ways in which her life is atypical are noted.

Great-Aunt Yeung lives in Kwan Mun Hau, one of approximately 20 Hakka villages in Tsuen Wan District. Kwan Mun Hau and some of the other villages are now entirely surrounded by the rapidly growing city of Tsuen Wan, with a population of over 500,000, but Yeung's story takes us back to the period before World War II, when the development of the area was just beginning.[7] The Japanese occupation of Hong Kong (December 1940–August 1945) marked a major transition in the lives of the villagers. Before that time, they, and the approximately 2,000 other Tsuen Wan natives, were virtually the only inhabitants of the narrow band of lowland between the highest mountain in Hong Kong and the sea. Within a few years after the end of the war, they were engulfed by waves of immigrants, primarily Cantonese speakers, from the nearby areas of China. Before the occupation, the men made their living by farming, fishing, cutting firewood, working in small businesses, and in some cases working overseas. Women worked in agriculture, grew rice and vegetables, raised pigs, and earned wages carrying loads with poles. In the 1930s, a few industries had been established, and these offered more regular employment to both men and women, although for the most part the work available was still heavy manual labor. Shortly after World War II, large-scale industrialization of the area began, changing very quickly the village economy and the people's standard of living. The life of Great-Aunt Yeung spans this period of extraordinary change.

Great-Aunt Yeung: A Hakka Wage Laborer

In Kwan Mun Hau, as elsewhere in China, villagers familiarly and respectfully address their elders with kinship terms. Those for women often incorporate their surname; thus Great-Aunt Yeung (Yeung Suk-p'o) is so addressed because she is an elderly woman whose surname is Yeung. She married a man of the Hung lineage of the village; her marriage was somewhat unusual in that she was her husband's second wife. Polygyny was not uncommon in Kwan Mun Hau, although it was a poor village, probably because women, through their labor, represented an economic asset.[8] Three successive generations of Great-Aunt Yeung's husband's family took second wives because so many of the men went abroad to work and thus earned more than most men who remained in Tsuen Wan.

Great-Aunt Yeung bore no children but adopted one daughter. She also refers to the first wife's children as "my son" and "my daughter." This sharing of rights in the children seems characteristic of those forms of Chinese polygyny in which the two wives are of nearly equal status instead of the second wife being a concubine or a mistress living elsewhere.[9] The very simple wedding ceremony of Great-Aunt Yeung indicates that she was originally considered to have inferior status. However, her substantial economic contribution to the family, her general competence, and her strong personality may subsequently have raised her family position.

Great-Aunt Yeung looks younger than her 76 years. She is unusually pretty for an elderly woman, with smooth skin, warm brown eyes, and a ready smile. Her pleasant manner is accentuated by her habit of frequently touching the hand or arm of the person with whom she is speaking, a gesture she shared with many of the older women. Like them, she wears dark-colored Chinese-style pants and blouse, but she never wears the black headcloth often worn by Hakka women or the flat straw hat with black cotton fringe. Many of the older women speak only Hakka or heavily accented Cantonese. She, however, can speak clear Cantonese, because while most of the others were born in Tsuen Wan or villages nearby, she was born near Canton.

She talked with us for many hours in the living room of her home.[10] She was a cheerful and willing informant, although conversations were made difficult by the presence of her noisy great-grandchildren and by the distraction of the large television set which dominated the room. Below the television was the household earth god shrine whose function was to protect the home; hung around the room were formal portraits of living and deceased household members, a constant reminder of the people who are part of her life.

"My mother was Cantonese, my father Hakka. His native place was Shaho, near Panyü, where the rice noodles come from. That place is famous for those delicate noodles. I can speak Cantonese because I was born in Canton. I was never sent to school, so how could I study? Some girls did go to school, and they even asked me to join them, but I couldn't. There was no need for girls to study then. I can only read simple characters and can't write. No one taught me. Who would have so much time? My brother had a chance to study for a few years because he was a boy. Now it is different; men and women are equal. My daughter studied for a few months at Tak Fan School, but she stopped because of the Japanese occupation. I was willing to pay for her education then, and many girls had the opportunity to study; my generation didn't.

"In Canton, I never did any farm work. I just stayed home caring for my younger brother and sister. After I got married, I had to farm. I was married at 18. My parents and I came here from Canton; we were very poor. We rented a house in the village of Muk Min Ha. My younger brother stayed behind. My father later went back to Canton and died there. At that time, around 1925, the situation in China was very chaotic.

There was a seaman's strike and civil war. Those who were not hungry considered themselves fortunate.

"There was no matchmaker involved in my marriage. My husband saw me and liked me, so he decided to take me as his second wife. He then discussed it with his mother. They sent his *paak leung* [great-aunt] to discuss the financial arrangements with my family; his mother didn't go. They agreed that he should give HK$400 to my father, and thus I was brought to his village. It was just like making a purchase! My father did it because of poverty, my husband because he liked me and because he wanted another person to help out. Men also take second wives sometimes because they hope to be able to add more sons to their branch of the family.

"My husband's family was poor, and my family was poor. The first wife may have had a banquet for her marriage, but even then most weddings were simple. For me, there were no wedding gifts, no ceremony, no banquet, and no dowry. I was not brought here in a bridal sedan chair. They just chose a lucky day, and he gave HK$400 to my father— that was all. The family invited a few close relatives to dinner at home, just enough to sit around one table. My parents came. There was no worship of the ancestors in the hall. I didn't even have to pour tea for my mothers-in-law, the two wives of my husband's father. But when my husband's older brother returned from Panama at Lunar New Year, I poured tea for him. He gave me a gold coin then like the red packet of money normally given to brides.

"The older wife of my husband had been a *saam p'o chai*, small daughter-in-law. She was brought into his household as a child, raised with him, and married him when they came of age.[11] She was born on the island of Ching Yi. Lots of people had laughed at her, saying that she had grown up with her husband and played with him and was just like his sister. On special occasions, she and I visited her family on the island. Her family also visited our family. We didn't visit at festivals; they came here when there was some special matter to discuss, such as an illness.

"I rarely visited my parents, because they went back to Canton after I was married. I went back to Canton once before the Japanese occupation and twice afterward. I never sent money to my family, because all the money I earned belonged to this household; my parents never sent anything to me, either. They were much poorer than my husband's family. Mother later came back here to live, and during the Japanese occupation, my brother and his wife also came here. I loaned him HK$10 to come, as I had worked for Texaco and had some money. When my mother lived here, I didn't visit her because I always had to work, but I knew everything that went on there. It's just as well. My mother was narrow-minded, irritable, and unpleasant, and I had nothing to talk to her about. During the Japanese occupation, she was sleeping one day in the market in a pork butcher's stall and was captured by the Japanese. She disappeared, and we heard nothing further from her.

"Generally the men taught school or worked elsewhere. Many worked in businesses. My husband studied until he was 15 or 16. He had quite a lot of education, because his father worked abroad and sent back money. When my husband was 20, he went to Hawaii as an indentured laborer and sent back money to the family. When he returned here and married me, he opened a shop. Then he became a teacher on Old Street in this village. In those days, a teacher was a highly respected person. He also helped with the farm work at harvest time. Unfortunately, he and his older brother then had an argument they could not settle. His brother was going abroad again and said that if one went, the other must go also, so they both went. My husband left after we had been married less than two years, and he died there when I was just 25.

"Nowadays, a woman would not be willing to remain a widow for such a long time, especially at such a young age. Since his family had large fields and houses and needed women's work, I decided to remain here to help raise the children. This family is really unlucky, because many women in it have been widowed at a young age. My father-in-law, brother-in-law, and husband all went abroad to work and died there.

"The older wife gave birth to three sons and one daughter, but two sons died.[12] I did not bear any children, so when I was 25, I adopted a daughter. She was two years old [Chinese reckoning] and could already walk. The first wife's daughter was married in Shatin, and she introduced me to the baby's family there. They were adopting her out because she was sick, or perhaps it was her mother who was sick. My mother-in-law suggested that I adopt a daughter, and she provided the red packet of HK$20. Even though the baby's family didn't request it, we gave the money because it was customary. It was as easy as getting a puppy or a piglet. I just walked over to Shatin to get her and carried her home on my back. I could have adopted a boy if I had wished to, but I never even considered it—adopting a girl isn't very serious, but adopting a boy is a very grave matter.

"Since my daughter now belonged to my family, she no longer had any relationship with her family in Shatin and never went to visit them. We continued to maintain contact with them, however. Sometimes they came here with steamed sweet cakes; sometimes I took them sweet cakes. When my daughter married, we sent a message to inform her parents.

"As soon as I was married, I began to farm and do the housework. The older wife also did this work. Before my husband died, I didn't go out to work for wages. After he died, there was no one to support the family, so I had to work outside. No one else helped our family—everyone in the village was poor. I worked for many, many years—from when I was in my twenties until I was in my sixties.

"The only wage work available then was carrying coal, charcoal, and steel with a pole. I carried coal and sugar, which was used for making wine. Tsuen Wan had 10 wine storage depots. I began drinking wine, although few women drank it then. I developed a taste for it working in the wine storage depot! I also carried salt and loaded it onto boats. The carrying of salt was primarily done by women.

"At that time, the weather reports were not reliable, and boats often sank. Sometimes I went with others to salvage rice from sunken boats. Two of us would carry the rice between us on a carrying pole, carrying more than 200 *catties* at a time. The rice could be sold, although at a much cheaper rate, or it could be dried and used for steamed sweet cakes. When I had the chance, sometimes I worked with two men and two women on a boat going to Lantao Island. The men rowed at the back of the boat and the women at the front, for the work at the bow was lighter. We carried cotton salvaged from sunken boats. We bought it for two dollars and sold it on Lantao Island for four or five dollars. We shared the profits and considered it very good to earn a dollar per day. All the people were from this village. Only one is alive now.

"After that [late 1920's], I carried cement for the construction of the Shing Mun Reservoir in the hills above Tsuen Wan. I had breakfast at eight in the morning and then worked, carrying six or seven bags of cement in a day. The bags weighed 180 *catties*, and each was carried up the mountain to the reservoir by two women. The bags were hung on a carrying pole. The overseer would not arrange for a fair distribution of the bags, so each women had to compete for the bags she was to carry. We grabbed the bags and sat on them. Fortunately, there were no serious fights, but sometimes we tore each other's clothes. There were no set hours for this kind of work. The overseers called us when work was available, and you could go home when you were finished.

"Carrying cement was very slow and tiring. The women coolies were paid 90 cents, the men coolies were paid a dollar. Men and women usually did different kinds of work. Even if both were doing carrying work, they would do different kinds, carrying different things. The cement workers came mainly from Kwan Mun Hau; a few came from the village of Hoi Pa. The people from the villages of Sham Tung Uk and Muk Min Ha did not do this kind of work. Those from Sham Tung Uk cut grass on the mountains for fuel which they could use or sell, while the people from Muk Min Ha carried the materials used in making incense for the incense mills near the village.

"I was 30 years old when the Texaco oil depot opened. The depot was opened near our village by an American man. I carried kerosene, wax, and the sheets of steel which were used to make containers for the kerosene. The steel had to be carried onto boats at the dock. You had to be very careful—if your hand slipped, you could drop it. You walked across a plank onto the boat, and if you slipped, you would fall into the water. Two women would carry more than 200 *catties* of steel between them at one time. Sometimes there was a lot of steel to carry and once we even had to work until midnight.

"Men and women did not get the same pay, because they did different work. Men poured the kerosene into cans, women carried them. Most people carried kerosene to the pier; some carried it onto boats. I got 90 cents per day for loading boats. The kerosene weighed 180 *catties* and was carried on a pole between two people.

"The carrying of steel was mainly done by younger women, usually those about 30 years old. After 40 or 50, no woman would do this kind of work; it was too heavy. Then they would carry only kerosene—no steel. Pregnant women couldn't do this kind of work; it was too dangerous.

"When I had no carrying work to do, I cut grass and wood for fuel. Sometimes people hired me to carry firewood; at other times, I cut grass which I myself sold for 30 cents per 100 *catties*. Most people preferred to do carrying work rather than cutting grass because it paid more money. We cut grass at the foot of the mountains and on the island of Ching Yi. We didn't cut it near the village, because the nearby hills were owned by the villagers. I never went alone to the island or to the mountains to cut grass; usually a few women went together.

"Even when I had no carrying work, I got up at four in the morning and brought water from the well. It took 10 trips with a carrying pole. If my clothes needed washing, I took them along and washed them. Then I carried water and pig manure to the fields. After that, I sharpened my grass-cutting knife, ate breakfast, and went out to cut grass. Sometimes around three or four in the afternoon, I ate another meal of leftover rice at home. Then I went out to cut grass again, or sometimes I rowed a boat to the island to cut firewood. I returned home at five or so and had to carry water again. After seven we had dinner, and then I milled rice and cut up vegetables for the pigs. I did this until ten at night, when I finally went to sleep.

"There was no time to stop working. There was no time to be sick; there was only time to die. During menstruation, we worked as usual. No one said we shouldn't go to the fields during our period. Generally, after the birth of a baby, a woman wasn't allowed out of the house for a month. She wasn't allowed to do farm work unless the family didn't have enough labor power. Then she would have to work even within the first month after the baby's birth.[13]

"Before the Japanese occupation, if we were sick, we still had to work. No doctor would be called; we just boiled herbal medicine to drink. We also soaked plants from the mountains in water, bathed in the water, and then went to bed to sweat out the illness. Once my period came when I was working in the mountains. I felt very sick and washed myself in a mountain stream. When I came home, I became so sick that my hair fell out and I turned yellow and was deaf. A person who was very sick could be sent to Canossan Hospital. They sent me to the hospital, but there were no beds, so I was sent back. Even when I was sick, I had to help with the rice harvest. I avoided the heaviest work. After I had been sick for a year, I fell down during the rice harvest and cut myself badly on the stubble. I felt utterly miserable. Finally my mother-in-law couldn't bear to see me like that, so she sent to Tai Po for some pills which cured me.

"When I came home from work, the children sometimes asked me for money, and I would give them a penny for marble candies. In my generation, when women worked, all the money they earned belonged to the family. Everything I earned was turned over to my mother-in-law. Before the Japanese occupation, when I carried steel and earned a lot of money, I sometimes kept a dollar for myself. I saved until I had HK$10 and bought a suit of clothes. This was more than 40 or 50 years ago.

"My older mother-in-law was the *tong ka* [household manager]. Generally someone from the older generation would be the manager, and normally it was a woman.[14] All the money the first wife and I earned was given to her because she was the manager. When I got work, I would inform her and tell her when it would start. She controlled all the expenses; no one could give her any advice. She had to decide when to raise animals such as pigs and how many to raise. The decisions concerning the planting of vegetable crops were less important. Some husbands gave money to the manager; some did not. If the family participated in a rotating loan association, the manager usually represented the family at the meetings. When we sold pigs, the purchasing agent would come to the house and bargain with her. People also came to the village to buy the pineapples we grew. They paid two dollars per 100 *catties*.

"No one determined the division of tasks in the family. We just did the work naturally; each person knew what to do. If I went out to work, the household work was done by my mother-in-law. The older mother-in-law cooked meals and cared for the children. During the harvest, she carried food to us in the fields. When I was first married, the younger mother-in-law took the older wife and me to the fields to work. We did all the farm work together. The mothers-in-law also took care of the pigs and watched the harvested rice, turning it as it dried in the sun. The older wife raked the fields and washed the clothes and sometimes worked carrying kerosene. She didn't have to carry steel or other goods, because she wasn't strong enough for very heavy work. She mainly did farm work, such as watching the cows and plowing, and led a more comfortable life than I. As for the children, the older girl had to help her mother, watching the cows and cutting grass, but the boy didn't need to. It was also customary that men did no household work. At night the children slept with their own mothers. Since I helped the first wife care for her children, they sometimes liked to sleep with me.

"At that time, we planted rice on the flat fields and vegetables on the hillside slopes. The quality of the flat ground was better. Our hillside fields were near the present location of the Texaco oil depot. We rarely sold any rice or produce. We planted broccoli and giant white radishes, which we preserved with salt for our own use. No one grew other green vegetables then; we didn't know how to grow them, and there was no one to sell them to. We grew cucumbers, corn, sweet potatoes, and taro. We ate sweet potatoes mixed with rice, and on rainy days we ate sweet potatoes alone. We used the shoots of sweet potatoes and radishes for the pigs, so we didn't need to grow or buy pig fodder. We also grew peanuts; we didn't use them for oil but instead for making paste.

"We had to buy oil and used it very sparingly. Our diet was very poor. We seldom had any meat. Sometimes we bought a few cents worth of lean pork and steamed it with eggs for the children. We seldom used any soy sauce. If we had it, we gave it to the children to mix with rice or congee. We bought fish or shrimp to cook with preserved vegetables, steaming them on top of rice. They were cooked without oil, and the dish had a very strong, fishy taste. We could also get oysters at low tide. Most of the time, however, we just ate preserved vegetables with rice. I could eat three large bowls of rice at a meal.

"Sometimes we were very hungry, but nothing could be done. Once when I was rowing a boat back from the island of Ching Yi, I felt that I didn't have the strength to go on because I was so hungry. But there was nothing to do except struggle on.

"We had few clothes to wear then, and those we had were made of rough blue cloth. We didn't make them ourselves. The weaving and tailoring were done by men. In the wintertime, we wore only two layers of clothing, but since we were young and working all day, the cold didn't bother us. We wore no special clothes in the rain; we just felt cold and damp. If it rained heavily, we couldn't go out to work. In the summer, we wore flat hats with black cloth fringe. This gave shelter from the sun, and when the breeze blew the fringe, it was very cool. We wore aprons to work in but only very simple ones. The generation before us made their own clothes from the hemp they grew. They stripped the outer covering from the hemp, dried it in the sun, rolled it in their hands to make thread, and wound it into a ball. Specialists were employed to weave this hemp into cloth.[15]

"Women were able to earn enough to support themselves, especially if they had some fields to farm in addition to their wage work. No work was impossible for women to do; we could do anything. A woman could support herself, her children, and her mother-in-law at some level. In our family, we supplied all the rice for the family's use from our own fields and labor and didn't have to buy any from outside.

"My father-in-law had sent money back from Hawaii to buy fields. He later became an opium addict there. In addition, our family had inherited fields from an uncle's family when the old people died without sons. We never employed any farm workers—we did it all ourselves. We even worked for others, so how could we employ someone? But we loaned our ox to others for plowing; in return, those people would watch the ox for us for free. Everyone in the village worked; we were accustomed to working. Most people had some fields. Generally, the people were very poor and did their own agricultural work. But even those with no rice or vegetables would not steal. If they had no fields, they would do farm work or other jobs for others. I sometimes had help from women farm workers. They were not real farm laborers, but just helped with the harvest. They were women from the village who would come to help out. We didn't contract them and didn't have to pay them; we just gave them meals. If they had no rice at home, we would give them some. If people in the village didn't have enough labor or didn't have an ox, others in the village would help them out or loan them an ox.

"People never stole our crops and never looked down on us because we had no men. There was no danger to women then. There were no hoodlums or murder or rape—not like now. It was very peaceful here. Women didn't have to worry; a woman could go out alone.[16]

"There was little entertainment for women or for men. No woman could go to the teahouse or gamble, and we didn't play cards. Now it's better; everyone can watch television. Then we could only watch Cantonese opera, a public performance sponsored by all the villages. Sometimes when I was free, I would go to Kowloon or even to Hong Kong to watch silent movies. I went to the Po Heng Theater in Kowloon. Sometimes I even went at night. I went by car; it cost 30 to 40 cents before the Japanese occupation. I went most often when I was 30 to 40 years old, usually in the company of several friends from work.

"No woman could buy or sell things like fields and houses that belonged to the family and were registered in her husband's name—these things are men's affairs. If a woman's husband were gone and her son still very young and there were no men left in her husband's family, a woman might have the right to buy and sell houses.

"Before the Japanese occupation of Hong Kong, no women bought houses of their own, either. Women didn't have that much money. Later they began to work in factories and earned more money. Then, when the

Japanese came to Hong Kong, some people needed money, so they began to sell their houses. Before then, no one would sell his house. When the Japanese came, I myself bought a house with my own money. By that time, I was the household manager.[17] I had met an old man who lived alone, with no one to care for him and nothing to live on. I sold the gold jewelry from my daughter-in-law's dowry to support him. Later he committed suicide. His son had left the area. When he returned, he said that the house had belonged to his father and his father's brother. We finally reached a compromise, and I bought the house. I had only HK$200 then, so I borrowed a few hundred dollars from others. I actually registered the house in my son's name. Later my son let his uncle's family live there, since they had sold their house and fields. It's always the case that when a woman buys property, she registers it under her son's name.

"I became the household manager when I was in my forties. My eldest mother-in-law was still alive then but very old. My husband's first wife didn't get the position because she couldn't speak Cantonese and wasn't so clever. It wasn't necessarily decided by my mother-in-law but was just the natural succession; the power was just passed on to me. When I became manager, all the money earned by the first wife was given to me.

"My mother-in-law had not wanted us to divide the household after my husband's death, so we continued to live and take meals together with my husband's brother's widow and her family. When she was over 50 years old, she ran away and married a seaman who lived in Shatin. After that, her daughter suggested that we divide the family, so we began to eat separately but still lived together. My eldest mother-in-law was still alive then. When we actually divided the family, we called in a male relative of my husband to mediate the division of property.[18] People related through women [ch'an ch'ik] do not mediate family divisions. We called him in to be sure it would be fair and equal.

"My eldest mother-in-law died around 1930; my younger mother-in-law died when the Japanese came in 1941. She died of diarrhea. She was more than 80 years old. Although we called a doctor, he said that nothing could be done and that we should prepare for her death.

"My daughter-in-law joined our family in August 1941. Relatives of her family introduced her to my son. He saw her before their marriage when she went to the next village, perhaps to visit relatives, but she didn't know she was being watched. On the day of her wedding, she was brought here in a sedan chair and kneeled and offered tea to us. She had already learned how to do farm work before her marriage.[19]

"My adopted daughter met her husband when he was working for my son, checking and repairing cars. She was working in a textile factory at that time. He is of the Lo surname, from the village of Hoi Pa. She liked the boy, but she cried from embarrassment when he first invited her to go to a movie with him. My son told her it was not a serious matter, so she agreed to go, but she said nothing and just sat and watched the film. I thought he was a good and honest boy. He had his own house, so they had a place to live and could be secure. Since he lived nearby, it would be convenient for me to help her. For these reasons, I agreed to her marriage. I looked after her when she had each baby and shopped and cooked for her. She had no mother-in-law. Every month she gives me HK$50 to go to the teahouse. I bumped into my son-in-law yesterday, and he gave me HK$100. They used to give me HK$200 at the end of each year, but now they have stopped because of the economic situation and because they have so many children.

"I did wage labor for a year or so after the Japanese occupation ended. I sold our old houses and bought new, better ones. I was regularly employed and was paid by the month. I carried cans of kerosene and loaded them onto boats. It was very oppressive inside the boats, and one could easily faint. My work was always interrupted by the family calling me back to settle problems. After we moved to new houses [c. 1950], I stopped working.

"Now my daughter-in-law has been the household manager for five or six years. She criticizes me when I watch television, saying that I am wasting electricity. If her husband had been my true son [*ch'an saang*] instead of the son of the first wife, she would not look down on me now.

"I have rheumatism now; it is very painful.[20] I had to work very hard when I was younger. Those were very bitter times—very hard. We had nothing. Our clothes and food were terribly simple. We had to carry heavy loads, like horses or oxen, and got no rest. As a result, all the bones in my body ache now.

"If you come back to Hong Kong again, I may not be here. I may be up on the mountain in my grave."

Village Life

The life of Great-Aunt Yeung after her marriage differs from the lives of other Kwan Mun Hau women only in that she bore no children and her family had no adult male present for many years. She also began her married life with fewer assets than most women who were primary wives. Unlike them, she received no valuable jewelry as a dowry and only one gift of cash, whereas other women receive many such gifts during the wedding ceremony. Such jewelry and money become their personal property.[21] She was able to gain a personal nest egg only from what she was able to put aside from her own earnings and, rumor has it, by setting aside money for herself from common funds when she was the household manager.

The prominence of women as household managers is not atypical in Kwan Mun Hau even though the buying and selling of houses and fields were normally men's affairs. There is some evidence for this division of economic functions elsewhere in China, although Cohen did not find this pattern among the Hakka people of Yen-liao.[22] Its prevalence in Kwan Mun Hau might be explained by the frequent absence of men through employment abroad.

The extent of Great-Aunt Yeung's economic contribution to her household is also not unusual. During the period before the Japanese occupation, the men were absent from many Tsuen Wan households for long periods; in other households, the men were an economic liability because they were opium addicts and stole their wives' earnings whenever they could. Even in households where the men were good and reliable wage earners or farmers, the women worked hard in both agricultural and wage labor. As Great-Aunt Yeung stated, everyone worked, even women from wealthier families.

The division of women's labor she describes, where the older women stayed home to care for the children, do household chores, and raise pigs, was essential in allowing the younger women to work outside the home. The same pattern helps make possible the employment of younger women in the People's Republic of China today. In Kwan Mun Hau, the burden of household work and pig raising was so great, according to many, that even when grandmothers were available, the children were given only a minimum of care. In those households where there was no grandmother, child neglect was sometimes severe.

The very difficult physical work done by Great-Aunt Yeung was not unusual for women in Tsuen Wan during this century, although I suspect that heavy physical labor by women for wages is a fairly recent phenomenon. Until the 1920s, there was probably little wage labor locally available for women, and they did not participate in the male pattern of temporary emigration in search of employment. As far as I know, women's economic contribution to that time was limited almost entirely to agricultural work for their own families and sometimes for others. The early- to mid-twentieth-century pattern of combining agricultural work and wage labor resulted from the peculiar economic conditions of the time, in that Tsuen Wan remained primarily an agricultural area but began to add small industries and construction projects. Since the late 1950s, agricultural land has been taken for urban development, and factory and even white-collar work is increasingly available for women. As a result, Kwan Mun Hau women need no longer work "like horses or oxen."

The way of life described by Great-Aunt Yeung is now almost entirely gone. The village of Kwan Mun Hau has been moved to new housing. It was previously at the edge of the city but is now rapidly becoming surrounded by high-rise housing and factories. The people's fields are gone, as are the clean air and pleasant environment. The landscape has been altered beyond recognition, concrete is everywhere, and smoke and automobile pollution make the hot summers extremely unpleasant. To the outside observer, the area is disagreeably noisy, grim, and congested.

More than 95 percent of the city's population is now non-Hakka immigrants, and Kwan Mun Hau people complain that they rarely meet anyone they know on the street. Despite this, the community life of Kwan Mun Hau and the other villages remains. Most communities remain intact, and despite their dramatically changed surroundings, the festivals and rituals continue within each tight little community.

Although there are apparent disadvantages to urban life, women express little regret for the way of life that has passed. They do miss the camaraderie they used to enjoy as they worked together; they miss the slower and more flexible pace of life. They state emphatically that they do not miss the hard physical labor, the endless childbearing, the lack of good medical care, the poor diet, or the illiteracy. They take great pleasure in the fact that their daughters and granddaughters can be educated and get relatively comfortable factory or office jobs with set hours and good pay. They feel no regret to see the end of the old system of arranged marriage, polygyny, and small daughter-in-law marriage. Fortunately, no serious decline has occurred in the respect for the aged or in the obligation felt by the young to support and care for their elderly parents. Daughters-in-law may not be as subservient as they once were, but most elderly people, like Great-Aunt Yeung, enjoy their last days living with their sons and grandchildren, caring for members of the youngest generation, going to the teahouse with their elderly friends, and watching television. They appreciate the leisure which they have earned, and they enjoy the respect of younger generations and know that it will continue even after their death.

Songs

During the time of Great-Aunt Yeung's youth, women and some men found relief from the hard work of daily life by singing. For women, singing also offered emotional release. In singing or keening at funerals, women expressed not only their grief for the dead but also personal grievances, such as an unhappy marriage, a cruel mother-in-law, or a greedy sister-in-law. Songs were composed by the individual women following a standard form which included repeated calling of the kin term of the deceased. Such songs were profoundly moving to all who listened;

even the men wept when they heard them. Only those accused by the singer of unjust behavior reacted with anger, and refuted the accusation, if they could, through a sung response.

Wedding songs sung by the bride and her lineage sisters were also individually composed within a traditional structure and, despite the supposed happiness of the occasion, have been called laments.[23] They expressed the bride's pain at leaving her family, her anger at those responsible for arranging her marriage, and her dread of the transition to come.

Other songs, more cheerful in content, were sung by women working in groups. One type was spontaneous—a humorous, teasing dialogue between individuals or groups of women and men, each trying to outdo the other in ridicule. The other type might be called a ballad; it was learned from other women. These often expressed the major concerns in women's lives, as is evident from these examples:

Song about a woman whose husband is about to go abroad to work.

I hold a golden cup with two hands, asking when you will come back,
I go along the upper road where there are many white flowers [other women],
Many, my husband,
I go along the lower road where there are many stones.
My husband, you are now leaving; when will you return?
When on the road you should not pick up the wild flowers,
Within the house there is already a plum blossom [herself].

Song about a woman whose husband has gone abroad to work with a group of friends. The friends return, but he does not.

Woman: Put away the hemp weaving, put away the stool,
        Waiting for my husband to return.
        He went with you but did not come back with you.

Man: Little sister, don't ask.
        Talking about your husband will make you very angry.
        Your husband has a relationship with a Vietnamese woman;
            it's very serious.
        During daytime they act as travel companions,
        At night they act as a couple.

Woman: Worship heaven, worship earth, so that whenever that Vietnamese
            woman becomes pregnant, the babies will die,
        So that my husband can more easily earn money and return.

Song about marriage.

Sister, when you marry it would not be good to marry a stoneworker;
The "het het" sound of the stonecutting would frighten people.
Sister, when you marry it would not be good to marry an educated man;
White pants and shorts are very hard to starch.
When you marry it would be best to marry a farmer.

Sister, when you marry it is best not to marry a farmer;
The upper part of his body stinks of earth,
The lower part of his body stinks of earth.
Sister, it is best to marry a pork merchant;
Then every morning you can have a bowl of pork soup.
Sister, it is best not to marry a stoneworker;
The "din don dik dap" sounds really frighten people.

Sister, it is best not to marry an educated man;
White shirt and pants are very hard to starch.
When I marry it would not be good for me to marry a farmer;
My upper body will stink of earth,
My lower body will stink of earth.
Sister, when you marry it would not be good to marry a pork merchant;
The "gew gew gew gew" sounds made by the pigs will frighten people.
Sister, it is best for you to marry a stoneworker.
Every night he would go to bed very early.

Song about a small daughter-in-law.

Older brother is poor, little sister is also poor.
We both work together, older brother.
Older brother does not have a good pair of trousers to wear,
Little sister does not have a nice headcloth.
Little sister, you struggle gradually to solve your problems,
Struggle for another year or two.
When you have sons, your life will be better.
I will struggle for another year or two; my son will be older.
When I take a daughter-in-law, everything will be good.

These songs were sung by a middle-aged woman with a remarkable memory and great patience. She permitted me to record them and many others.[24] Such songs are no longer sung; only the funeral songs are still heard in the village. Women no longer work in groups, so they have no opportunity to sing together. Likewise, the situations depicted in the songs—the large-scale migration of men abroad, the arranged marriages, the small daughter-in-law marriages—no longer exist. For these reasons and because of the distractions of television, movies, and radio, the old songs which were so meaningful to the women in their youth are now being rapidly forgotten.

PART II
Taiwan
and
Hong Kong

Part II contains lives of younger women in Taiwan and Hong Kong. To begin with, a methods chapter discusses the fieldwork of the three authors.

6

Doing Fieldwork

By Lydia Kung, Linda Gail Arrigo,
and Janet W. Salaff

Introduction

The following sketches of fieldwork situations discuss entry into the field, sample selection, and development of rapport. They also describe the interaction between fieldworkers and their respondents as well as the strains and rewards of doing fieldwork as a form of data collection.[1]

The costs of doing fieldwork include psychic ones; some alienation and distance from one's own culture appear to follow almost inevitably from an intense fieldwork experience.[2] Some researchers return to their own culture enriched by the view they attained from outside it. Others become intensely critical of the roles and values they learned in their own culture. Fieldwork experiences are rewarding, though, because of the human relationships that develop. Fieldwork also provides intellectual stimulation and experience in solving problems and collecting data at the same time.[3]

Lydia Kung

The two lives I present in this study were chosen from among several women whom I interviewed at length over a period of many months. I did not originally record their lives chronologically, but I have arranged the data by topic and in chronological sequence. In addition, I have allowed these women to speak for themselves, without my interpretations. Writing of such methods in anthropology, Edwin Ardener has argued:

> When we come to that second or "meta" level of fieldwork, the vast body of debate, discussion, question and answer, that social anthropologists really depend upon to give conviction to their interpretation, there is a real imbalance. We are, for practical purposes, in a male world. . . . Those trained in ethnography evidently have a bias toward the kinds of models that men are ready to provide (or to concur in) rather than any that women might provide. If the men appear "articulate" compared with the women, it is a case of like speaking to like.[4]

Ardener adds, "To the degree that communication between ethnographer and people is imperfect, that imperfection drives the ethnographer in greater measures towards men." But the problem here is not merely technical, for there is an analytical side to it as well: "If the models of a society made by most ethnographers tend to be models derived from the male portion of that society, how does the symbolic weight of that other mass of persons . . . express itself?"[5] Although my study of Taiwan's garment workers deals specifically with women, Ardener's remarks are germane in that he directs attention to the way in which the relationship between an ethnographer and her subjects may affect her interpretations. This process of interpretation is, moreover, particularly central to my study of women.[6]

Field data are obtained in specific contexts, and the nature of those contexts should be made explicit. It is not only the anthropologist who observes, for the informant is also an observer, and the informant's reactions cannot be dismissed. The anthropologist has a particular role or roles, and people respond accordingly. For their part, women may have a particular definition of themselves that they wish to convey, which in turn may be influenced by their understanding of the investigator's motives. (For instance, I am college-educated. During our early meetings, one informant apparently wanted to make sure I was aware of the extent of her education.) How an ethnographer and people present themselves to each other, then, is relevant. Attempting to discover what is concealed, however, raises issues of what is culturally defined as private information and the range of subjects about which an outsider can legitimately ask.

Taiwanese factory women, for example, responded comfortably to questions concerning wages and expenses but were less open about the amount of money taken or sent home. This is a more sensitive area, because it is an index of the overall financial status of a family. Mothers of factory women generally did not hesitate to share such information among themselves; indeed, norms of what constitutes an acceptable amount sometimes emerged in this fashion. But female workers, already keenly aware of the circumstances that brought them into the factory, were usually reluctant to cite specific sums until a very familiar relationship had been established.

My sample consisted of 82 women whom I interviewed informally. I also analyzed questionnaires from approximately 450 other women. During the first half of my stay in the field (January–June 1974), I lived in Sanhsia, a market town about an hour's bus ride from Taipei, the capital city of Taiwan. There I spent time with residents of Sanhsia, Ch'inan, and Ch'ipei, two nearby villages, concentrating on women who lived at home and commuted to factories in the vicinity. I usually spent my days interviewing their families (most often their mothers and grandmothers), since the factory women were available only at night and on Sundays (provided they did not work overtime). I was usually accompanied by my research assistant, an unmarried native of Ch'inan. A number of my informants had been her classmates in primary school.

Our conversations were generally in the women's homes, in a room where we could be by ourselves except for small children who wandered in and out. Sometimes we met outdoors. Television is a popular pastime on Sunday afternoons, and occasionally we found several young women watching together. In most instances, they were neighbors, cousins, co-workers, or friends, and under these circumstances our questions were directed to the entire group. We used these opportunities to generate discussion and to pursue differing viewpoints. From time to time, we accompanied women (or asked them to join us) on trips to P'an Chia, another larger town, or to Taipei.

A number of families in the Sanhsia area were involved in cottage industries, the most common being the assembly of plastic flowers and the mending of fishnets manufactured by a local firm. Because some daughters were expected to assist in these activities in their leisure time, we sometimes talked while performing such tasks. In more formal settings, private and community rituals were observed and recorded; betrothals and weddings, in particular, afforded the best opportunities to draw out personal feelings about marriage and speculation about the future.

Because other anthropologists have lived in the area, many residents had some idea of an anthropologist's activities, and our visits from house to house and our presence at villagewide events did not seem entirely strange.[7] I do not mean to deny the effect my presence may have had, but at least our activities could be placed in a perspective which was familiar to the residents of those communities. I described myself as a student with research interests in the young people and the industrial growth of Taiwan.

What motivated village informants to spend time with us and to answer our questions? Although the women understood that I was there to carry out a research project, many of them also regarded our calls as social visits—temporary diversions—where conversation ranged over a number of subjects (life in the United States, shopping information about Taipei, movies, grievances about jobs). Since we did not take notes in their presence, it is perhaps not surprising that our visits often ended with women urging us to "come and chat again." If these women perceived themselves as informants, I doubt that they were altogether certain of which types of information I considered significant.

For the second half of my fieldwork (July 1974–January 1975), I collected material at one of Taiwan's largest factories, which I shall call Western Electronics, located in the city of Taoyuan. In the course of the year, I had occasion to visit many foreign- and Chinese-owned factories. Western Electronics seems typical of the largest. It is an American-owned firm that employs some 4,000 female workers and several hundred male workers. About half of the women live in company dormitories. I obtained an introduction to the management, explained my research project, and received permission to carry out informal interviews in the plant during working hours. I lived in the company dormitories. (My assistant remained in Ch'inan, and I returned to the Sanhsia area once a week.)

In the plant, my usual practice was simply to pull up a chair next to someone after speaking with her group leader or foreman. (Group leaders oversee 10 to 20 other women, are promoted from assemblers, and are sometimes no older than the workers they supervise.) Conversations also took place in the cafeteria, in eating places near the factory, in the recreation center, and during Sunday excursions to nearby scenic spots.

I also attended, along with newly hired women, a two-day orientation and training program given by the company. With this as background, I had excellent opportunities to follow up the adjustment of newly arrived women, many of whom were working for the first time. I worked for a few days in various sections of the plant to obtain firsthand experience of assembly line work and to forge some initial ties with workers. I met other informants through the three trainers who were responsible for the orientation sessions. All three had once been assemblers themselves.

These contacts developed into others when, for instance, women who were friends of one informant stopped to listen and later joined our conversation. At other times, I simply walked into dormitory rooms accompanied by a dormitory supervisor, who introduced me. In these settings, I began by explaining my interests; the fact that each woman was among roommates no doubt reduced any discomfort they might have felt. (Admittedly, however, no one was likely to adopt this procedure as a way of meeting people!) Again, the group setting was valuable for promoting discussion and exploring differences of opinion. Where I felt that the presence of others inhibited the expression of some points of view, I tried to return to the subject when I was alone with an informant. Overall, I aimed for some representativeness in terms of background, age, education, work position, and work experience.

I customarily began by asking where a woman came from, how long she had been at Western Electronics, whether she had classmates or friends there, and what the composition of her family was. Inquiries about the dormitories and the company, and about each woman's likes and dislikes invariably stimulated lengthy comments. Because the factory women were so sensitive to educational level as an indicator of social status, they were no doubt conscious of my college background; it probably made the strongest impression on working students, who are highly motivated to obtain their high school diploma. I think my move into the dormitory helped to reduce any distance that may have been caused by differences in education. Although Taiwanese factory women resent the condescending attitudes of Taiwanese office workers, clearly I was not employed in that capacity. I believe that I built relaxed relationships with the workers because they were convinced that I was not being paid a wage by the company.

One of the attractions of leaving home for a distant factory is the chance to meet a wide variety of people. Taiwanese women soon discover, however, that their contacts are largely limited to other factory workers and that their prospects do not match those of the heroines they see in movies and novels. In this regard, my background probably heightened their curiosity and increased their willingness to talk. In any case, the factory and the dormitory are characterized by high turnover and new faces, so my presence was perhaps only slightly different. Talking with one's co-workers is the best part of the job, since it relieves the monotony. My talks with the women were probably perceived as an extension of this.

Women complained about boredom in the dormitories after work hours. A minority enjoyed an active social life, but most workers spent their leisure time reading, writing letters, talking, or napping. It was not difficult, therefore, to fit my interviews into their routines, although it was possible to speak with working students only on the job or during the summer, because their schedule left them little free time. As in Sanhsia, I used both Mandarin and Taiwanese for interviewing, and I recorded the information as soon as possible after each conversation.

In some field situations, the anthropologist comes to be regarded as a potentially useful intermediary with employers or government officials, and it is conceivable that some women spoke to me hoping that I would communicate complaints about the dormitories and their work to the appropriate offices. However, I do not believe this to be the case, since they seemed to hold extremely modest expectations of improvements. Although my activities certainly did not conform to any of the ideas that factory women hold about school-related work and they surely did not know what dissertation research for graduate school entails, at the same time, none of my informants thought of me as part of the management. The only concrete assistance I could provide was in the form of English lessons, and these were important only to the women attending evening school.

In writing the two lives in this volume, I have quoted wherever possible from the statements of the women themselves. These cases may seem to dwell on expressed values rather than actual behavior; this is because in part my interest has been in how the women interpret their experiences and the world beyond the home. The women develop ideas about how the world works; they reflect upon and evaluate their circumstances. Women act according to their perception of an event or situation; their perspectives are therefore important data. In this light, these excerpts from the lives of two factory women can be viewed as a beginning in understanding how each women perceives her work and behavior.

Linda Gail Arrigo

When I flew to Taiwan for Christmas vacation in 1973, I found Taipei markedly different from the city where I had lived as a girl from 1963 to 1967. The downtown now sparkled with neon lights, and plastic and aluminum covered the old wood surfaces. The streets of the movie district were thronged with young people, even couples openly holding hands, as if a new youth culture had emerged overnight. A malodorous but grassy-banked drainage channel had disappeared beneath a treeless four-lane thoroughfare. In what had been outlying agricultural suburbs, the peaked eaves of just a few grand old farmhouses could still be seen as they stood stranded among tile-faced four-story apartment buildings.

The business streets were lined with prosperous-looking trading companies. Outside the city were new industrial parks with mammoth plants flaunting prestigious corporate names. The local market offered a plethora of foreign brands, and a walk through side streets and even country villages revealed women busily machine-knitting sweaters, assembling plastic toys, and packing Christmas bulbs for piece rates that rarely netted the worker more than an average of US25¢ an hour.

In the summer of 1975, I tried to find an American priest I had first met in 1967 when he was setting up a new dormitory for factory women. He had welcomed my research, because he was hopeful that my work would help him understand them. But the new Catholic administrator of the dorms was more cautious and expressed considerable doubt that I would be able to live among the women and adapt to their meager accommodations. He eventually acceded to my request, though, and I was able to move into a large regular dormitory room. There were 12 women to a room; each had a narrow bunk, a footwide closet, and a desk and chair. A large vacant room and one bathroom facility with five toilets and three showers, rarely all in working condition, adjoined the four dormitory rooms. I immediately learned that in a hot climate, a board with a towel on it is a far more comfortable bed than a spring mattress. I maintained my office, with a bed and personal effects, within walking distance to the dormitory and lived in each room in turn.

The women in the dormitory were almost all electronics assemblers. Most were from villages in central or south Taiwan, and about half were attending night school at the secondary level. They ranged in age from 18 to 22, and although I was only five years older than most, they called me "Elder Sister Chen" as a gesture of respect. It was only after we became close that they used my first name.

Four or five of the women were curious about where I came from, what countries I had visited, why I was in Taiwan, why I spoke Chinese well, how I dared to leave my husband at home by himself, and why I was still going to school after marriage. Searching for some way to build rapport in our first encounters, I handed around colored postcards from Japan and the United States. When I told them about my family, they quite naturally told me about theirs, where they lived, what their fathers did, why they had come to Taipei. They criticized some of my personal habits that were different from their own—for example, they said that I should take hot showers rather than cold, even if the weather was muggy; after I got a skin fungus, I found they were right. They seemed amused when I could not get clothes clean washing by hand, and I often felt helpless and awkward under their scrutiny. But they also took care of me in a more intimate fashion than Americans would have. A few times, I awoke in the sweltering heat of a summer night to find Yu-yun, whose bunk was pushed next to mine, gently fanning both of us through the mosquito nets.

Initially I sought a sizable sample of subjects for life histories. Before I came to Taiwan, I had outlined an extremely ambitious plan. I thought if I could listen to one life history a night and spend two or three hours recording it during the daytime, I could easily reach a quota of 50 unstructured life history studies to supplement the nearly 1,000 anonymous questionnaires that I had collected. My topic was family relations, and I wanted to find out about conflicts between parents and daughters, feelings about marriage and sex, psychological modernization, and fertility ideals.

After I met many of the dormitory residents, I told some in detail about my research, asking them rather formally if they would later tell me about their lives. The women were mildly interested in hearing about my research, but they did not see how it related to their own lives. They responded to questions in abbreviated format—where they were born, where they attended school, how many people were in their family—but they said little about psychological motivation or interpersonal conflict. When I probed on these topics, they still did not respond. I finally perceived that I was inquiring into very intense feelings about parents, marriage, and sex. Moreover, these were defined as private issues and were discussible only within a small, intimate group. These were not topics for discussion with outsiders. I eventually came to share their definition of privacy and absorbed the reticence of Chinese women.

My roommates continued with an active routine of work and recreation. In the long summer evenings, they chatted until the lights were turned out at midnight and sometimes after. Asked directly about why she sent money home, Hsiu-mei replied, "You owe your parents your body. You were raised by them. So you must repay them and be obedient." But in a discussion with roommates, she gave a lively account of how the daughter in her family who didn't work was left home to mop the floors and scrub the clothes and was still looked down on by her other brothers and sisters. She also told how her mother waited by the factory gate on payday or borrowed money from the daughters that she never repaid. Some women secretly went to school at night, against the wishes of their parents, who thought that paying tuition for women was a waste of money. The traditional statement was, "Daughters get married and belong to someone else; education is useless for housewives." Negotiation of remittances seemed acted out in such indirect struggles and interactions. At other times, the women teased each other about having a boyfriend (few would admit to having one). If a match were in the works, hard facts were exchanged about the education, career, and earnings of the man. This was in some contrast to the ethereal words of the romantic Mandarin songs they sang—"Love is everything for a woman but only part of life for a man."

It gradually became apparent to me that my roommates, like other people, talked freely about their inner feelings and experiences not for the abstract sake of science or for direct material gain but for the satisfaction of interacting with others who cared about them and did not judge them. It became clear that I needed to appreciate the "insider" limits to revealed information that they valued. They needed to trust me not to use their information against them. But this process of gaining trust, accordingly, could not be scheduled mechanically, as I had anticipated in my interview time frame.

In practical terms, I found it exhausting to maintain a pleasant mask and to communicate friendly curiosity when I was inwardly fuming that I had not collected enough data for the time expended. It was counterproductive, too, because the women felt my impatience and detachment and then seemed to withdraw. On the other hand, when I finally began to enjoy my newfound friends' company, activities, and other aspects of their lives, I found that my understanding of them increased as a matter of course.

From these realizations, I evolved a different style of interaction—a low-key general expression of concern, a contentment at spending long hours in outings and casual conversation without an immediate end in mind, and a willingness to listen to each woman's problems whenever they arose and to try to help if I could. As I restructured my own concepts of time and work, I began to feel happier. At the end of the summer, when my most diffident roommate suddenly sat down and told me her life story, unsolicited, the feeling that she trusted me was as important to me as what she said.

The general approach I developed may be called participant observation. I feel that the life history method, pursued in this interactive fashion, enabled me to attain the flow and process that are necessary to understand the women I met.

I thought more about these problems after I returned to Taiwan in June 1977 and developed time-deepened relationships with people. Women I had known before became even closer to me, because I had come back to them, as I had said I would, from a place so far away. I was also confronted with outcomes I had not suspected from some women—a rough-featured tomboy now moonlighted as a "coffee shop" girl after her factory shift. One woman became a particular challenge to me. Articulate and self-possessed, she gave me two elaborate but disparate accounts of what she intended to do in marriage; one was restrained, the other overtly promiscuous. Both accounts had sharp observations on sexual politics, hidden power plays, and assumptions about male-female social inequality. My Taiwanese research assistant asked what a wife should do if her husband has an affair with another woman; this woman replied in the normative fashion, "Keep the hearth and turn the children against him." To me, whom she considered by now a nonjudgmental insider, she said, "The wife should get a boyfriend of her own." Gradually, the common psychological basis of her two accounts became apparent to us. She struck poses, and each account reflected a possible strategy. Sometimes a third persona surfaced briefly, one that was emotionally vulnerable and defensive. It is not my task to choose one over the others but to report all three, and indeed her three apparently disjunctive sides fit together to make a complex whole.

I met very few people who approached this degree of complexity, but I suspect that there are more personalities like hers among persons who have violated cultural ideals. Most of the workers were young women whose lives had not yet reached any particular "turning" or crisis. When they felt like communicating, they were straightforward and sincere; they had nothing to hide. However, occasionally they had to choose among alternative options, and they would waver between two explanations in the midst of deciding. The options they considered explained their dilemma to me far better than just knowing the outcome of their decision. Older unmarried women, especially those past the usual age of marriage, often explained away their perspective by saying, "My views are very different from most people's. It's no use talking to me if you want to know about general marriage ideas." They perceived their own views as quite different from the prevailing ideology and were able to rationalize the variance. I considered their rationalization and reconciliation with the norm as important as their variant views.

I contrast the life history method to any method that asserts some fixed truth about an individual. I believe instead that it is the normal state of human life to be caught between conflicting forces. In my belief that I could learn at least as much about causation from a few examples of lives as from massive statistical correlations, I began to collect the nearly 30 life histories that are represented by two women in this volume.

My interest in life history flows from my desire to obtain representation from all kinds of people whose lives appear to explain the deeper workings of the social system. I focus on regions of social and psychological conflict. The life history method lends itself to this concern, because people who suffer conflicts are usually very willing to talk to a sympathetic listener. Those whose lives are running along smoothly seem able to chat but not to reflect deeply about their situation; thus they teach me less about a society than those in conflict.

My experience leads me to conclude that association with a few persons over an extended period, the minimum being six months, is generally necessary to reveal social causation. Naturally I complement my intensive studies with more limited observations on and comparisons of a larger number of persons. Two considerations prompt this lengthy interaction—the human need for friendship and my desire to be present when events occur that might cause a person to reflect on her life by talking with her friends. Such events unfold randomly, and it is important to be there during such life crises, because it is difficult to elicit the same emotional responses at a later time.

In trying to understand the views of various women, one of my techniques is to challenge them by presenting a contradictory viewpoint—"But what would you do if—!" I then support them by listening attentively. After hearing a number of different responses, I often understand the range of reactions, and at that time I may play a conservative or a liberal part as a mild devil's advocate. I try this technique on occasion with my respondents, but of course it is not a mechanical exercise to be used repeatedly with any one person. It is most important to express one's own opinions sincerely, and this happens most easily when one shares one's own life experiences in order to solicit the experiences of the other. The exchange can continue quite successfully even between people of very different life experiences and very different views.

It is apparent to me that I am able to become intimate with a large proportion of women who are in conflict with or the victims of traditional values and social structures. I suspect that I provide a psychological escape for them and that they are a psychological release for me also. Thus, in an emotion-laden moment, a woman whom I had known for three years lamented over her loneliness and stated that she could not find anyone to discuss her pregnancy with. I asked her, "Then why can you tell me?" She shrugged as if I should know already: "You are different. You won't deride me about these things as they would" (as she gestured to an unseen audience in the room).

Although I seem to attract people who are experiencing considerable social and psychological pressure, it is also clear that there are many so-called deviants in Taiwan, far more than usually acknowledged in the press and other mass media. These exceptions are generated by the system, but in trying to escape ostracism, they perpetuate the conspiracy of silence about the oppressiveness of their society. Seeing me as outside the system allowed my friends to break their silence.

In recording the lives of my respondents, I placed myself openly in the interview format. My presence was a real factor in the disclosure of their problems, and I feel that the context of this disclosure should be apparent to the reader. My research approach is not cost-free, however, and exacts its emotional price. Nevertheless, I cannot distance myself from the concerns of my respondents. From my own experiences in the field, I believe that genuine understanding of social causation and interaction is possible only with the researcher's concern for the society she studies and that the process of learning about a society is influenced by that society.

Janet W. Salaff

The two lives that I present in this volume were collected in the course of research that emphasized substantive problems. I investigated changes in women's status in the family and community as a result of their increased earning power with the industrialization of Hong Kong.[8] I always kept in mind, however, C. Wright Mills' admonition that social scientists undertake "the study of biography, of history, and of the problems of their intersection within the social structure."[9]

I pursued my interest in the lives of particular women over a long period of time. I went to Hong Kong for initial fieldwork in 1971 and met some of the women who later became my respondents and friends. Most of my research was carried out during nine months of 1973, when I met with the women I had known since 1971 and several others as well. With all of them, I was able to establish repeated close contact in both formal and informal situations. Between 1974 and 1976, I went back to Hong Kong every year and always resumed my ties with these people.

The result is a panel study, which means that individuals were contacted over a period of time. The panel study is often used to predict reactions of individuals and then test evidence against the original predictions. Sometimes the respondents themselves make the predictions, for example, their marriage age, basis of marriage choice, and life-style expectations. In other cases, the researcher makes the predictions. Both approaches are used here.

My relationships with these women encompassed some six years of my life. The repeated contact, heightened in clarity by the intervals of separation, enabled me to determine which issues were likely to be problematic to them. Their views regarding work after marriage could be compared to their actual behavior. The life of Wai-gun's family after the death of her father contrasts markedly with their life before his death. Rainbow's hope to strike out on her own proved unrealistically romantic within the Hong Kong context. Her failure could easily surprise a woman coming from a North American background, where such expectations would be reasonable and realizable. (The understanding of this was part of my own crosscultural education in becoming aware of my own social and cultural assumptions.)

It was also possible for me to see the several respondents as a fugue. I spoke with one at length about her personal life experiences, then asked another how she would have acted in similar circumstances (maintaining anonymity). This form of role-playing and role-testing provided a wider range of potential experiences and data upon which I could draw than the actual reference to attitudes and behavior of only one person.

Environmental settings provided yet another essential factor for my study of roles and personality. These evolved naturally as I developed rapport with my respondents. I began to be included more and more in their activities, beginning with the night school English classes where I met them, moving on to coffee dates, picnics, and beach parties, and eventually visiting their workplaces, "hanging out" in their homes and neighborhoods, and taking part in hospital calls on ill relatives, temple events, marriages, celebrations, and family crises. In these contexts, I was grateful for the training which helped me to see these situations simultaneously through my own eyes, my respondents' eyes, and the eyes of those who beheld us. The three perspectives of time, comparison, and varied environment combine to create more balanced life histories.

My intensive interview method was feasible largely because of the availability of rich demographic data in census reports and population registration statistics. These provided socioeconomic and demographic profiles of the entire population, establishing the base lines of marriage age, family size, education, and labor force participation by age and sex. These government reports freed me from the necessity of collecting descriptive materials from a larger number of women, and I was thus able to give more attention to theoretical issues. The demographic profiles also pinpointed particular problems that should be studied by in-depth methods, such as the high rates of marriage within the same speech group, or the apparent direct relationship between marriage age and the status of the bride's occupation.

The Hong Kong census reports and Department of Labour Annual Reports showed which occupations were most frequently held by young women, and I drew my sample from these—factory work, sales, service, and semi-professional jobs. I also paid attention to the size of the firm to be certain that these were in line with the documented averages for employed women. I selected women from large and small families. My final sample included 28 women, all unmarried, aged under 30 (with most 20 to 24), and living at home at the time of our contact. The families in which they grew up were large: 19 belonged to families with five or more surviving children. In seven of the 28 families, fathers were absent and mothers headed the household.

My preparation for fieldwork included experience with the standard, short-term interview, which lasts for several hours at the most. I had not anticipated the kind of contact that lasts over many years or that the unfolding of my own life would intertwine with the lives of my respondents in such a way as to enhance my intellectual perceptions of role and personality in life courses. As my field visits continued over several years, I naturally went through a series of life cycle-linked social role changes—from a childless woman to a mother with an infant to a mother with a young child. These changes placed me in different role relationships with the women and their families. In 1971, as a young married woman, not yet a mother, and unaccompanied by my husband, my position more closely resembled unmarried than married women in the Hong Kong setting, and I could easily adapt to the roles and activities of my unmarried respondents. However, in 1973, as a young mother, I found that my role had altered. At that time, it became easier to interact with older members of the respondents' families, including their married siblings and mothers, because we had more common ground than before. It simultaneously became more difficult for me to go on "double dates" and other excursions popular with unmarried women; consequently, family outings replaced these activities. Thus the inevitable adoption of new roles and thus status provided different gains and losses of vantage point for fieldwork.

I was a nursing mother when I first brought my seven-month-old daughter Shana to the field. For almost a year, she accompanied me everywhere I went, watching over my shoulder from her snug backpack. At first, it did not occur to me that Shana's presence would greatly influence my investigations; she was with me simply because I did not want to part with her.

However, to my great surprise, Shana became one of my best assets, a special kind of research assistant. She fitted perfectly into the Chinese cultural proclivity to pamper small children, and people's defenses dropped. My openness in bringing my child to my respondents indicated my non-judgmental acceptance of their milieu, and they responded in kind. Shana played with other children, let them carry her about, and was perfectly happy eating the family fare of rice gruel, noodles, and bean curd. These homes provided a kind of extended family environment for both of us and child care without which I could not have carried on my work.

Shana was a universal stimulus to conversation about child care and motherhood expectations. Because people treated her as one of their own, I came to understand the variations between families in views about child care, especially differing viewpoints on childbearing between modern daughters and traditional mothers.

However, Shana has her own life cycle, too. When she returned to the field with me as an older child, she was unwilling simply to be my adjunct. At four, she preferred a more structured play situation and entered an Anglo-Chinese neighborhood playschool. Again I learned a tremendous amount through her experience, this time about Chinese women as teachers for small children. Shana has already reserved a place for herself on my next field trip, and I expect that the level and degree of her participation will change through each stage of our development.

As my intellectual interests evolved over the past decade and I became increasingly concerned with understanding the operation of colonial rule in Hong Kong, these themes became more integral to my work and to interpreting the impact of broader political and economic institutions on the lives of the women I met in Hong Kong. Additionally, my perception changed of my own academic and professional roles as separate from my concern for my respondents when I came to know them better over a longer time. My initial use of the standard interview of a few hours did not elicit the deeper commitment to them developed by our longer-lasting relationships. Thus the questions I asked and the way I perceived earlier installments of each story began to reflect an increased appreciation for complexities and the insight I had from my deep attachment to them. Our personal closeness never became confused with cultural sameness but led instead to the multiplication of cultural bridges. We never erase our own autobiographies. It is this longer exposure and the interaction between us that made possible the writing of these lives and that continually adjust and refine my interpretation of social interaction within broader political and economic contexts.

7

Taiwan Garment Workers
Wang Su-lan: Filial Daughter
Teng Hsiu-ling: Middle Sister

By Lydia Kung

Introduction

Wang Su-lan and Teng Hsiu-ling are among the first Taiwanese generation of young women to be employed on a regular basis in industrial enterprises. As a generation, this group figures prominently in Taiwan's labor force. Women, for instance, are 59 percent of the workers in the food processing industry, 79 percent of the workers in the textile sector, 85 percent of the workers in the apparel industry, and 65 percent of the production employees in the electrical equipment and supplies industry.[1] Large numbers of women are also employed in the service sector. As one of the women put it, "Taiwan is changing from an agricultural society to an industrial one," and she places herself in that transition.

The factory where Wang Su-lan and Teng Hsiu-ling work is located in the city of Taoyuan. With a name made familiar through the media, it draws workers from all areas of Taiwan. The company enjoys a sound reputation for its dormitories and other facilities and thus appeals to women who must live away from their family. There are eight four-story buildings and one older unit that house female workers. A spacious recreation center adjoins the dormitories; it is equipped with a library, snack bar, lounge with television and radio, beauty shop, sports facilities, and auditorium. The path from the dormitory complex to the plant is lined with small stalls offering noodles, fruit, and snacks. On payday, vendors come to display clothing and other articles.

Factory work enlarges the sphere of social contacts for women workers, and all of the factory women I interviewed in Taiwan felt that friendship on the job was the most rewarding aspect of their employment. All enjoy some leisure activities with co-workers, but the frequency of outings is severely limited by cost, distance, and schedules. Personal autonomy has increased the most in the area of dating and marriage. Although the women are not always satisfied with their job opportunities, factory employment does mean that a woman is in regular contact with a larger variety of people than a woman who remains on the family farm. Female workers have more opportunities to meet men and do not need to rely on go-betweens or family members for introductions; women consequently have the freedom to choose some of the men with whom they become acquainted. Wage earning in a factory does not, however, automatically transform a woman's attitude towards independence.

Unlike working students or women who pursue new experiences for their own sake, factory employment is not a strategy for achieving any well-defined personal goals for either Wang Su-lan or Teng Hsiu-ling. They have not come to regard their occupation as a viable or desirable alternative to marriage. They may speak of themselves as self-supporting, but they foresee that factory work will be terminated at either marriage or childbirth. They note at the same time that factories prefer to hire young women. (As many women point out, factories are now filled with young unmarried women, with married women being the minority.) Many have long ago abandoned the hope of continuing their education.

It is not necessary for parents to develop a new set of values to allow their daughters to work. Parents retain preexisting expectations with respect to the wages of their daughters. They continue to believe that daughters are lost to others at marriage, that daughters ought to repay the cost of raising them, and that family interests take precedence over daughters' wishes. Daughters may be employed some distance from home, but those activities that affect the family's well-being, that is, household income, continue to be subject to family supervision.

As for the working women themselves, the notion of a financial debt to their parents and the sense of obligation from filial piety constitute a large part of their rationale for working. Even if daughters were given some control over the disposal of their earnings, it remains to be seen whether alternative channels for investment exist outside the family. Customarily, older Taiwanese women are able to invest their money in loan associations, become money lenders, or buy livestock, but these are not activities young women adopt. Education, in contrast, *is* perceived as a means to upward mobility, but not all families permit women to use their wages for this purpose. In strictly economic terms, most factory women are capable of supporting themselves at a standard approximating that at home, provided their dormitory and meals are subsidized in whole or in part by the firm, but only a minority work to become self-sufficient for the purpose of leaving their family. Finally, most women believe that even if they cannot earn enough to increase the family income substantially, they should work so as not to be a drain on family resources.

Predictably, women who have spent years living in a dormitory far from home become emotionally more independent from their family; this is not, however, necessarily accompanied by a reduction in their economic commitment. They feel similarly to women who live at home that an increase in how long they work and contribute to the family income does not bring with it a commensurate desire to play a greater role in family decisions or an expectation of more tangible returns.

There are, however, some women who adopt an earthy, critical resistance to factory life. Teng Hsiu-ling is such a person. She moves from place to place, perceiving the limitations of every job and unable to settle at one. Her awareness results only in personal flight. She can make no impact upon her workplaces to change them for the better, nor can she change the character of her own home and/or job fulfillment.

Wang Su-lan: Filial Daughter

The Wang family lives in one of the new boxlike dwellings of the community of Chinan on the road to Taipei. Each small house has the same pattern—a living room in front, bedrooms, an eating space, and a kitchen at the back which opens onto a small rice paddy. This block of houses is recessed from the main road. The families share a common courtyard which serves as a play area for children, a work area for drying rice and vegetables, and a place for neighbors to chat on summer evenings.

Wang Su-lan looks younger than her 19 years. She ties her hair back and generally wears a skirt and blouse, believing that dresses make her look too grown-up. She is shy but mingles easily with her neighbors, and in the beginning she seemed puzzled that my research assistant and I should take an interest in her life, which she considered quite unremarkable, uneventful, and ordinary. Why should we, who were older than any of her friends, want to associate with her? Nonetheless, her proximity to my assistant's house made brief exchanges and, later, lengthier conversations seem natural. Su-lan's mother is on good terms with the neighbors and spoke readily about various family matters.

The Wang family is not large—Mrs. Wang is a widow, and Su-lan has an older brother age 26, an older sister age 21, and a younger brother in lower-middle school. Her older brother is a metalworker who lives on his shop premises, returning home every two or three days. Her sister is unmarried and lives in a factory dormitory in Sanhung on the outskirts of Taipei. This leaves Su-lan with most of the housework that her mother cannot finish. When she returns home from the factory each evening, she feeds the chickens, helps prepare dinner, and does the family laundry. Su-lan is fond of novels and wishes she had more time to watch television, but her mother insists that she be in bed by ten, in order to rise at six-thirty to catch the morning company bus. Once Su-lan comes home from work, she rarely goes out again.

Su-lan began working immediately after primary school. She wanted very much to go on to lower-middle school, but her mother explains, "Su-lan did well in school, and it wasn't that we didn't want to let her continue; there just wasn't enough money. I realize that girls who are better educated are able to find better jobs, but once a girl marries, she belongs to other people. Besides, if Su-lan had gone to lower-middle school, it would mean that she would not have been bringing money home. Now her older brother tells her she can afford to attend night school, but she says she is no longer interested. Her older brother also wanted to stay in school, but now he feels he is too old. So he says that if his younger brother wants to go to college, he will manage it somehow." The youngest son is the only one who has progressed beyond elementary school. Younger siblings, especially sons, stand the best chance of attending secondary school, because the earnings of their older siblings, particularly sisters, make tuition payments feasible.

Su-lan turns over all of her monthly earnings to her mother, who then gives her a frugal allowance. Her company, Eastern Textiles, provides uniforms for its employees, and Su-lan often makes her other clothes. She dares not attend the more expensive films in Taipei and instead goes to the cheaper local theaters. Su-lan sees only five or six movies a year. "I don't go too often because my mother says it's a waste of money," she says. When my assistant jokingly suggested to Su-lan that she retain a portion of her earnings, since she is the one who receives the pay envelope each month, she demurred, "That's impossible. People can read figures, and my mother would ask. I could never get away with it." Later, in a more serious vein, Su-lan said she felt that turning over all her earnings to her mother is only right and proper: "After all, our parents raised us. If we don't give them money, who else should it go to?"

Dormitory living can be expected to bring the first break in a daughter's filial piety. It is not factory work itself but the fact that Su-lan's sister has lived away from home for the last several years that gives her more control of her earnings. As Mrs. Wang says, "When my eldest daughter, Su-fang, first began working, she gave me all her earnings. If she needed money for something, she would come to me. But now things are different. She's been working and living outside for a long time, is less obedient, and wants her own way. She holds out NT$400–500 a month for herself and only gives me what is left. She is not like Su-lan, who still gives me all her wages and asks me when she wants spending money. Su-lan is more filial." Mrs. Wang complains that she must dispatch her son to Su-fang's dormitory to make certain that her monthly contribution is forthcoming.

Su-fang has remained at the same factory for four years, however, showing a remarkable degree of stability.

Su-lan is not particularly close to her sister, who returns home every other Sunday, dresses more fashionably, and is more sophisticated. "She's offered to take me swimming with her friends, but I've never had the nerve." Su-lan speaks of her sister without making judgments or showing envy, saying only that she has no desire to see what dormitory living is like. "I prefer being able to come home every day. Even if I were interested, my mother would never allow it, because I'm the only daughter living at home. When Su-fang first finished elementary school, she stayed home for several months doing chores for my mother. Then a relative took her to a family in Shulin who wanted a babysitter, and later another villager brought her to her present factory. That's why she's accustomed to living away from our family and doesn't mind it so much. If I were the one to move so far away, I could never manage. I don't have the courage."

Although her sister's factory is only an hour's bus ride away, Su-lan perceives that as a formidable distance. (In contrast, the more adventurous factory women I met eagerly look forward to traveling from one end of the island to the other.) Su-lan voices other reservations about dormitories: "With so many people living together, the situation is bound to be disorderly. The women do as they please, they may not get along, rooms can be noisy, and so on." Generalizing for other women, Su-lan concludes, "If one's family were nearby, everyone would prefer to live at home."

Su-lan does not complain about her load of housework except for occasional yearnings for more time to watch television. Although the prospect of acquiring a new daughter-in-law to relieve the burden of chores looms large in her mother's mind, Su-lan dares not voice her own feelings about this expectation.

Obtaining a daughter-in-law preoccupies Mrs. Wang with calculations of expenses for the engagement and wedding. "These days a wife can cost up to NT$80,000 or NT$90,000. My son has hardly any savings, and if he has no money, who will marry him? When a daughter marries, you can at least use her bride price to get a daughter-in-law! But this wouldn't balance out for us, because if I let Su-fang marry, that would mean losing her income. So I wouldn't want Su-fang or Su-lan to marry early." Mrs. Wang has begun to press her son to set a date, and in order to raise the necessary funds, she proposed starting a credit association or two if needed. "That way we can be sure of getting about NT$60,000. That should be enough, and we can pay it back with his sisters' help."

The financial and psychological strain that the impending engagement and wedding would impose on the family is compounded by Mrs. Wang's persistent threat to return, in spite of illness, to her arduous job as a manual laborer at a construction site. Her children object but their mother repeatedly raises this possibility, especially after lay-offs at Su-lan's factory. "Some of the neighbors say I should be satisfied since we already have three wage earners in the family. But Su-fang spends too much and doesn't bring enough home. She has even declared to me that compared to other girls in the dormitory, she is considered filial! She leaves me no choice but to go back to work. It's really hard carrying those heavy loads; sometimes my legs shake when I'm going up steps. *My* money is earned the *hard* way."

During this period, Mrs. Wang kept a close eye on the exact sum Su-lan received each day. Su-lan's work is sewing collars on shirts. She and other production workers at Eastern Textiles are paid by the piece, and when there are few orders to be filled, they are given only a minimum base wage. Eventually Mrs. Wang suggested that Su-lan join her cousin at another garment factory, where the base wage was higher. Su-lan was reluctant to make the move, worrying that she might not adjust to a new place, that she would be assigned to seaming cuffs (which is slow and particularly difficult work), and, finally, that she didn't have any friends there.

Mrs. Wang openly expresses her agitation over her daughter's low income. One day, after Su-lan had gone on a reunion outing organized by her elementary school classmates, Mrs. Wang complained to Mrs. Li, an elderly neighbor, "I told her not to go, but she insisted." Mrs. Li said, "She's a big girl already; it wouldn't be right to scold her. Anyway, she turns over all her money to you and is so obedient besides. You aren't earning any money now, so you should treat her better."

Mrs. Wang countered, "It's not that I want to be so strict. But with me not working and her bringing less money home, I lose my temper more easily. It isn't as if we had lots of money. I had to give her NT$100 for the trip plus another NT$100 as spending money. Soon her company is sponsoring a trip south, and that means another NT$100 for transportation, more for expenses, and maybe even a new dress. Where is all that money going to come from? She's still young; she's got lots of opportunities to play later on. We never had such chances when we were young!"

But Su-lan rarely participates in such outings. Her short evenings are largely taken up by chores and television, and she is usually at home on Sundays as well, listening to music or watching television with her sister or her cousin, Pei-ying. Su-lan has few close friends in the village. "Finding someone who can be a close friend isn't easy. Once off work, people either go home or go to school, and if it weren't for Pei-ying, there wouldn't be anyone I could talk to when I'm home."

Su-lan's leisure time increased during the recession, and she spent the daylight hours wandering along the streets of Panchiao and Taipei, restless and frustrated: "People at the company say that many important government people, even Madame Chiang Kai-shek, have invested money in the firm, so they reason that it won't be allowed to go out of business. But here it is only Monday, and they told us not to come back until Thursday. It's hard sitting at home with nothing to do." She describes the problem of irregular work. "Those in the dormitories of our factory are the worst off; if they have to go without regular work for just one month, they're forced to find another job because they have to have money to eat. Now there are only six girls in our section, whereas there were nearly 30 before. The company tries to persuade us to stay, but without work, how can they expect us to remain? The managers tell us that things will improve, but they don't sound as if they believe their own words. Women from the south ask for leaves of absence, saying that they just want to visit their families, but everyone knows they don't intend to come back. That's just a way of quitting politely."

With other girls from her section, Su-lan made the rounds of firms in the area but found nothing that would have been a substantial improvement. Moreover, because no one was willing to make a change alone, the end result was that all of them remained where they were. A number of women at Eastern Textiles have managed to find positions in smaller places, but Su-lan sees the risks of fly-by-night operations: "In those smaller places, work comes in spurts. Sometimes there's a lot of overtime, and then again they can go bankrupt the next day."

Su-lan herself is faced with the social shame of being personally faulted for being out of work. When she is home, she avoids going outside during the day, and when she returns from the factory early, she enters by the back door. "With no work these days, I try not to come in through the front, because people will ask what I'm doing at home. Then I have to explain that there's no work, and just listening to myself is hard to take."

When the effects of the recession were just beginning to be felt, Su-lan sought comfort in the sheer size of Eastern Textiles. "It's too big to go out of business; if it goes, then the whole country is in trouble." The stability and reputed economic soundness of the firm explain why Su-lan has never held another job and why, prior to the recession, she had no plans to change factories. If she were to move to another garment factory, her work would be much the same, but she would have to adapt to new people and strange surroundings. Su-lan adds, "Even if I wanted to change jobs, my mother probably wouldn't allow it, because Eastern Textiles provides buses, which is convenient, and my mother wouldn't want me running around."

As for taking up another line of work entirely, few alternatives seem attractive to her. A classmate obtained a job as a waitress in Taipei, but Su-lan objects, "Girls who become waitresses soon behave in a very casual way with male customers, and it's easy to be deceived. The pay may be a little higher, but the bad influences and habits last a lifetime. There must be other jobs available, so why would someone go into that line of work? With an ordinary job, you earn a bit less and the work may be harder, but at least you lead a happier life." Su-lan makes similar remarks regarding two young women in a troupe which provides entertainment at funerals. "I can't understand how they can exhibit themselves in front of so many people! They could very well go into factories. Whatever would lead a girl to get involved with that type of work?"

Although Su-lan is aware that by most standards factory work is low in status, she does not dwell on this, nor is she prone to reciting her dissatisfactions, as many of the other women workers do. It is also difficult for her to predict her future. "I really haven't given much thought to how long I will remain at Eastern Textiles. One can never tell about the future, so what good does it do to try to think about it? The company has money to hire workers, and it pays me for my work, so I just do what they assign me." Expressing no sense of self-direction, she is concerned only that she is earning something by what she considers respectable means.

One certain event in the future is, of course, marriage. But Su-lan, who considers herself too young to date, would not take my questions about marriage very seriously. She would, however, like to continue working after marriage, provided her mother-in-law helps at home. "Nowadays most girls prefer not to have to do housework, and if it's possible, working outside is easier than doing housework."

Other girls her age do not share her negative view of dating. Her co-workers go out with the "disorderly" and "ill-mannered" male workers at the factory. "Those girls just want to go out and have some fun, but because they're so young, they may be easily misled, and it's always the girl who loses in the end."

Su-lan does not perceive herself as a modern working woman. She accepts her role in the factory without reflection and finds on-the-job gratification only through casual co-worker relations. She appreciates the piece-work organization and its fair degree of autonomy from the supervisors. Her relations with group leaders and foremen seem satisfactory to her because of their absence of close contact. "With our type of work, we have little to do with them. We don't need to talk to them much, so relations between us are neither one way nor the other. Supervisors and workers who've been in the same section longer may know each other better, but they don't know much in the way of personal matters. Besides, the workers aren't afraid of supervisors, because how fast we work affects our own pay more than it affects them. That's the good part about this job—you just rely on yourself, and there's no need to flatter the group leader or the foreman."

Similarly, she does not expect special treatment from her employer. "It's only in a small factory that the management can look after its workers. In a company this size, with so many workers, it isn't possible for the management to see to our needs. There are so many managers and supervisors as it is—how could they have time to show concern for us workers? That's why some girls would rather go to a company that pays higher wages; they feel that if a firm is willing to pay more, it means that the workers are more highly valued."

If the location of the factories were remote from Su-lan's community, it is probable that she and women of her age would remain home until marriage, leading a fairly restricted life. In evaluating the options that wage earning makes available to them, however, it is essential to remember that their ability to choose among alternatives is often contingent on gaining their parents' approval. This must be borne in mind to avoid over-estimating the actual extent of change that factory wage labor has introduced into these women's lives.

For instance, leaving school to begin work was not a decision these women made on their own. Initially, they lacked realistic conceptions about the job market. However, because factory employment for young women is becoming more prevalent and companies are disseminating information more systematically through recruiters, recent middle school graduates are somewhat better informed than the women who preceded them. It is primarily women from this younger group, rather than Su-lan's contemporaries, who assert that it is best to learn as much as possible about a firm before seeking a job there and who stress the maturity that independence brings. This attitude is in marked contrast to Su-lan's; she never uses the terms "independent" or "self-reliance" in reference to herself. Factory employment has never fostered aspirations of independence in Su-lan.

Teng Hsiu-ling: Middle Sister

Teng Hsiu-ling remarks that she has done virtually every kind of work imaginable, a statement that accurately sums up the past 10 years of her life. In 1974, she was 24 and had been employed at Eastern Textiles for almost three years, the longest time she has spent at any single factory. She has been exposed to a far greater range of environments than most women her age, and after piecing together the sequence of her jobs, the impression is of someone moving impulsively from place to place with little direction and surprisingly little parental interference.

Hsiu-ling accompanies her words with quick gestures and acts on the spur of the moment. Other women say she is too outspoken. Her older sister is an equally forceful personality; the only one in the family who is cautious is their mother, a small laconic woman, who barely acknowledged our presence. Hsiu-ling's father is a coal dealer who conducts his business from one room of their house. Other family members living at home include three sons, two older than Hsiu-ling and one younger. The eldest brother had married and moved to Taipei. The Teng family house, situated on one of the two main streets in Chipei, always seemed dark.

Hsiu-ling left home to work almost immediately after elementary school, when she was sent to live with a family in Shulin, another market town. Her duties there included helping in the family-owned store, babysitting, and housework. Her next position was similar; she stayed with a family that had a dressmaking business. Between child care and housekeeping chores, Hsiu-ling tried to learn sewing skills. "I'll never forget one incident—I was supposed to watch their twin daughters, but once when I wasn't looking, one of them fell and injured her leg. Her father became very angry with me, telling me that I was careless and irresponsible. After that scolding, I wanted only to leave. By that time, too, I knew I had no knack for sewing. My second brother had told me to go there in the first place, saying that girls should learn dressmaking. What did I know? I was only 14 then. Finally I became homesick, and when it was obvious that I wasn't learning, my brother let me come home."

She next went to Taipei to serve as personal maid to three bar hostesses. She shared their flat in a modern district bustling with tourists. Hsiu-ling had no complaints about the work itself. Her employers, themselves young, were not overly demanding and treated her well. "The only part I didn't like was the fact that there were always foreigners hanging around or other men who came to play mah-jongg. I couldn't sleep because of the noise. Besides, people kept saying that if I stayed there much longer, I would soon be in the same type of work as they were." She left this job but remained in Taipei and worked as a maid for a doctor's family. "That only lasted a few months. His wife was very picky and fussy, and I couldn't stand her. She was so condescending, and I had to eat in a different room after they finished their meals. Considering the work involved and my age, though, the wages were high—NT$40 a day."

Hsiu-ling subsequently returned to Chipei, where she stayed home for several weeks before heading for Taipei once more. "A girl I knew in Chinan had gotten an introduction to a restaurant, and we went there together to work as waitresses. The restaurant owner had some rooms nearby for his employees, and that was all right because the rent was very low. But a waitress job is almost like being a prostitute. Some men are rude and make jokes at your expense. Some are members of gangs, and you have to be careful not to offend them or else they may decide to 'fix' you."

She then went to work in a store. "Being a shopgirl isn't as easy as it looks. Some people think we just sit all day, but they don't understand that our hours are different from everyone else's. One also needs a great deal of patience, which I didn't have. Customers will pick and choose, bargain, and then end up without buying. Besides, there's only so much a salesgirl can do; the product either sells itself or it doesn't." During this period, Hsiu-ling and several other shopgirls shared rooms provided by their employer. "The girls from the south soon decided to move out to a place of their own, saying that our boss imposed too many restrictions on us. Those girls always helped each other; when someone from their village came up, they would help her find a job or let her replace one of them, so they could go home for a visit."

At 18, Hsiu-ling took her first factory job; she began in a textile mill close to home. She soon decided that she could not tolerate the cotton dust from the spinning machines. "Another problem was that all of us worked rotating shifts, alternating every week. Just as you were getting used to one sleeping schedule, you had to begin another." She changed to Eastern Textiles, where she was again assigned to the spinning section. Her first stay at this factory was brief: "I developed nosebleeds, and my third brother said I had better quit before things got worse."

Hsiu-ling then learned how to operate a knitting machine. These have become virtually ubiquitous in the Taiwanese countryside. A family may own one or several of these machines, depending on their capital, volume of business, and how many workers their living room and any additional rooms can accommodate. Workers are not difficult to find, because hours are flexible and machine operators (both male and female) are paid by the piece and can work well into the evenings, raising their wages when they feel like it by a burst of effort. Hsiu-ling did not have to go far to find such a position, and for a few months her place of work was a neighbor's house several doors from home. Three other women worked there, and she recalls having enjoyed learning to use the machine: "I finally felt as if I were acquiring a skill." The reason for her departure in this case, she claims, was her employer's wife. "She was always coming by to watch us. She expected us to sweep the floors, and that's something I don't do even at home. Two of the other girls didn't get along with her either, so the three of us left together. Another reason we left was propriety. Our boss would often talk and joke with us during our breaks, and once he treated us to a movie. The woman next door began to gossip about us, saying that we weren't decent and didn't behave properly. It just wasn't worth the bother to stay on."

Hsiu-ling began to show some stability with her position in a toy factory in Sanhung. This company employed 20 women, most of them from southern Taiwan, and the owner returned periodically to his home district in the south to recruit additional workers. Hsiu-ling applied for a job after reading an advertisement, and her two years there passed quickly. She even brought another Chipei girl to work in the factory.

Overall, she has pleasant memories of the people there and enjoys reminiscing. "Twenty people aren't very many, and maybe because of this we all got along very well, including the boss and his wife. Once I was sick, and his wife brought me special dishes and not the food the other workers were eating. When they saw that one of us seemed moody or unhappy, they would ask us what the problem was. But most of the girls were from the south, and I gradually found that I couldn't always get along with them. They've done farm work at home, so they are accustomed to hard work. Even in Sanhung they maintained the same habits; they would sometimes work until midnight and then get up very early the next morning to start over again. I just couldn't take it. They managed to produce a lot more than I did, and it appeared as if I were the lazy and inefficient one. They were also very frugal and hardly ever wanted to go out, and that left me with few companions.

"But actually the main reason I quit was because of something else. Before the New Year holiday one year, the boss didn't tell me when we would start work again, although later I discovered he told the others. Not letting me know was the same as not wanting me to work any more. He came here after New Year's, asking me to return, but I wasn't about to; he only came to me when he couldn't find anybody else. Well, in any case, factories are all the same; they all use people. It's true—they just use our labor to make money. I once went back to see them, but there had been some changes, and most of the girls were new. The boss will always be boss, while we're only workers." The expressions of concern from her employer that Hsiu-ling had valued in the beginning were not enough to offset what she saw as a basically exploitative relationship.

Hsiu-ling returned to the garment section of Eastern Textiles. When asked if she had any intention of leaving, she replied, "It's hard to say. One thing is certain—I won't go into an electronics factory. That kind of work is all right if it's for a short duration, but if one stays longer, the soldering fumes are harmful to one's health. If it's a new type of job entirely, that's not good, because you don't know anything in the beginning and have to learn from scratch. I've already done too much running around; changing jobs one more time probably won't satisfy me. Besides, I've been at Eastern Textiles for almost three years, and while the work is only so-so, I'm used to things here now."

Hsiu-ling finds her current work situation unrewarding. "Many girls say that we're wasting away our best years at Eastern Textiles, because by the time we get home each day, it's late and there's no opportunity to go out with friends. It's as if we were shut up inside all day, selling part of our lives just to earn some money." She complained several times about the frequent overtime, and I asked about the possibility of making her feelings known to her supervisor. She responded, "Look at it this way—there are lots of people who've been at Eastern Textiles a long time, and they don't dare say anything. Who are we, who've only been there a couple of years, to say more? So we just complain to each other, and in the end, it's not even worth discussing."

Hsiu-ling enjoys television serials but wishes there were more women in the neighborhood who would accompany her to movies or join her in other activities. "Because I've been away from home for so long, I don't know the people here well, and I feel bored and restless when Sunday comes. Although I have sisters, the three of us don't get along well, because each of us has very definite ideas."

Hsiu-ling's older sister was 33 at the time I knew the family, and even though matches had been suggested, she had no plans to marry. She was using her spare time learning to chant the texts used for ritual occasions at a nearby temple. Hsiu-ling resents her younger sister, Li-ching, an adopted daughter. As a legitimate offspring, Hsiu-ling feels that she should be treated more leniently then Li-ching. "My younger sister has a much better life than I do. Some people don't know and think I am the adopted daughter rather than Li-ching! Ordinarily, parents treat their own daughter better than an adopted daughter, but in our case my mother treats Li-ching better—much, much better. If Li-ching wants to go out, my mother never says no, but I have to stay home and cook. She goes south to amuse herself while I'm supposed to 'play' in the kitchen! When we were small, my mother wanted to let Li-ching go on to middle school, but it was Li-ching herself who didn't want to. As for me, I wasn't smart enough to do well in school, and our family didn't have a lot of money, so I wasn't given the chance to continue school. Now Li-ching is interested in school, but it's too late and there's nothing to be said. Mother also pays less attention to how much money Li-ching brings home; even if it isn't much, she doesn't seem to mind. With me, Mother expects the same amount each month. The reason my mother is so kind to Li-ching is that Mother was an adopted daughter herself, and from the time she was a little girl, she had to do more around the house and was scolded more often by her foster mother than her stepbrothers and stepsisters."

The strained relationship between the sisters is why they never took jobs at the same factory and why Hsiu-ling was so ready to leave home at such an early age. To resolve the strain between the sisters, the family granted considerable freedom to Hsiu–ling in her job decisions and mobility.

In 1974, Hsiu–ling had no idea of how long she would be working. "A person can never tell what circumstances will be like in the future, so thinking about it doesn't take you very far. I just take each day as it comes. But after a woman marries and has children, she can't work because her family is more important; children need their mother's care. As for whether I'll have a job after I marry, I guess that will be up to my husband, but since I don't even have a boyfriend, it doesn't make sense to talk of such things."

Two years later Hsiu–ling married a man she met through a mutual friend. They now live in Taipei, where her husband and his brother own a small store. Hsiu–ling spends her time minding this shop.

8

Taiwan Electronics Workers
Lim Li-suat: Adopted Daughter
Tsai Chen-hwei: Divorcée

By Linda Gail Arrigo

Introduction

Taiwan's working women rank themselves by family background, education, and income. In workplace and dormitory, they form mutually exclusive social groups, from the least advantaged women—those who are only primary school graduates from poor rural homes and have given up on further education—to those who can spend all their limited salary after paying tuition, to those with good clerical jobs, quite likely obtained through connections. Many women explained to me that it is shameful to be poor or from a poor family: "It is not good to let your associates know about it, or they will look down on you." Even women whose income is comparable are further divided over small discrepancies in schooling or social status: "People will laugh at you if they know you are an adopted daughter."

The women assembly workers and low-ranking clerical workers frequently complain about their tight budgets and sparse living environments, haughty treatment and even sexual exploitation by managers, and how difficult it is to get a good office job. But their main concern is how to get a husband of good disposition and multiple assets, which they view as an escape from all these oppressions. By common agreement of the women workers in discussion groups, sufficient assets include a monthly income of at least NT$10,000, the salary of a skilled blue-collar worker or an office worker. However, they also desire a husband who is refined in manner, not one who does hard labor and comes home stained with sweat and grease. Best of all is a man who is a government employee or teacher and thus has a stable, secure, lifelong job with health insurance and other employment benefits.

By estimate of the Taiwan Provincial Family Planning Research Institute, there are twice as many single women as single men of marriageable

123

age. Accordingly, there are increasing numbers of young women who cannot live up to the dictates of traditional custom that every woman must marry and who are stigmatized for their unwitting failure. The factory dormitory that I studied holds a fair number of women who are near 30, especially among the secretaries and professionals. What will happen to them later I do not know.

Intense competition for spouses under a regime in which male purchasing power places highest value on female virginity is the only way I can explain the viciousness of the women's recriminations against those who have lost their chastity or who are suspected of promiscuity. The young women in the dormitory are hostile toward the older unmarried women and divorced women living among them, as if their misfortune were an infectious plague.[1] The life of Tsai Chen-hwei in this book illustrates this amply. The prevailing morality denies that women have sexual needs, and women who appear to give away their sexual goods arouse the ire of those who are seeking to sell theirs at the high price of marriage and lifetime support. Thus women become the caustic enforcers of restrictions on each other. These interactions—the jockeying for position among women of different class backgrounds and the aspersions of sexual impropriety—are an indirect cultural expression of the local political economy.

The political economy was revealed through my interviews with dormitory supervisors and personnel managers about recruitment, social background, and life patterns of female workers. Personnel managers were most concerned about turnover, efficiency, and labor costs and knew little about the personal lives of their workers. They stated offhandedly that young women would work docilely for less money than men and that it was not necessary to provide for long-term career advancement or security. They believed young unmarried women to be more industrious, taking less time off for family responsibilities. Employment of young unmarried women obviates the necessity for maternity benefits for married employees. The physical examination at hiring even includes a urine test for pregnancy! The recruiting managers establish close connections with junior high school principals all over the island, and thus each crop of graduates, especially those from remote rural areas, is channeled into employment in the industrial zones. When labor needs are especially pressing, the Ministry of Education assists recruitment by allowing "work-study" for those who have not yet graduated.

Since 1974, a new wage system has grown up, at least in textiles and electronics, the main export industries. As wages rose to keep pace with mild inflation, salary increases became variously named performance bonuses, which often constituted as much as 20 percent of total wages. Lunch and transportation allowances also ballooned. The performance bonuses are regulated and can be denied for a multitude of reasons, including tardiness of over five minutes and taking sick leave. The performance bonuses and allowances are also excluded from calculations of hourly payment for overtime work and year-end bonuses. Depending on whether managers wished to reduce or expand the labor force, bonuses can be given strictly or freely. Strictly enforcing the performance bonus rules can result in a labor cost savings which I estimate to be as much as 5 percent; some workers will also get angry and quit without severance pay. When export orders are up and peak production is sought, performance bonuses can be given freely, and their selective distribution still functions as an informal punishment for those who refuse to work overtime. Payment for overtime may actually be lower than wages plus bonuses for regular worktime.

Such means of adjusting labor costs have been especially important since the 1974 oil crisis, because production orders have been more uncertain and production planning shorter since then. The life conditions of the Taiwan female worker—her migration, separation from family, and physical surroundings—are intimately and increasingly tied to the world market.

Lim Li-suat: Adopted Daughter

One September night in 1975, when I was visiting as usual in the rooms of the factory dormitory, I asked the women about their reaction to a recent talk on marriage compatibility by a psychology professor. In the course of the discussion, one woman in a school uniform gave an eloquent account of what being independent meant to her. "As for me, my home is not far away, but I want to live here. Here we can be free. When you live at home, you have to turn all your money over to your parents. When you want to go out, you have to ask them. What you want to eat, what you want to do, is beyond your own control. Here we come and go as we please, eat what we want. Of course, my freedom is limited by my economic means, but within these limits, I feel I have control over my own life and responsibility for myself." This was Lim Li-suat, known as A-suat to her friends.

After a two-year absence from Taiwan, I ran into A-suat in June 1977. When I visited her dormitory room, she was reading, just for amusement, from a textbook of classical Chinese with phonetic guides and explanation prepared by the *Kuoyü Daily Newspaper*. She said she likes to read about ancient history, because one can learn about how people behave and society operates. I asked if she had studied modern Chinese history. She replied, "Yes, I have studied a little. There isn't much of it in the textbooks. . . . Once one of my history teachers, a young teacher, said not to believe everything we read in the books. He also told us not to quote him outside the classroom. Maybe after a long time we will be able to know the real present-day history."

I asked her what she does besides work, if she still went to night school. She said that she had graduated from high school just last month but was staying on at the electronics company because about a year ago she got a promotion to the position of personnel and materials manager for one section. She manages about 60 people; some are retired military. Her section is more mechanized than most; the workers just watch the machines, so there are no female assembly workers in her area. Her work is fairly leisurely, and she can take off an hour for lunch or leave for home early if her work is finished for the day. She has several different tasks. Aside from keeping track of attendance and advising the line leaders, she requisitions the raw materials for the day and prepares reports on the cost of the product, taking into account both labor and raw materials.

As for what she does besides work, she says, "I have joined the social service group that my teacher started. It got going just a few months ago. We do things like go to see children in hospitals and orphanages. I am also studying child psychology. You have to study it in order to do social services properly. Every Sunday afternoon, we go to see the children in the hospital. It is pretty hard to do. The family is usually around the child and is not very cooperative in our presence. We try to bring along interesting objects and think of games to play with the children. It is very hard to make them smile; they are usually sullen. You feel it isn't worthwhile to come. But every once in a while, a child will say something clever and be glad that you came, and then you feel that they are learning and you want to come again. Sometimes we go to orphanages. The children are very dirty if they have not already taken a bath when we come. If not, you have to keep them at arm's length, or you will get black splotches on your clothes. They are very naughty, not at all obedient. When we bring candy or toys, they snatch them from us and fight with each other. For the older ones, there isn't much hope of making them behave better, but for the younger ones, we hope that if we give them some love, they will learn good behavior. I like social work; we must be concerned about our society. I'd like to be a teacher."

A young woman came in to see A-suat. She had four beautifully watercolored folders with inscriptions like "A drop of love . . ." on them. They were to be used for name rosters in a blood donation drive. A-suat discussed how to staple in the blank lined paper for name lists. After the other woman left, I explained that I was interested in society too and was researching the role of women in industrializing countries. I asked her to come to visit me in a few days.

A-suat arrived at my house slightly early. She was very well dressed but said she had just come from work and that these were her regular clothes.

She wore a tailored white skirt, very high white heeled shoes (the expensive kind), and stockings that were faintly white in sheen. She is not very tall but is well proportioned, with a slight swell of bosom. She has short dark hair and a curly permanent. When I first met her two years ago, she wore a neat khaki schoolgirl uniform and a Dutch boy student haircut. She has beautiful skin, and she wears glasses most of the time. She often has a slightly stiff good-little-schoolgirl expression. Her voice is shrill and a little rasping. Her responses are quick, and she speaks intelligently. It is easy to see why she was promoted from the ranks of assembly workers.

I served some grapes. She asked about my husband and child, whom she had heard about two years earlier. I liked her, and I told her quite openly that I had freed myself from marriage and was going about my own goals of social research, although sometimes I missed my child. I am glad to be free. This seemed to touch something in her, and suddenly she began to talk about herself with intensity.

"I am free, too. I am free, floating around with no relatives or friends to care about me and to depend on. These last few years I keep feeling as though I am floating. I feel free and independent, but it is also a little frightening. In this society, it is difficult to explain yourself if you don't have relatives. Friends think you should have relatives to care for you if you are a good person.

"I am an adopted daughter." A-suat said this starkly and simply. I asked her to explain. "I don't have a happy relationship with my adopted family, and I don't really belong to my real parents. So I have nobody."

"What does it mean if you are an adopted daughter? Why should that matter?" I sat back with studied relaxation, watched her intensely, and waited patiently for her reply.

"People look down on you," she said with a pained grimace.

"Like who? Why should they look down on you?" I asked gently.

"Like my eldest younger brother. He said to me, 'If you have money, you can make a dead man work for you.' It means he looks down on me. He said that even though I have been his elder sister for many years and took care of him when he was little." The lines of strain around her mouth deepened, and she seemed to speak very quickly so that she wouldn't cry. I was perplexed by the Taiwanese idiom and surprised that she was suddenly exposing what seemed to be deep personal feelings. I asked her what he meant.

"It happened this last Chinese New Year's. All children go home to their parents at Chinese New Year's. So do I. When I got home, my eldest younger brother was already back from military camp; he is in military service now. I always help take care of the house. I saw that the wallpaper in the front room was discolored and peeling, so I measured the room, gave my youngest little brother some money, and sent him out to the store to buy the wallpaper and some other things for Chinese New Year's. Then my eldest younger brother said to me, 'If you have money, you can make a dead man work for you.' He really hurt my feelings, but since we never got along very well anyway, I didn't make much of it and just went about my preparations and the wallpapering.

"The next day, I got up and took a walk around where we live, which is in the suburbs but nearly outside the city. I saw a pretty pagoda and hiked to it and went in. It was a pagoda for holding bone urns. It was a little scary, and I left right away. I mentioned it when I went home, and my eldest younger brother said I was bringing bad luck to the house, especially on the first day of the new year. But how was I to know it was a bone tower? I left as soon as I found out.

"In the afternoon, I was watching television by myself, and my brothers were playing poker. My little brother started crying because the others owed him some poker chips and wouldn't hand them over. He screamed and cried for a long time, and finally I couldn't watch TV anymore, so I went over and told my brothers to give him the poker chips. They didn't pay any attention to me; my eldest and second younger brothers didn't even talk to me. My little brother kept screaming. I got angry and told them, 'If you don't listen to your elder sister, you can give back my red money gift envelopes!' I didn't really want them back—I just wanted them to pay attention to me. Maybe I shouldn't have said that, but they were really being mean. My eldest younger brother said to me, 'Who cares about your lousy money!' and a lot of other things too. My mother came over and scolded *me* for making a fuss on the New Year, and she told me to go back to watching TV. But she also picked up the package of cookies I was eating and put it away."

A few minutes earlier, A-suat's eyes had become very shiny. Now a few drops welled over, stopped at the bottom edge of her glasses, and slowly marked wet streaks down her cheeks. I gave her a tissue, and said something lighthearted in the hope that she wouldn't be too overcome and embarrassed and stop talking. But she was so immersed in the experience that she continued immediately.

"I always cry when I think about it, even though it is already half a year ago. My roommates think I am too sensitive. . . . But how could my mother treat me like that? I couldn't protest that I had worked for her for so many years, taken care of the children, and done the housework. I just started bawling and went to my bed and wrapped myself in the blankets and cried all night. My eyes got swollen. Nobody came to call me or talk to me.

"The next morning, as I was waking up, I heard my father and eldest younger brother talking in the front room, near where I was sleeping. My eldest younger brother said he was going back to military camp early, that he didn't want to stay at home. Then he said to my father, 'She's got such a temper. She's studied too much; she's gone crazy.' My brother said it right where he knew I could hear! When I heard that, I was beside myself, really anguished—I put myself through three years of junior high school and three years of senior high school, all working in the daytime and studying at night! They didn't help me at all! How could I be crazy? I got angry and started crying again, and I came out and asked my brother how he could talk about me like that. He left. My father said some things to calm me, then he said what my brother had said, repeated it directly to me—'You've studied too much, you're mentally ill.' I couldn't stand it any more. I threw my things together, and I left. It was only the third day of the New Year, and there was no electricity or hot water at the dormitory because everyone was away, but I didn't think of that—I just left.

"I cried and walked, wandering in the direction of the bus stop. Tears were running down my face. I walked and cried. Then a young man on a motorcycle asked me the way to Chia Chuang College. I pointed the way but didn't talk to him. He kept saying politely that he didn't know the way and would get lost, so would I please get on the motorcycle and direct him? He was very gentle and polite, and the college was just a few bus stops away from where I was going, so I got on. I kept crying to myself. He didn't say anything. After about 10 minutes, I looked up and saw that he wasn't going the right direction for Chia Chuang College! I shouted and made him let me off. In another few minutes, he would have carried me far off the main road! He left without saying anything. He looked like a polite young man; how could I know he was a bad man? I felt worse and cried harder.

"I took the bus all the way back to Hsinchuang, near my dormitory. I didn't have anything to do, so I went to a movie. It was an American movie. The theater was half-empty. I cried as I watched the movie. I didn't have anyplace to go, so I sat through it again. A man was standing near me in the aisle, and finally I noticed that he was wandering closer and closer. I kept watching the movie. But then he came very close and faced me. He exposed his private parts to me! I couldn't stand to look; I almost threw up! I was very frightened; I stood up and left the theater in a hurry. How could two bad things like that happen in one day? That never happened to me before.

"By then, the sky was beginning to get dark. I wanted to go back to the dormitory, but the electricity and hot water were turned off. I was afraid to be by myself in the dark. Only a few people were left who didn't go home because their homes were very far away in south Taiwan. If I talked to the other workers, they would want to know why I was back already when my home was just on the other side of the city.

"Finally I got on the bus and went back to Tatze. When I got home again, it was eight o'clock. I knocked on the door. My mother opened the door and said, 'Oh, you're back'; she didn't ask where I had been. My eldest younger brother was home, too. We all went to bed. The next morning, my eldest younger brother got ready to go back to military camp, and my mother got up early and fixed a special breakfast and fussed over him. She didn't prepare any for me. When I left, she didn't say much to me or tell me to come back again soon. It was still a day before the end of the New Year's holiday, but I just stayed in the dark dormitory."

During most of her narration, A-suat's arms were tightly flexed, and she ate only a few grapes. A tear trickled down periodically. Now her arms and cheeks relaxed somewhat. I asked her about her current relationship with her family.

"Ever since I was little, the neighbors always knew and remarked that I was an adopted daughter. I didn't know why it mattered that I was adopted; I lived with my family and did everything like their daughter. Why do they always have to mark me a 'yang-nü' [foster daughter]?

"After a few weeks, I went back home again briefly. When I was going to school, I could manage to save only a few hundred dollars and send it home every month or so to buy some extra things to eat at New Year's or other festival times. But since I graduated from high school last June and also got promoted, I can afford to send more money now. I took some money home on Sunday. My mother wasn't there, but my father said that my mother told him to tell me that the household didn't need my money anymore. My father repeated what my mother said without any particular expression. He just does what my mother says. I really feel separated from my family; they don't care about me. Since then, I send money home by post office money order rather than by going myself, because they look down on me and I am afraid they won't take it. Am I not part of the family?

"I wanted to give my third younger brother NT$1,000 to buy a watch, because he just got a very good grade on his senior high school entrance examination and will get into Chien Kuo High School. I felt pained that he might not take it. But my second younger brother, with whom I get along better, told me not to worry and took the money to give to our younger brother."

I asked A-suat if she helped pay for her younger brothers' education. She said that they were all allowed to go through junior middle school before working; she recently paid NT$1,000 a semester toward her third younger brother's tuition. I asked her if her family might want to ostracize her because there is some question of inheritance. She said that they are poor and don't have any land to split up. Moreover, when she was 20 and went to live in the dormitory and work, her parents told her quite clearly not to expect any *chia chuang* (dowry and wedding furniture) from them.

She would have to save up for her dowry from her own earnings. I asked A-suat how she felt about that. She said it was all right with her; she didn't seem resentful about it. I queried her on the specifics of her early life, and gradually the following came out.

"When I was two years old, my real parents, who live in Sanchungp'u, gave me to my foster mother. At that time, my foster mother didn't have any children. But later she had five boys. I was 13 years old when the last one was born. At first we lived on Yenp'ing North Road. We were very poor. My mother worked near Yuanhuan. When I wasn't in school, I had to take care of the baby. The summer that I was eight, I had to carry my little brother all the way down to Yuanhuan at noon so my mother could nurse him. He was so heavy; I had to walk almost an hour to get there. Later we moved to Tatze.

"After I graduated from primary school, I couldn't go to school anymore. At that time, there wasn't any middle school available. At first, I worked as an apprentice in a garment assembly factory in Hsinchuang. I made only NT$200 a month. I lived at home and brought the money back to my parents. I worked there for almost three years. Because I was only an apprentice, I made hardly any money, but at least I learned a little about making clothes. We were very poor then, too. When I was about 11 or 12, I remember that my mother, my eldest younger brother, and I had to work every night until midnight, peeling water lotus seeds for a restaurant. We worked like that for a long time, but we still didn't have enough money to buy food. We didn't have any vegetables or meat to eat. We didn't even have enough rice, because our credit at the rice shop was bad. Everyone in our family had white tongues—white on the sides. I don't know why it was like that, but when we didn't have enough to eat, our tongues got white. After my eldest younger brother went to work, our financial situation got a little better.

"My uncle ran a rice shop, and his son helped him. When his son went into military service, my uncle hired me to help, so I quit the garment factory. I worked in the rice shop nearly three years; I still lived at home and gave my wages to my mother. Then my cousin came back from military service.

"By then I was 20. I wanted to go back to school, so I found a job as an assembler at an electronics company. That job allowed me to go to school at night and also provided a dormitory and some tuition assistance. My family wasn't happy that I wanted to go. Probably they would have been happier if I had stayed at home and earned money and kept doing the housework. My father said, 'It is useless for girls to get education.' But I went anyway. When I needed money for my tuition, I borrowed it from my real elder brother in Sanchungp'u. I have two real elder brothers. But I have never been close to my real family, because I have seen them only once or twice a year since I was little. When I go there, they are very kind and polite to me, as though I'm a guest. When I borrow money from my real elder brother, I pay it back right away."

I said, "I thought that since you just graduated from school you must be about 20. I didn't know you were already 26. Are you concerned about marriage?"

"I am afraid to get married. My life is very free at present, but of course everyone has to get married. Some people say that old spinsters get bad tempers. I think maybe it is true. It really troubles me that recently I've been losing my temper for no reason at all. Last week, I was watching television in the central lounge near my dormitory room. A co-worker stepped on my toe, but I didn't say anything, just glared at her once. Then she bumped me and said, 'Miss, don't you talk?' I don't know why I got upset. I got up and ran to my room and lay down on my bunk and cried in the blankets. My roommates must think I'm overwrought—to cry like that over nothing.

"But I am really afraid to get married. I look at my parents, and I think I never want to get married. They have been fighting ever since they got married. When I was little, they said they wanted to get divorced, but then they didn't, and they had so many babies. They don't even care what they say in front of the children. My mother has the temper of a tiger; she bosses my father around. Recently he is developing a little more self-respect. I would rather not get married than get married and live like that."

Tsai Chen-hwei: Divorcée

I first saw her at a bus stop in October 1977. She was a plump but handsome young matron, perhaps 35 or more, with a scholarly mien beneath her black-rimmed glasses. Her hair was combed conservatively, flat tight curls framing her face. She wore a staid maroon-gray knit dress. She was a pleasant-looking woman, probably one of the neighbors, I thought, and I asked her the time. Soon I gave up waiting for the bus because it was hot and dusty and I would be late for my appointment. When I hailed a taxi, I asked if I could drop her off on the way. After a moment's surprise and hesitation, she smiled and got in. The taxi had to take a long detour around a blocked section of the road, and we readily struck up a conversation; I was immediately gratified by her straightforward openness. Her name was Tsai Chen-hwei, and she was a Hokkien-speaking native of Tainan, although from her excellent Mandarin, I would not have known.

Chen-hwei said that she had just arrived that morning from Tainan by all-night train and had already signed up for work at the local electronics company, a mammoth foreign-capitalized plant. I told her that I knew some people at the dormitory and gave her what useful information I could about the area. It was plain that she was not accustomed to dormitories and that her life had not taken the usual course of long residence with and service to husband and children. The others at the dormitory were mostly young unmarried women, "girl children," as they still call themselves, age 18 to 24. I invited her to my office-residence the next morning for a chat and an outing, since she didn't have to start work yet, and she happily agreed. I talked a lot about myself, especially since I was relieved to have someone other than naive young maidens to converse with; it was easy to talk to her, because she accepted things without surprise or judgment. She got out of the taxi in a residential district not far from the center of Taipei.

When I got home at seven that evening, I was surprised but glad to see her there. Late that afternoon, the company had told her that the staff member who arranged for dormitory accommodations was absent and that she should come back in two days. She had a friend who lived not far away, but her friend would not be back until midnight; in the meantime, she was hoping just to have someplace to sit down.

Her friend was married to a construction worker, and the couple lived temporarily in buildings as they were being built. Every day I saw laborers like her friend's husband, plastering glossy ceramic tile on the faces of apartment blocks. They were a symbol of the rapid industrialization and urbanization of this area of outlying Taipei, the main metropolis of Taiwan. When I had first come here 15 years ago, only a few blocks of gray tile-roofed houses backed the one main road down the valley, and emerald paddy fields lay in neat squares from the river to the hills. Now row after row of concrete four-story apartment blocks marched toward the hills, engulfing farmhouses and what had been market streets. Asphalt spread everywhere, stopping short only at ditches that used to be streams; now they were filled with refuse and black sludge. Gleaming, massive factories have been imposed on the paddy land; they mingle with the puffing smokestacks of small commerce and industry. The roar and dust of heavy trucks and buses rise from the main thoroughfare, now a four-lane highway; in the late afternoon, the bus stops are crowded with students and young factory workers coming home or leaving for night school.

Chen-hwei asked about my occupation, and I explained in general terms that I am a social scientist interested in modern women's lives and current social problems. She asked if I had any children, and I guessed from the inflection in her voice that she had children too. I showed her pictures of my son. Eventually, quite unself-consciously and cheerfully, she began to tell me about herself and why she was coming to work in Taipei.

She had two children—a boy one and a half years old, and a girl two and a half. She and her mother lived in Tainan, and her mother took care of the daughter. She was coming to Taipei to work and to see her son. Why was her son in Taipei? Her smile had a touch of melancholy. "I got married when I was 27, almost 28. I met my husband through an introduction. He worked in Taipei, so we exchanged letters and met only a few times before we got married. We never had any period of romance. It wasn't long before I found out he had a violent disposition. He was 35 when we got married and was used to living by himself. He lived in a bachelor apartment, part of his company dormitory. He never made any allowance for my living with him and did what he wanted without talking to me. He made NT$7,000 a month. This was a fair salary, but he put it in his savings account and never gave me any, even for food or the expenses of the house. I used up all my private money that my mother gave me. Then he got me a temporary job at NT$3,000 a month for three months. Once he gave me his salary together with mine and told me to deposit the money in his account. I did, and then I couldn't get any back from him.

"I had my first child at the end of my twenty-eighth year, my second near the end of my twenty-ninth year. I am 30 now. When I was pregnant, I always went home to Tainan. My mother took care of me, then I delivered at home. So I did not live with him for very long.

"When I came back, I stayed home to take care of my children. My husband constantly abused me, scolding me that I couldn't make money and I didn't love or care for our son well. But he didn't provide any money for me and the children. Once my daughter got sick, and I wanted to take her to the doctor, but I didn't have any money. He wouldn't let me go to the doctor until she became seriously ill and other friends said it had to be done. He wouldn't even let me go out of the house; then he abused me until I had no choice but to leave. He is so ferocious and single-minded that there is no way to talk to him. I gave up."

"What does he want to put all that money away for? Doesn't he make good wages and get free housing?"

"His parents live in Malaysia, even though they are Taiwanese, and I think he wants to save enough money to move back there. So he just throws his wife and family on the rubbish heap.

"My second child is a boy—a beautiful boy. When he was a month old, my husband came down to Tainan to see him and took him! I shouldn't have agreed to the divorce so easily. But he abused me until I was just glad to get away. He was afraid that I might ask for money for settlement. He said that I had no economic capacity, certainly not enough to support two children. His brother has only four girls, and my son is the only grandson to continue the line of descent, so my husband wanted him. I couldn't stand to be abused anymore; with his violent temper, there was no way I could reason with him. I didn't get any compensation from him. Even if I had made a court case, he would have said that I had no economic capacity. We went to the police office and put our seals on the divorce statement. He paid NT$2,000 for half the fees, and I paid NT$2,000, too. I never want to go back to him, there is no emotion between us. But my son—!"

"When you were young—20 or so—didn't you ever go out and meet men? How did you happen to marry somebody you hardly knew?"

"When I was 20 . . . I rarely went out. I wasn't like young women today; I didn't know how to play," she sighed. For the moment she would say nothing more.

I thought of an unmarried woman, Miss Chia, whom I had met two weeks before, and could well imagine how Chen-hwei may have looked before marriage—perhaps not very different from afterwards. Miss Chia is 27 now. When she was little, her father was a poor farm tenant in Taipei district. After primary school, at age 14, she went to work at a garment factory in Keelung for five years. By then, her brothers had started a business, and her father had gotten compensation under government regulations for the rights of tenants when the paddy land was sold as a site for high-rise apartments. Miss Chia had gone through six years of night school for junior and senior high while working at an electronics company and occasionally doing accounting for her brothers. Finally, at 27, she began to have time for recreation and male companions. She frequently goes on hikes and outings, but her anxiety is clear that she has not yet found a steady boyfriend. Chen-hwei bore an uncanny resemblance to Miss Chia—calm, self-assertive, scholarly in manner (including spectacles and literary quotes), stodgily conservative in dress, with an outdated coif of ear-length, tightly curled hair.

It was about nine o'clock, and we were still sitting across from each other on my red plastic sofa. Chen-hwei had drunk only half a glass of cold water and had not touched her tea. She was still talking quietly. As if to deny her apparent calm, she said, "I have been telling you my life for so long. It's all right for you, but my head is spinning with all the things I must decide." I was surprised she didn't appear close to exhaustion, because she had been on the train all the previous night. It was apparent to me that her friend didn't have any place for her to sleep, so I urged her to bed down in my quilts on the sofa, which was quite comfortable.

"But one of your housemates is a man, right? How could I sleep in the front room with a single man in the house? I would never be able to sleep. I would just stare at the ceiling." She laughed ruefully to herself. "First I go to stay by myself in a hotel, then I sleep in a house with an unmarried man.

What would people say? I am getting worse and worse—just like a divorced woman. If you are unmarried, people won't suspect and scold you so much, but if you have been married and are not with your husband, the people who see you say that you are doing something sexual, something illicit.

"When I came two months ago, I arrived by train about three o'clock in the morning. I needed to rest for a while, so I went to a small hotel. It cost NT$90 a night. When I tried to check in, the daughter of the owner said to me gruffly, 'We don't really welcome single women here.' I said, 'I am a tired traveler; why can't I stay?' 'Single women aren't safe. They bring in their boyfriends in the middle of the night, or they steal everything in the room and then run off.' I wouldn't do anything like that! I don't know how the hotelkeeper's daughter could say such crude things to me. I was frightened all night. Then I got very sick with intestinal cramps. I couldn't pull together the courage to ask my husband if I could see my son again. I felt very sick. So I went straight back to Tainan on the train the next day."

Chen-hwei became disheartened. It was already late at night, and she had no certain work, no residence; she didn't have much money. Her sadness weighed on me. "I spent all afternoon wandering around where my husband lives. I wanted to knock, but every time I got near the door, I didn't dare. It's very bad, the neighbors must say that I am crazy, that I have come back to Taipei without any legitimate employment, and who knows what I am doing to support myself? I already divorced him, so what am I doing hanging around?

"I came from Tainan with just one thought—one thought drove me here. I want to see my child. I don't care about the job; I just went to sign up anyway. There is no place for me to live. My ex-husband will never let me see my child. I may as well go back to Tainan. I'll go back to Tainan tomorrow."

Having heard her story, I wouldn't let her settle for that. "Why do you want to give up so fast? You just got here. Wait until you've settled in and are a little rested. You don't have to work at the company to live in the dormitory, and it only costs NT$300 a month. If you do work, you can make enough to break even, and then you can work things out gradually. Come on, if you won't sleep at my house, let's go now and you can sleep in my bunk at the dorm. My friend Yuan lives there. She got run out by her mother-in-law four years ago, but now she works and supports herself and her daughter." I encouraged Chen-hwei a little more, then she looked happier and acquiesced, "OK, let's go to the dormitory."

The dormitory is a huge structure; its modernistic exterior, softened by the surrounding trees and garden, conceals its poorly maintained plumbing, the leanness of its facilities, and the masses of uprooted young women within. As dorms go, however, it is a pleasant one. I led Chen-hwei down the corridor past the sign that said "Non-residents please stop here" and up to the third floor. There were 12 bunks and metal study desks in each long room and one cavernous sitting room for every four bunk rooms. The sitting rooms were empty except for flaking mirrors, a circle of wooden chairs, and an old black-and-white television. There was a flock of young women in front of the TV; I recognized only a few because of the recent turnover. Many of those who had graduated from night class senior high school had departed recently; and their places had been taken by a shipment of 17-year-olds from Suao in eastern Taiwan. I was very conscious of Chen-hwei's burden of age, which was more obvious from her manner than from her appearance.

We entered the last bedroom. My friend Yuan was reclining on her lower bunk at the far end of the row. There was only one other woman present, studiously clicking her abacus as she practiced. All the other roommates were work-study night school students who wouldn't be home until ten-thirty. Yuan got up, welcomed me with a broad affectionate smile, and commented that she had visited my office a few days before while I was still down south. She was wearing a long white nightgown with a pink flower fringe, and she looked very tall and pretty. Her skin was fair and smooth, her eyes brightly twinkling, and she had a stylish new hairdo, short and loosely curled. Perhaps because her smile filled out her face more, her jutting front teeth were no longer conspicuous. She looked younger than in the wedding pictures I had seen, taken when she was 23.

I said, "This is my friend Chen-hwei. She just came from Tainan, and she signed up to work at the company." Chen-hwei sat down quietly. Yuan and I sat close together on her bunk, and I was pleased that she gave me a hug and held my hand. She took out a book of photographs of herself and her nine-year-old daughter on their recent outing. Her daughter was wearing a frilly white dress and riding a merry-go-round. I held the photographs so that Chen-hwei could see; her eyes gleamed a little more, and she smiled silently. Yuan seemed to sense Chen-hwei's feelings and her awkwardness and prattled on about how well her daughter did in school and what they were going to do next weekend.

I mentioned that Chen-hwei hoped to move into the dormitory, and the two of them discussed whether she would get the company subsidy, which had recently been suspended. "How old are you?" Yuan asked point-blank of Chen-hwei as if talking to an old grandmother. She was hesitant and added, "Your skin is dark, and you look mature. You know the company won't take applicants over 35." Chen-hwei answered that she was 30 years old. "Huh! I'm five years older than you!" Yuan puffed. She squeezed me again affectionately. It seemed that the two of them were going to be friends.

Chen-hwei asked about my occupation again. When Yuan explained that I studied the lives of modern Chinese women, Chen-hwei voiced her uncertainties about my motivation for spending so much time with her. "So 'sociology' means that she gets our application information as soon as we go to the company, I suppose?" I laughed with Yuan somewhat uneasily. "Gee, I sure wish I got paid by the company. Americans make a lot of money there. Unfortunately, I'm just a sociology researcher on a low salary. For me, sociology means people—people like yourselves—not emotionless statistics." Chen-hwei seemed satisfied—perhaps even pleased—by that explanation.

There was no empty bunk in Yuan's room. Yuan and I led Chen-hwei to another building. I was going to give Chen-hwei my bunk, which had the mosquito net and bedding already set up; however, I was apprehensive that my roommates there would be inhospitable. Some were clerks, accountants, and full-time students, and they were often contemptuous of the factory assemblers from other parts of the dormitory. In the sitting room, the room captain, Chin Feng, a short, sharp-faced mainlander of about 30, was sitting silently in front of the television with cucumber slices stuck to her face; other girls were sitting at their desks reading. Chin Feng was known to persecute new boarders she didn't like, to give long monologues on making hot Szechuan-style pickles and bumming movie tickets off gullible old soldiers, and to talk loudly and dance limberly around the dorm room when there was an audience to watch. When I went in, I made a point of saying "This is my friend from Tainan."

After Chen-hwei was settled in a hot shower, Yuan and I went out on the unlighted balcony alone. Yuan confided that her estranged husband was planning to remarry and would probably finally make a divorce settlement, five years after the fact. She added enticingly that she might get remarried within a year, too. She wouldn't say more, just giggled, but she promised that I would get a piece of the wedding cake. Then she was serious. "If you want to be happy, you must *k'an k'ai* a little [look at things more philosophically]," she said. "You cannot pay attention to all the prejudices in society or all the things people might say about you. I didn't understand that before, but now I've learned. You must develop a thick skin and deaf ears. You just have to live and enjoy your own life."

We hadn't been talking very long when the illuminated doorway was momentarily blocked by a stocky figure, then the door was forcefully slammed shut. After a moment, Chin Feng opened the door halfway and beckoned me to enter. Pointing to Yuan, Feng said ominously "Is that the friend who wants to take your bunk? We know about her; she works in the factory. She's a shameless hussy. Everybody in our part of the factory dislikes her." Steady though rather cowed, I said that my friend from Tainan was a different woman and that she was in the shower. Feng replied curtly, "Very good. We will take good care of her."

I quickly took Yuan's arms and led her to the corridor. Yuan snorted indignantly, "Huh! She's the one who always walks into the plant swinging her hips and wearing short skirts. And she has the nerve to say that about me! *San-pa san-pa-teh!*" (This is a derisive reference to overly forward, independent, and, by implication, promiscuous women, literally "three-eight".) Yuan stalked back to her room angrily.

Although still somewhat stunned by the confrontation, I considered that by dormitory rules I should say a word to the house mother, Sister Li, about an overnight guest. Her door was open, and she was sitting at her desk conversing with a teen-ager in a student uniform. The paint and curtains in her room were new and fresh. Sister Li asked me to sit down; I had talked to her only a few times before. She was a young nun, perhaps 30, from some isolated mission in the south. As usual, her white habit and veil were clean and severely starched. I said that I had given my bunk to a woman who had just come by train from Tainan last night and that she would check in tomorrow. Sister Li had probably seen us walk by earlier. Her pleasant expression faded as she queried, "Is your friend married?"

"Perhaps she has been married," I hedged.

Sister Li's cheeks flattened and her thin lips pressed together. I suspected that she did not approve of me, but my presence at the dormitory had long preceded hers. "The directors have been discussing this matter recently, and we have decided that in the future married women will not be allowed to move into the dormitory. We are concerned that since they have had certain experiences, it is not good to have them live with unmarried girls. Married women may say crude things and influence the behavior of the young girls."

I thought of Chen-hwei—her bypassed youth and her flattened-down hair. She had come to the dormitory to protect her virtue! What could she tell young women that would incite promiscuity? Perhaps her story would tell them the unjust and oppressive side of the system of marriage laws and economic opportunities that they would otherwise encounter naively and unresistingly.

"Oh! My friend is from the south; she's very conservative. She just needs some help right now. Anyway, isn't it good for unmarried women to know some married women, so they can foresee problems? How can you discriminate against some women just because they have been married?"

"It's not that we want to discriminate against them," Sister Li continued evenly. "Does your friend have children? You see, we want to encourage married women to take care of their children—to live up to their responsibilities. It's best for them."

"Probably my friend doesn't have any children," I lied. I was touched by the irony of Sister Li's concern about women who might abandon their children, especially as it was so inapplicable in this case. It would probably have been futile as well as a breach of confidence to impart the full particulars, so I commented instead on the beautiful new wall hangings that Sister Li had put in her room. She seemed as pleased as I to end the interview with some lame pleasantries. Somewhat agitated that Chen-hwei might be harshly rebuffed if she ran into Sister Li, I sought and finally found a more receptive house mother in another building. By then it was midnight. I walked back to my office and went to sleep.

The next morning, Chen-hwei visited me again. She was irrepressibly cheerful, and I couldn't help thinking that she already looked five years younger. She had left her small bag of clothing at the dormitory and would begin work at the factory the next day. She had worked at an electronics company for several years before she was married but had voluntarily quit during the mid-1974 electronics industry slump. She had worked for about three years on microscopic circuitry and had become extremely nearsighted. "There isn't any way one can make much money as a worker," she explained. "Like me—I don't have much education or skills, and there are so many of us after the same jobs." (Chen-hwei had stopped just short of graduating from high school, but she casually interjected so many literary allusions into her speech that one would think her a college literature graduate.) "Now I am older and already near-sighted. The companies think that the younger women have more nimble fingers, so it is difficult for me to get a job at all. People like me can go nowhere," she said amiably. She would be making NT$3,000 a month at the factory if she got all her bonuses and NT$2,500 if not. She had to live at the dormitory because living elsewhere would be prohibitively expensive. Chen-hwei had about NT$400 to live on until her first paycheck, two weeks away.

Earlier, when she had talked about going to stay at a hotel, she mentioned suddenly having become seriously ill, so I asked her about her health. "I've had problems with stomach and intestinal infections for some time. Just after I had my second child, I got a cold, but my husband wouldn't help me or take me to the doctor. Later I took all kinds of Western medicine instead of eating proper month-after-birth replenishment and Chinese medicines. When my intestinal problem acts up, my stomach squeezes together and is very painful for two or three hours. Finally I went for a thorough diagnosis and got better treatment. The X-rays cost NT$1,000! I've been taking antibiotics for the last six months, but those have side effects too; my lungs get irritated easily."

I realized that Chen-hwei didn't have any bedding, so I lent her a mat and a blanket until her own arrived. I reminded her to see the one house mother I had recommended and none other.

Two evenings later, I went to stay at the dormitory and stopped by to see Yuan. She took me to the room where Chen-hwei had been assigned a lower bunk. Chen-hwei was resting under a new mosquito net. Yuan and I sat down on the adjoining bunk, and Chen-hwei told us about her first day at the factory. She was lucky to get a kind supervisor who reassigned her after the fumes in one area bothered her lungs; she was pleased to be working again. "When the girls in my work line ask me why I'm working and where my husband is, I just tell them he's dead," she said cheerily, irreverently crooking one finger in the Chinese hand sign for death. "I don't like to lie, but it's a lot simpler that way."

"I do it too," Yuan laughed, raising one hand in the same sign. They seemed to find it a great joke.

In the weeks following her move into the dormitory, however, Chen-hwei began to be despondent over the vicious attitude of the younger women toward her. One threw her new washbasin and toothpaste in the toilet. One of my friends, who had previously been kind to her, suddenly lashed out at her. This girl had emotional problems of her own, and she took it out on Chen-hwei. As Chen-hwei was subjected to these emotional pressures, she became more and more dependent on me, until, frankly, she became a nuisance. She required continual reassurance from me and became paranoid that people were talking about her—which, unfortunately, was true. She seemed constantly seized by nameless terror—what will people think? Will they say I am a bad woman? She transferred to a different company and tried to live outside by renting a decrepit room for NT$350 a month. When she was later able to live at our dormitory under a company subsidy, she transferred back. All the same, she faced the continued threat of being expelled because she had been married.

After a few weeks, she had saved some money, which she said would influence her former husband to let her see the child, and she got up enough courage to visit. Her ex-husband was silently hostile, but he let her see her son. The son didn't recognize her and cried. She went to visit a neighbor, who sympathized with her and said that she would try to help Chen-hwei find a better husband.

Around this time, Chen-hwei became engrossed with visiting temples and asking the gods for assistance. Something kept pulling her back in particular to the Chih Nan Kung, a very old temple perched high on a mountain outside the city. There she had found a small black bronze Maitreya Buddha which she said had appeared to her in a strangely disturbing dream the night before she first met her husband. She recalled the dream and its circumstances.

When she was 26, she decided that she might as well marry and allowed an older maiden aunt to arrange an introduction to a civil servant. On the night before the introduction took place, Chen-hwei dreamed that her aunt took her to a temple near Taipei to burn red and gold paper spirit money before a black Maitreya Buddha image. A man in a dark suit and tie approached. She knew it was the man to whom her aunt would introduce her, but he turned his face away and refused to speak to her. Chen-hwei awoke startled and upset but tried to forget the dream. When the young man arrived at her home and talked with her parents, she hid and came out only to send him off, like a girl in an old Chinese novel. However, he had looked all right to her, and it also appeared that she would have an easier time with him because they would live alone, not with her mother-in-law. So she did not object to the marriage arrangements. They went out two or three times, but she was too shy to talk very much.

After the marriage ceremony, Chen-hwei moved to her husband's apartment in Taipei, taking only personal clothing and the small fund of private money traditionally kept by Taiwanese women. Neither bride price nor dowry was transferred in the wedding; it was a "modern" marriage.

Now she hoped for a good omen in her discovery of the black Maitreya Buddha and sought its protection. Twice, she stayed overnight in the dreaming quarters for pilgrims at the temple, but she did not get the answer she wanted. She visited temples in the nearby hills every weekend; one temple fortuneteller encouraged her by saying that she had already passed the most unfortunate part of her life and that the future would be better.

We often visited the temples together. One afternoon, we sat for hours among the mounds and semi-circular balustrades of the ornate graves in the Taiwan Air Force Cemetery. Chen-hwei expressed her doubts that she would ever marry again. Suddenly she admitted sexual need and plied me with questions about sexual physiology. She said she had never experienced orgasm. "Linda, now I need a man," she stated forthrightly. "I've had two children, but I've never had a romance with a man . . . what does it feel like?" There were few secrets and little embarassment between us.

Not too long after, a friendly neighbor set up an introduction. It was a miserable failure, and another was planned. Chen-hwei had begun to look younger in manner, perhaps from being around the younger women in the dormitory, but her clothes and hair were still drab. She spent endless hours at my house making tentative improvements, asking me to apply small bits of makeup and then creaming them all off, saying she wanted to show her true self. For whatever reason, the second introduction was successful. Kung was a man of 34 who had never been married and was not up to her ideals in education or income, but he treated her kindly. She was like a 14-year-old going out for the first time.

During these months of our temple visiting and the introduction to Kung, the situation in Chen-hwei's dormitory gradually came to a head. She told me some of the things the other women had said. "Once when I was waiting to take a shower, I said to the girl in front of me: 'Miss, I don't mind if the water isn't so hot. Why don't you let me go first?' She got angry and snarled: 'You old lady, everybody knows you are thrown-away goods!' Last week, I overheard one of my roommates say to another: 'She was married to one man and divorced, and now she has taken up with a second. It's just like cheating the second!' These little misses go out with a different boyfriend every day. But who knows, 10 years from now, when they are as old as I am, that they won't be just like me? They are children and don't understand. I smile at them, but they turn their faces away."

The dormitory house mothers soon moved to expel all women who had ever been married. They put up a large red poster in the downstairs hallway stating that all ever-married women must be out within a month. The house mothers admitted that the ever-married women were quiet and obedient and caused no problems but insisted that such women would give the young girls a jaundiced picture of married life. Apparently, more and more divorced women were applying for residence in the dorm, and the tide had to be turned. A kind of witch-hunt followed to expose those who had been married; those who were divorced or widowed had ID cards which said "single," and the house mothers had to question those suspected under the guise of counseling or pick up information from their roommates. About 10 women were identified among the 800 residents, and it became general knowledge both that they had been married and that they were the targets of harassment, such as flashlight bed checks after midnight. Demoralized, most of the women left quietly. A widow aged 25, employed as a cement carrier, had previously kept her secret to herself but slit her wrists at night in the toilets. Fortunately, the physical injury was not serious. Chen-hwei resisted for a while, and Yuan, who had never hidden the fact that she was long separated from her husband, held on for a year before giving up. Both moved to distant, dingy private rooms and took other jobs.

Chen-hwei is still undecided. She says that she is afraid to marry again and afraid that another birth will kill her. She is perhaps fearful of losing her freedom. She and Kung have developed considerable mutual affection. He is pressing her to marry him but still expresses the usual prejudices about her having been previously married and not a virgin when they met. Thus Chen-hwei is caught between the censure of others and her own ambivalence.

Conclusion

Lim Li-suat, adopted daughter, and Tsai Chen-hwei, divorcée, may not be completely typical of women in factory work in Taiwan, but they are by no means unique among the women I met. Their situation illustrates the pressures on women's roles in modern Taiwan society—at the intersection of rigid traditional family roles and the opportunities and escapes for women brought by industrialization.

Tsai Chen-hwei is one of only a very few divorced women among the adolescent electronics workers, yet her story starkly illustrates the social problems in the wider society. The marriage squeeze, tightening over the last five years, has made it inevitable and already apparent in my sample that increasing numbers of women will be unable to marry or will be abandoned by their husbands, who can easily seek another mate. In the past, women who lost their husband often had little choice but prostitution, but women who worked in industry as teen-agers now tend to return to that work, because they are familiar with it. Chen-hwei is atypical but not unique; I encountered several people like her in my tours of factories and dormitories.

Of the nearly 30 women I came to know well, four were adopted daughters; three of them had tragic histories of family rejection. As Margery Wolf, Arthur Wolf, and Chieh-shan Huang have so well described, female adoption was prevalent in traditional Taiwan for two main reasons—to acquire brides for the sons of the family in later years or to "lead in," according to common belief, the birth of sons.[2] At the turn of the century, in some areas of northern Taiwan, up to 70 percent of wives were adopted daughters. The practice has also been reported in other areas of South China, such as the lower Yangtze valley region.

One of the other adopted daughters I knew and her sister had been raised in the prosperous household of a primary schoolteacher to marry their "brothers." When it became apparent that the matches would be rejected by all the children, the two adopted women were denied any further household resources. A-suat represents the "lead-in" variety of adoption. Whatever the reason for adoption, adopted daughters were traditionally assigned a subservient role.

The cases of A-suat and Chen-hwei express poignantly what is a general truth about the traditional Chinese family—women have no permanent home in their parental family. Among the unmarried working women I knew, most of the few already over marriageable age had strained or alienated relationships with their parents, frequently against their own wishes. Chen-hwei knows that she can visit only briefly with her mother, although her mother cares deeply for her. "It would be bad luck for the marriage prospects of my brother. People would talk," Chen-hwei says, "if a divorced daughter came home to live."

The ostracism of daughters seems to be based in part on the view that they will be a drain on household resources and that they may claim inheritance. Traditionally, Chinese women have no right to inheritance.

In my research, I never met a woman who expected a share of her parents' property, even if the question was raised when the estate was being divided. This is in spite of Taiwan law, which purports to give daughters and sons equal inheritance rights. Whether a daughter receives a dowry is totally at her parents' discretion. The young women workers who have migrated in order to earn a wage, especially those from rural and poor families, seem, in addition, to have suffered from a distancing from their parents because of their many years in the factory dormitory. Usually they expect and are expected to make their own provisions for the lesser expenses of a "modern," less prestigious, wedding. A-suat is an example.

Now that industrial work is generally available for women, wage-earning daughters who contribute to their natal family's budgets are often encouraged to delay marriage and seem to be more valued in the family than before. This still does not grant them long-term enfranchisement. For sons, parents figure long-term costs and benefits, including an old age with a devoted and plentiful patrilineal line; for daughters, they balance immediate costs and benefits. This is the maxim that I derived from the life histories I collected. It is borne out in the cases of A-suat and Chen-hwei.

9

Wage Earners in Hong Kong

"Rainbow": The Café Culture
Wai-gun: The Garment District

By Janet W. Salaff

Introduction

Transnational corporations are increasingly seeking foreign labor for the low-cost production of goods to sell in the major capitalist countries. Many less developed countries not only provide such a supply of labor but also constitute potential new markets. In Hong Kong, Malaysia, the Philippines, Singapore, South Korea, and elsewhere around the rim of Asia, international hotel chains and an extensive hospitality network have created the environment for a mass influx of visitors; tourism has become one of the two or three largest industries. The transnational corporations and their splashy advertising penetrate new markets, wielding slogans designed to create local demand for factory-made consumer goods among the young people newly employed in the medium and large factories of the area. The molders of the "Pepsi generation" invite indigenous youth to enter the wage economy, work where they wish, date freely and marry a mate who attracts them, and, most of all, buy what they fancy. In short, young people are being urged to make economic decisions independently of their family.

The sale of overseas goods, mass advertising campaigns originating abroad and inspired by Hollywood or pop culture, and a vast tourist presence have characterized life in the British Crown Colony of Hong Kong for over two decades. Hong Kong is well known as an offshore location for transnational corporation manufacturing in growth industries like electronics and more traditional indigenous ones like garment work. For example, Toko Denshi Seizo Company employs 700 workers to manufacture electronic components; YKK Zipper employs 250 women in its Hong Kong manufacturing plant; Matsushita has established a subsidiary where 100 schoolchildren weld together transistors for radios; and for many years over 1,000 women passed daily through the gates of the multistory Fairchild Semiconductor factory. Domestic and overseas Chinese capital finances the textile and garment factories of Apple Jeans and Dorce Knitwear, where women stitch the garments for the region and the northern hemisphere.

The impulse for young women wage earners in Hong Kong to act independently of their families is becoming irresistible. It is still unclear as to what extent traditional Chinese family life will be altered by capitalist economic forces. What impact does the Western and Japanese commercial and political presence have on the way of life of Asian youth? Which Western mores and norms can be assimilated without harm into the family system, and which must be resisted by the family to avoid its own destruction? Preliminary answers to these questions are suggested by the life histories of two young women who toil in the bustling industries and spend their leisure time in the cosmopolitan atmosphere of urban Hong Kong. These life histories help clarify the widely debated impact of the developed world's contemporary influence on indigenous social structure and culture.

To understand the range of responses available, we locate the Hong Kong Chinese family in the family wage economy.[1] Each member works in concert toward goals set by the family head. Both young women introduced here—"Rainbow" and Waigun—were trained from childhood to function in the domestic and work life of the family and to follow its rules and expectations to the letter. Each learned early that her life is inextricably interwoven with family fortune and that survival and success depend on the integrated contribution of every member. The family loses when daughters cast off their internally defined responsibilities, and young women are admonished that they will forfeit much by a premature exit from the family.

But colorful magazines, stimulating advertising, and the pulsating beat of Western pop music all urge young people to pursue their freedom. Considerable tension thus exists between the morality of the family wage economy, with its "family first" creed, and that of the burgeoning cash economy promoted by the corporations. Each woman here resolved in her own way the conflict of family needs versus personal desires.[2] Each response was shaped by economic background, family structure, and individual personality. The dual portrait derived thus illustrates a complex range of responses to the challenge of Western-induced social and cultural change.

Ultimately, however, the two women and their families still conform to a recognizable family wage economy; the family essentially remains in control. Hong Kong is by no means unique in this respect, as related interview studies show.[3] This does not imply that capitalist industrialization and superstructure do not influence indigenous social structure and culture; it demonstrates only that we have much to learn about how a politically torpid but economically active society like that in Hong Kong adapts to outside socioeconomic influences.

"Rainbow": The Café Culture

Rainbow takes her picturesque name from the popular song, "Somewhere, Over the Rainbow." Her birth name is Choi-hung. She was first dubbed with a Christian name by a secondary schoolteacher, a conventional practice in Anglo-Chinese education. Many Chinese girls keep these first names, but some later reject them as alien. Equally uninspired by traditional Chinese culture and staid Christianity, Choi-hung borrowed her name from Hollywood.

Rainbow quit secondary school in 1973 to become a head waitress at the Café do Brasil when she was almost 18. She is the most Western-looking Hong Kong young woman I met; on our first outing, she donned boys' sneakers and blue jeans with ragged bottoms instead of the modish, bell-bottomed Apple jeans her friends were purchasing in the Jeans-East boutique in Tsimtsatsui. Her long hair curls under at her shoulders, and her shell necklace suits her place of work. Her English slang puts her reasonably at ease with Western men. Her adoption of Western couture reflects a profound tension in her life—her responsibility to her family versus a long-standing effort to maximize her own growth space and individually paced way of life.

Rainbow is the firstborn of the five children from her father's second marriage. Her father's primary wife lives in another part of Hong Kong with her 40-year-old son and his family. Because she has a son to support her, the first wife receives no regular allowance from Rainbow's father, although she receives the customary "red packets" and gifts at major yearly festivals.

Rainbow's father is an ivory carver. His workshop fills one of the three ninth-floor apartment rooms in a mixed working-class residential and factory area between North Point and Shaukiwan. The walk-up flat was built in 1964 during one of Hong Kong's prolonged water shortages. Since seawater was used in construction, its pitted and cracked cement walls are unstable. Several other dwellings erected during the same period have collapsed, and this one looks three times its age. Nevertheless, the family was glad to relocate there from its previous squatter shack on a Shaukiwan hillside. Because there is no elevator, in 1973 the family paid only HK$200 rent per month for their bedroom, kitchen, bath, and living/workroom suite.

"Railway flats" line the main stairwell of Rainbow's narrow tenement. Her front door opens into a dingy bedroom with a pair of bunk beds facing each other. The windows admit so little light that I could make out only the outlines of the furniture; I had to rely on a naked overhead bulb to illuminate my way. To the left was a bright corner with three clean windows, to which a visitor is at once drawn. Two workbenches are fitted into the corner nooks—one used by Rainbow's father, the other by her 16-year-old brother. Suspended next to the window is a birdcage. A rooster strutted up and down the corridor, and hens clucked from their coop under the kitchen sink. A dog and several cats rounded out the domestic menagerie.

A Venerable Craft

In 1973, on my first visit, Father returned at ten from breakfast in a teahouse, toting the caged bird which he had taken there for fresh air and attention. Father was cheerful and outgoing, and on my second visit, he invited me to attend his sixtieth birthday party banquet the following evening.

He was keen to tell me of his life as an ivory craftsman, which he began as an apprentice in Canton: "Nowadays, young people don't have the patience to apprentice for five years, like I did. They usually train for only three years and then consider themselves journeymen." Father executes the designs and has trained his children to help him carry out the simple, routine jobs, such as ivory burnishing. When I visited, only his first wife's son practiced ivory carving as a trade; the rest of the children devoted only their spare time to understudying Father. But Father's eyesight was already failing, and soon either his children or someone else would need to take over his work. He was quite reluctant to seek an outside successor, and this would have been difficult to accomplish in any case, because so few people are interested any longer.

Father therefore considered his sons as the only possible inheritors of the trade, his suppliers, and his clientele. Because Rainbow is female, she was not the one to carry on Father's handicraft, of which the family was so rightfully proud. Nor was she anticipated to be the family breadwinner after Father could no longer carry on his trade. Instead of training this capable eldest daughter in the intricate skills of design, carving, and fine finishing of the pieces, Father treated Rainbow as an extra hand to perform rough work under his supervision.

Home and Family

Mother had long worked outside the home in unskilled jobs in garment workshops, such as snipping threads from garments before they were pressed by a more skilled worker. She worked a full nine-hour day, seven days a week. As first daughter, Rainbow was saddled with sizable family responsibilities, so she intermittently left school for six months at a time to keep house and care for the younger children. She hauled water, washed and dried clothes, chopped wood for the cookstove, and prepared meals. "I could barely reach the pole to hang up the clothes," she recalled. Until she was 12, she would return for a semester in school, then drop out again. When Father taught her to burnish ivory, she joined him at the workbench, while her younger sisters assumed the major housework burdens. As a result of her patchy schooling, at age 12, Rainbow was several years behind her contemporaries.

In Rainbow's home, the unique characteristics of all the family members were visible. Sixteen-year-old brother worked on ivory by the light of the window after school. His tools occupied one side of the workbench, his books the other half. I read the titles—*The Old Man and the Sea* and several Japanese novels in Chinese translation. A thoughtful lad, he liked to climb the hill behind his home and play melodies on his flute while he gazed out over the horizon. Brother was ranked quite low in his class in his Anglo-Chinese secondary school, perhaps because he preferred reading these novels and other self-assigned material to the rote memorization of texts which is a hallmark of Hong Kong education.

Mother was taciturn and ventured only a quiet "hello" when I entered the home. She murmured a polite apology for not serving "enough good food" at the luncheon I shared with the family. She never engaged in conversation with me, nor was she interested in demonstrating her cooking skills, like the other mothers I knew. Rainbow confirmed my impression that Mother was much less social than Father, a rather despondent, even angry, woman.

Rainbow herself always behaved quite autonomously, had never been afraid of adults even when she was small, and was prepared to quarrel and even defy her elders. "I'm like Mother. We both argue with people and sometimes shout at them. Several years ago, Mother even moved away from home for a while after a dispute with Father."

Rainbow also shares the stubborn independence of her father, whom she did not hesitate to confront when the occasion demanded. Rainbow did not openly resent helping her family until at adolescence she learned to identify and protect her own interests. In accordance with custom, Father tried to block her from attending secondary school and cited his real or imagined need for her to work full time in the shop. Father saw no way that his daughter's higher education could help her carve ivory, and his ambitions were limited to the family artisan enterprise. The labor power of his eldest daughter was far more useful to him in the short run than a better educated Rainbow would be in the future.

When Rainbow was 14 and still responsible for the care of the three youngest, she decided to risk a bitter clash with Father by enrolling in a secondary school. When he remained predictably adamant, she left home with the three siblings in her immediate care. She set up house in a vacant squatter's hut on the Shaukiwan hillside, where her family formerly lived and where she still knew the neighbors. She enrolled in morning classes and left her charges with a neighbor. Each afternoon, she sent the children to primary school, and she trudged off to work a nine-hour factory shift to support her unlikely brood. This lasted six months, during which Mother visited the hut regularly but concealed its location from Father. She reported on the children's well-being, but she was not skilled at negotiation and could not bring together the strong-minded father and daughter. Father could not bear having his family so divided, and eventually family unity became more important than sticking to his original dictum that girls should not be educated. When Father's will was finally broken by Rainbow's daring maneuver, "He begged us to come home," she recalled proudly. Since her return home and resumption of schooling, she has guarded her own interests even more vigorously. At my suggestion that family needs could be assigned priority over her own, she quickly retorted, "I have *already* repaid the costs of my upbringing to my family!"

Rainbow's independence also manifested itself in her resistance to the compulsory religious training at the English-language missionary school she attended. Denominational institutions offer many inducements for their students' conversion, and Christian students have a greater likelihood of receiving scholarships to upper- and post-secondary schools, of obtaining employment in mission-related organizations, and of participating in a plethora of church-based youth groups. Rainbow turned her back on all these opportunities, "No, I didn't convert, because I'm strong!" she boasted.

She finally left school not over theology but because she was "not really scholarly" and was more interested in earning money. She felt that it was right and proper for her 16-year-old brother to continue school even if his grades weren't high, because he, in contrast, had the aptitude. In succumbing to the temptation to leave school and earn money, Rainbow made a choice endorsed by her parents, the major benefactors of this decision. This sacrifice of the daughter's long-range chances in favor of short-term gains for the family, especially for the brothers, typifies the narrow range of opportunities of Hong Kong elder daughters.

"In spite of all our quarrels, I love my family, and I enjoy living at home," Rainbow countered when her co-workers and friends asked her to move out and live with them. There was still a communication gap separating Rainbow from Father and Mother, but she nonetheless preferred the home environment, partly because Father has become more understanding and less severe and demanding of her. "Maybe it is advancing age that has changed him," she reflected. "He's much more tolerant and accepting of me now." Father must have realized that he could keep his daughter at home by turning a blind eye to her social life, dating, and private banking of part of her income.

The Café

The petite Café do Brasil is located in the Ocean Terminal, Kowloon's star tourist and shopping attraction. It serves coffee, fruit juice, cakes, and pastries but not the wide range of snacks available in other coffee shops. The café offers fragrant, freshly roasted and brewed Brazilian blend, ranked by some as the tastiest in town. Other coffee shops, with larger kitchens and tables, sell soft drinks, ice cream, and light snacks of spaghetti, omelets, chicken, and hamburgers, plus the obligatory egg rolls and fried rice. In the Café do Brasil, already a minor institution in Hong Kong, friendly liaisons and business appointments take place, and the emphasis is on subdued discussion rather than eating. To its Chinese clientele, the café offers an alternative meeting place to the small noodle shops and teahouses specializing in rice porridge and pastry snacks, where patrons are required to vacate the table as soon as the meal is over.

Rainbow signed on as a waitress as her first job after leaving secondary school. Only three young women work at the café, and the one with the most seniority automatically becomes head waitress. Eventually Rainbow became the most senior. She worked from nine-thirty to five, with every other Sunday and one day each week off per month. Her work consisted of labor-intensive coffee preparation, which requires lugging 100-pound sacks of beans from the storage room behind the kitchen area to the grinding machine at the counter, grinding the coffee for the day, brewing the coffee to order in individual small glass pots, cutting and serving the prepared cakes with the coffee, and billing the customers. It is not complicated work, nor are the hours overly long, but she was always on her feet.

As head waitress, in 1973 Rainbow earned about HK$800 per month in basic salary and tips. With her seniority, she received 50 percent more of the tips than the other waitresses. Nevertheless, she professed to dislike her work. Switching from Cantonese to English, she emphatically declared, "This is a lousy job!" She resented in particular having to walk around pouring refills while another waitress then presented the customer with the bill, because she considered the work undignified. She was annoyed by the paternalism of the Portuguese manager, who required petty services from the other waitresses (taking his broken shoes to be repaired or fetching his daughter's purchases from Ocean Terminal shops). One of her workmates left the job because she considered the café a hangout for young men prowling for women, but Rainbow did not find this in itself objectionable. "My dislike of the café is not caused so much by the customers. It's not a costly place. If I were working in a more expensive spot, it would be much worse. The more expensive the place, the more complicated it is. All those pimps patronize high-priced restaurants, not the café."

Rainbow worked primarily for the wage, and since her tips flowed from pleasantries to the patrons, she knew how to chat smilingly with the middle-class Chinese and overseas habitues of the café. Her tips afforded her some independence from Father, to whom she never disclosed her precise income. She donated HK$300 to her family monthly and banked the tips. She also developed a life-style to suit her milieu and her independent spirit.

Rainbow knew, however, that she could not stay on at the Café do Brasil. She was almost 20 in 1974, and restaurants prefer to hire teenagers. The main reason she remained at the café through 1974 was her inability to land a better-paying job. She had already saved HK$2,000; when she succeeded in banking HK$1,000 more, she had promised herself a year or so of traveling (she had no idea that such a sum would cover only a month, not a year, abroad). When she first discussed her plans with me in mid-1973, she expected to visit a boyfriend in England. She never did. By June of the following year, she was thinking of traveling through Southeast Asia with girlfriend employees at Ocean Terminal shops and nearby restaurants and bars. Two months later, however, she was considering marriage.

Father had only an inkling of Rainbow's plans, but he disapproved of what he knew. She was prepared to defy him, stating emphatically, "I have already given much of my life to my family and my money as well! Now I want to live for myself!" Again using English for emphasis, her voice rose with excitement. "Anyway, youth must be *free!*" She finally left the café in late 1974 and lived at home on her savings. Under the mistaken impression that Rainbow had been temporarily laid off (a common occurrence in Hong Kong), her family did not complain about her temporary lack of contributions to the budget. At the time, it was hard to predict whether she would resume work elsewhere or embark on one of the trips about which she had long been dreaming. She herself had not yet chosen between work and an adventure. She was certain only that "I need to enjoy myself and rest for a while before I decide anything."

Peer Relations

Greatly influenced by the fashionable atmosphere of their workplace, Rainbow and her co-workers normally spent much of their wages on clothing, which they sometimes purchased at fancy boutiques. Although they wore uniforms in the café, the latest fashions were anticipated and admired in their circle.

The family relations of these shopgirls were affected by the values prevailing in the work and leisure environments. Rainbow's workmates were even less close to their families than she was; a number had already moved away from home to share rented rooms. As Rainbow explained, "Their parents can't do anything to prevent this, because the women are old enough to look after themselves."

It may appear unremarkable that waitresses in a big city rent rooms together, but the factory workers I knew did not believe that women in their early twenties merited physical separation and personal independence from the family. Factory women generally moved instead directly from their tightly knit family to marriage. Although their evening classes, weekend parties, beach outings, and picnics helped them consolidate a separate identity, they engaged in these pursuits while living at home.

At the time I wondered whether the service workers were decisively influenced by their working atmosphere or whether they entertained strong ideas of independence at an early date, which then led them to the cafés and department store counters, which then reinforced their earlier inclinations. Rainbow manifested her independence before starting at the café and then strengthened it with her wage packet and new contacts. She did not join her co-workers for lunch at restaurants but economized by bringing her own lunch to work. This resulted in good-natured but nonetheless stinging taunts of "stingy" and "anti-social." She said in her offhanded manner, with a shrug, "I have my own goals, and I do what I think is good for me. I don't care about them and their criticisms."

I met several of Rainbow's friends on one of our beach outings in 1974. Most worked in bars and nightclubs; some were also models and entertainers. They interacted easily with the non-Chinese men they met at work. They conversed about the relative merits of the hi-fi which one Western fellow who was present had just purchased. They discussed the modeling engagements of another man. One woman had just recently changed her job, and the discussion turned to nightclubs and the various atmospheres and humorous incidents that had arisen between the bosses and the women.

Rainbow's friends spoke up-to-date English slang and dressed in a style acceptable only to non-Chinese. They wore bikinis purchased in a tourist boutique rather than the more modest two-piece bathing suits sold in Chinese stores near their homes. But although they dressed "in fashion," they exhibited none of the modish languor often seen in sportier and wealthier circles of Hong Kong women. And while they adorned their bikini outfits with silver bangles and Indian bead necklaces, they played catch with beach balls and tossed sand at each other vigorously with the same healthy abandon as the factory women. After swimming, they decked themselves out in semi-transparent Indian muslin shirts without bras and floor-length dirndl skirts. (Wai-gun, the subject of the next life history, would have been shocked by this costume, for she wore at least two pieces of underwear even in the hottest weather.)

Despite the substantial amounts of money they spent on clothing, Rainbow and her companions still contributed to their families. Thus their expensive life-style, combined with the reduction in income because of wages taken by their family, left them perpetually dissatisfied with the pay at ordinary factory and clerical jobs. It was understandable that some of them were eventually attracted to the better-paying jobs in the hundreds of bars catering mainly to tourists, including, at one time, scores of thousands of American servicemen sent to Hong Kong for rest and recreation during the Vietnam war.

To the uninitiated, these bars with their garish, glittering exteriors may all seem the same, but Rainbow's friends assured me otherwise. "Some owners think they possess you," one said, "and I would hate to work in such a place." She introduced me to her companion, a young Australian photographer whom she had met in the bar, and pointed out that some bars would have tried to prevent her from dating him outside working hours.

Rainbow also dated men whom she met at her café. Her most recent boyfriend was a man whose work temporarily took him to South Korea but whose family, of mixed Portuguese and Chinese ancestry, lived in Hong Kong. She told me that she was engaged to him and proudly showed me his photos and one of his letters from Korea. "He loves me," she stated as simply and romantically as any North American teen-ager. She wanted to marry him when she turned 19. Her father was ignorant of this plan and had originally opposed her dating at all. He feared that when she married, she would withdraw her income from the family. When he realized that she was dating non-Chinese, he relented by urging her to marry a nice Chinese boy and settle down. Rainbow explained that he preferred her to marry at a young and more controllable age rather than take the risk that she might marry out of the family and her culture altogether.

Rainbow believed in the power of love to build a relationship between husband and wife that would whisk her away from the tedious environment of parental and in-law obligations and the daily drudgery of meeting those family obligations. She was trying to find a young gallant to transport her out of the narrow confines of family-centered Hong Kong life to the wider world of travel, exploration, and adventure. For a dissatisfied but untrained girl in the service sector, marriage is almost the sole alternative to the bar girl circuit.

A Woman Bows to Social Expectations

Rainbow struggled to evade the demands of her family by responding to promises of love, affection, and nurturance. In the second major escapade of her youth, in 1975 she left her home. This time, unlike the first, she was not prepared to return. She followed her heart, withdrew her savings from the bank, and joined her boyfriend. They lived together in South Korea for a year, then he was reassigned to Hong Kong. When they returned, Rainbow was pregnant.

They married, and Rainbow moved into her husband's family home along with his married brother and sister-in-law. The wheel of material demands and obligations turned for Rainbow just as for most young mothers. There were no household conveniences, and Rainbow washed all the diapers by hand. She awoke at night when her son fretted, prepared all meals for her husband, and, since her Chinese mother-in-law often played mah-jongg outside the home, was also burdened with cooking chores for the entire family.

Rainbow sighed complainingly as she recollected her experiences during 1977: "I wish I hadn't run off with him, because life as a mother is so hard compared with that of a coffee shop waitress." But then she smiled down at her chubby, healthy-looking boy trying to inch off her lap onto the rug to practice crawling. "Well, he's a wonderful baby!" she acknowledged, revealing both warm maternal feelings and the awareness that frivolity was at an end.

Summary

No other working-class woman I met manifested so clear and forceful a desire to break away from family cares, actually taking action on two occasions. I wondered where this remarkable trait of Rainbow's originated. Was her position in the Café do Brasil chiefly responsible for fostering, or at least furthering, this determination? As we became closer friends from 1973 to 1975 and I learned the context of her quest for latitude, I realized that she had much in common with Father long before she began at the café.

Father, independent and headstrong, preferred to run his own shop rather than work for others. Rainbow, also independent and headstrong, not only earned a better wage by servicing tourist customers but also came to believe that their life-style held the best opportunities for her. Her instruction at an English-language secondary school, while incomplete, further opened her to Western ideas. When Rainbow entered a job which introduced her to many like-minded friends in the entertainment and service trades, she found that they spent their leisure time on self-centered pursuits, such as clothes, jewelry, and popular music. Rainbow's job setting and her close personal friends stimulated her to think of her individual needs as gratifiable and worth attending to. Rainbow's close contact with Westerners actually strengthened in her the family artisan heritage of fierce pride and independence.

Rainbow was obviously juggling the tension she felt between her obligations to her family and herself. She acknowledged the legitimacy of her debt to her family, which in her eyes she had fully paid, and justified her late adolescent breakaway by citing the time and energy she had lavished on them during her teens. This duality was quite unusual among the women I interviewed. As the most modern person I met, Rainbow was the only one who had turned around the terms of the demanding Chinese family obligations by asserting that she had already redeemed her debt and was now due some reciprocation. But the exception proves the rule, and although she was trying to pull away from her family obligations, Rainbow used them to justify her independence as a young adult. That she followed through with her independent goals in the face of parental disapproval is a remarkable testimony of her strength of character and the encouragement of her peers and work environment. But girlfriends alone cannot come to the rescue of a Hong Kong married woman, and once having left, Rainbow no longer had the workplace and wages to support her resolve to keep clear of family bonds.

Wai-gun: The Garment District.

Wai-gun's life was shaped by her position at the head of seven brothers and sisters in an impoverished family. Her contribution to the family economy has always been central. As for other working women, family structure and domestic economic pressure forged a conscientious and capable daughter. Nevertheless, no woman's personality is completely conditioned by such structural factors. Wai-gun firmly believes that existence promises some purpose beyond obtaining and using material goods. Although she could not quite articulate to me her goals and purposes in life, she never hesitated to seek answers. During the time I knew her, Wai-gun deepened her search and widened her previously individual exploration of her cultural roots as a Chinese woman into a political search for the direction and stimuli for broader social change.

Home and Parents

In 1973, Wai-gun's family lived in an apartment in the huge Ngautaukok Resettlement Estate. A single room 10 feet by 12 feet housed the seven children and two adults of Wai-gun's family. A cotton curtain subdivided the room. A windowless inner area contained a pair of bunk beds, curtained for privacy, and each wide enough for two people, and a bureau. The outer area was a bedroom/living room with another double bunk bed, a cluster of shelves with a family shrine and some objects that had gathered dust for years, a television set, and a small refrigerator for bottled drinks. Atop the television rested the phone. Two windows in the outer room faced the courtyard; flourescent lights mounted on the ceiling were the only source of interior lighting.

Mother, aged 42, had always been employed, but her health was deteriorating, making continued labor more difficult for her. When the children were small, she assembled plastic ornaments at home for a small Chinese company, straining late at night under the dim lights. She blamed this work for "ruining my eyesight and health." When her last child was old enough to remain home unattended, she took a better-paying factory job in a Chinese company, cutting metal into pieces for kettles and cups; this job did not require good eyesight. "It's not a complicated job. The task is easy to learn and clean, although quite arduous," she explained. Mother was often tired and ate foods valued for their nutritional properties, such as liver, gallbladders, ginger, and snake meat in winter in an effort to bolster her run-down condition.

While Mother was away at work, the children kept house, cooked their meals, and prepared the family dinner. Mother said, "It's not very good for the children, you know. They are left unsupervised, but what can I do?" Although she had left the countryside almost two decades earlier, she still considered herself an illiterate woman of the soil. She lacked the means to generalize her urban experiences, so, in her view, factory work in itself in no way broadened her life. After sweating for nine hours in the factory, she returned home immediately and could rarely afford the time to visit relatives and friends.

Mother was frustrated by the conditions in her factory. Once, when her hand was cut during work, she reported the injury to the foreman, only to be summarily sent home without pay—a violation of the Hong Kong industrial compensation ordinance. She therefore justified her subsequent passivity: "It doesn't do any good to report such treatment higher up. Shop floor managers speak with two mouths—one to the workers and one to the supervisors. Powerful officials like them will pay no attention to an illiterate woman like me."

Father worked an exhausting shift in a factory, manufacturing cast iron weights. He favored the piecework wage system by which he was paid. But although piecework has the advantage of permitting a strong worker to earn a greater income through extraordinary exertion, it penalizes the weak. In 1972, Father underwent an operation for a cancer of the liver; his gallbladder and half his liver were removed. Care in the government public hospital was virtually free, but his factory did not pay sick leave and there is no government unemployment compensation in Hong Kong. Father could no longer draw a full day's wage, which means that the earnings of his children became even more important.

Father's strong personality dominated the family scene even after his hospitalization. A blunt man, he spoke his mind to anyone who would listen. In his view, everyone in Hong Kong was out for himself, so it was useless to try to organize the workers. Under such conditions, "They could never get together!" Father dominated most family decision-making, from the education of the children to the choice of everyday household purchases, including the television set, which represented the combined labor of three weeks for Father, Mother, and Wai-gun.

Father's paramount role in the family and his outspoken views also influenced his children's thinking about Hong Kong society. Wai-gun acquired her father's essentially defensive verbal adroitness, but fortunately she was spared his self-centered pessimism. As a woman, she did not measure herself and her achievements in strictly economic terms, however, and had adopted more idealistic goals.

Family Relations

From age 12, when she began wage labor alongside her mother, to her acceptance at age 13 of her parents' decision that she withdraw from school, to the assumption at around age 20 of her role as principal contributor to the household budget, Wai-gun served the family dutifully as eldest daughter. When I asked about her feelings on having sacrificed her chances for education and independence, she replied, "Well, I am part of the family, too. I must share the responsibility for running it!"

For several years, Wai-gun's contribution to the family income was sizable; in early 1973, she earned around HK$400–470 per month, 36 percent of the family budget. After her 15-year-old brother began employment as a delivery boy on a 7-Up truck, his first job after middle school, her share dropped to a still substantial 28 percent. Other children entered the work force two years later.

The frequent economic crises that arose from the illnesses of her parents gave Wai-gun's stable earnings a particular importance. Despite this, she was seldom consulted by her authoritarian father: "Purchases? Schooling and jobs for the younger ones? Father is really obstinate and makes these decisions. He says that my mother is 'just a peasant woman' who doesn't know how to shop for goods. Father selected the television set, but it turned out to be a lemon! So now we just grin and suffer his purchases. Even though I put money into them, I don't choose them."

Wai-gun's central economic role in the family did not confer the right to a voice in the family's long-term affairs. She did not know how much Father earned. However, her role did give her a clearer perspective. Despite her father's decision-making monopoly, Wai-gun felt that she could weigh his actions on her own scale and did not have to take him as seriously as in the past. If the consequences of his decision-making were tragicomic, as in the case of the faulty television set, she could chuckle from an emotional distance.

Work also gave Wai-gun the right to spend HK$80 every fortnight on personal needs. For Wai-gun's birthday, her mother gave her HK$10 to buy whipped cream cake and barbequed pork for the whole family. She also spent HK$20 of her own money on a new blouse and shoes, her main summer clothes purchase that year.

Wai-gun felt completely free to pass her spare time as she chose, mainly with friends, and she performed very few domestic chores. Household chores were done by her siblings; Eldest Brother hauled water—"He is the coolie of the family," I was informed amidst peals of laughter—two younger sisters washed the dishes, and the younger brothers had no tasks. Father did more housework than Wai-gun, since he increasingly took time off from his job because of his ill health. He purchased food for the family and for his wife's and daughter's lunch boxes. He also prepared dinner when his wife worked overtime.

Wai-gun's sibling relationships illustrate the rapidity of life-style change within a single generation. She was very close to Eldest Brother, two years younger than she; they frequently went places together and took each other's photographs. One Lunar New Year's Eve, they set up a stall at a local night market and sold neckties. On another occasion, they went to a film together. Yet Wai-gun and her sister Ying-gun, five years her junior and the third child in the family, were never very close, in part because the difference in their ages created substantially different experiences and outlooks. Ying-gun dropped out of school at around age 13, despite the fact that the family wanted her to continue. Even though she was young enough to be considered child labor, she took an assembly job at the Fairchild Semiconductor plant. She preferred the independence gained from employment. Although as a learner her earnings were too low to be of much help to the family, she supported herself while living at home and spent her pocket money on entertainment and fancy clothing like bell-bottom trousers and stacked shoes. Wai-gun was openly critical of her sister's spending in the youth culture. It was not legitimate for Wai-gun to chafe openly over her own sizable contribution to the family purse, but her purchase of a Chinese lute and folk music lessons, to which her parents objected, and her reproach of Ying-gun's spending habits reminded them all of the opportunities which as Eldest Daughter she had sacrificed for her family.

Education

Wai-gun had attended a rooftop primary school run by the government in her resettlement estate. To encourage attendance, schools like this one accept all youngsters from surrounding districts, regardless of aptitude or achievement. There is no entrance examination, and as a rule all students move easily from one grade to the next to make room for newcomers. The schools are crowded, with an average of 45 children per room. Classes are held in two shifts—in the morning from eight to one and in the afternoon from one-thirty to six. Government-run primary schools like this one have a low standing in the community and are generally believed to be less rigorous than missionary or other private schools, which cater to families of somewhat higher income, require entrance examinations, and maintain lower student-teacher ratios.

Wai-gun characterized the teaching style as the "stuffed duck" method—students are crammed with facts, like grain is force-fed to Peking ducks, so that they can pass the secondary school entrance exams. She hated rote education, and she willingly accepted Father's decision that she should drop out after graduating at age 13. Given her family's impoverished financial circumstances and their need for her earnings, Wai-gun was grateful for the little schooling she had had. At that time, it was the norm that working-class children in Hong Kong would leave school early. In her last year of primary school, Wai-gun had already limited her study time in order to assemble plastic flowers with Mother.

Wai-gun explained, "My brother went to school longer because he's a boy. With only a primary school education, it was easier for a girl to get a job than for a boy. He has the responsibility to rear his own family in the future, and further education is more important to him than to me."

"But women certainly work after marriage," I said.

"Yes, I know that large numbers of women are now working, but these numbers were much smaller six years ago. Anyway, a woman's job is second to a man's even now," she countered.

The factory job that Wai-gun obtained was considered a good spot for a daughter but a dead end for a son, because he would eventually have to support his own wife and children. In the patrilineal family, moreover, sons are expected to continue their economic contribution to the family coffers through the lifetime of their parents, whereas the daughters' economic input ends at marriage.

"How did you feel about quitting school?" I asked her.

"Well," she replied, "I am part of the family, too. Two of us cannot attend secondary school in the same year, and my brother is advancing, so they especially need my labor now."

Eldest Brother's Anglo-Chinese secondary school, operated by the Church of Christ of China, had a good reputation. His school fees were contributed by a Canadian family under the auspices of the International Children's Association. He finally left his studies for a job as a delivery boy that paid little more than Wai-gun's.

Of all the children, Wai-gun had the aptitude and drive to continue school, and it is ironic that although she dropped out to support her family while Eldest Brother was in secondary school, he preferred to play soccer and basketball and to earn a living. Wai-gun later deeply regretted her lost schooling and tried to recoup the deficit during eight long years of night school.

Wai-gun's passionate interest in China, its culture, and political history awakened after she left primary school. She took evening classes in European history, English literature, and liberal arts subjects, all of which were taught in English. She lacked the time to do homework, and her grades were barely passing. Because her school was run for profit, it encouraged everyone to re-enroll year after year and advanced them no matter how they performed on the tests. I once looked at Wai-gun's history book and grammar tests and found them quite difficult, with few adaptations for use in Hong Kong.

Wai-gun saw learning as a broadly defined, dynamic experience extending outside the classroom and into society. In 1976, Wai-gun finally lost interest in acquiring her elusive diploma and, without renouncing her idealistic view of the importance of learning, dropped out of evening school. Her creative energy then began to flow in channels better suited to her character and aspirations.

Work

When I met her, Wai-gun had held four jobs, beginning with home plastic flower assembly at age 12 and garment sewing in a small workshop the next year. She then joined numerous other 14-year-old girls on the assembly line at Fairchild Semiconductor, piecing together electronic circuits. She had also sewn seams in brassieres in a large West German-owned factory.

Wai-gun's dislike of the piecework system in the undergarment plant was unusual for a young and potentially fast worker and revealed a perspective that extended beyond her individual self-interest. She recognized that piecework discouraged solidarity among workers by creating a breach between the younger, stronger ones and the older, less dynamic ones. Piecework automatically weeded out older women workers, like her mother, whose health was run down by the system until low earnings forced them to quit.

Wai-gun also objected to the control such methods of pay gave the employers. Her company set an unofficial maximum of HK$25 per day. When a worker mastered shortcuts which enabled her to attain this maximum, the management reduced the rate for each piece, thereby keeping wages below the ceiling. Employing a scientific management approach—timing the workers' motions with a stopwatch and blueprinting their physical work flow for economy—the foreman often arbitrarily and without notice changed the piece rates. In Wai-gun's words, "In our factory, employer-worker relations are awful. There is a German woman walking around the room all the time. When she sits in front of you clocking your speed, it makes you really nervous. They also 'pick stones from eggs' and find tiny faults in our work. We pretend not to understand English. When they speak to us, we pay no attention. If they hand us work to redo, we just put it aside and make repairs only when the stitching is really poor."

Wai-gun also found this job dissatisfying because the fast assembly line pace and rigid work rules forbade conversation. She especially disliked sitting at the sewing machine all day. "You can't even go to the washroom except at your break. We must take our lunch sitting at the bench," she complained. On the other hand, Wai-gun also said, "I don't have to think about the work while I do it. I can think about other things instead!" This aspect of her work, and her much-needed paycheck accounted for her acquiescence to the deadening routine.

However, certain management actions occasionally provided the spark that triggered an expression of pent-up resentment. Wai-gun described a one-day sit-down strike in her factory to protest the management's decreasing the wage without first informing the workers. The factory was not unionized, but a spontaneous feeling of ill will spread through the shop. People whispered the plan as they passed by each other's workbenches. Everyone took part except the well-paid section of workers who operated the multi-purpose sewing machines. The management was forced to raise the wages slightly. But, according to Wai-gun, "It was only a gesture! After that, they returned to their old habit of cutting the workers' wages without informing them. This shows that the bosses are very smart. They know how to drag the issue out until our 'organization' disintegrates."

Wai-gun, who considers the interests of workers opposed to those of management, had also joined a spontaneous strike by the unorganized workers in the Fairchild Semiconductor plant in 1970. The dispute concerned differential pay rates for shift work, an accepted North American practice but one that was considered unfair by the Hong Kong workers on the day shift. Wai-gun recalled, "The strike failed, probably because we were not united enough. For one thing, we didn't know each other well enough beforehand. For another, the leaders were too weak. We elected them just because they were the most vocal, but they were too excitable and lost their tempers during negotiations, giving management the impression that we were immature and naive. Management knows that ours is not complicated work and that new workers can be easily trained. So they fired those of us who worked up to the highest wage ceiling without giving us the required one month's notice or one month's extra wage. They summoned us to the office to do it and let us wait for three hours in a cold, air conditioned room without sending anyone to talk to us. It was a damned cold way to lose a strike."

Wai-gun's untutored and instinctive identification with the sporadic worker protests in the factories where she worked reflects not only a passionate commitment to social betterment but also latent leadership potential. She could probably be a capable section leader, which would give her a more skilled, more secure, and more satisfying position. But despite Wai-gun's clear interpersonal skills on the factory floor, she was reluctant to seek promotion by currying favor with the foreman. To her, the slight pay increase was not worth the increased responsibility and estrangement from her workmates.

Although Wai-gun feels that workers are exploited by capitalists, she is pessimistic about the long-term prospects of uniting the proletariat and attributed the collapse of the Fairchild strike to subjective divisions among the workers. She felt that the workers' position would remain poor even under socialist rule or, as she put it, "even if the color of the colony is changed to red," referring to the common expectation that someday sovereignty will revert to the People's Republic of China.

Peers

Like most other working daughters I met, Wai-gun also engaged in recreational activities and joined evening and weekend classes as a means of broadening her skills and locating like-minded friends. Peers provide a psychological counterweight to formidable family obligations. The chance to confide without fear of criticism for self-centeredness or disloyalty and the freedom to engage in activities without regard for family rules of hierarchical deference were attractive to Wai-gun. She was most attracted to activities which helped her find her cultural heritage as a Chinese. The search for national roots is difficult in a culturally undernourished and politically restricted city like Hong Kong, but Wai-gun followed her populist bent for many years and found other young people who shared her interest.

Wai-gun and her best friend Shing-wa teamed up with a young man, about age 25, who lived in the same apartment block as Wai-gun. Unmarried, mainland-born, and with his family still in China, he rented a half-room apartment from friends who had been allocated it but had moved elsewhere. The trio exchanged rings and swore to become "blood brothers and sisters." "This is a fictive kinship relationship of solidarity that was common in traditional China," I was told by Wai-gun. Sworn Brother shared his intellectual interests with Wai-gun and taught her calligraphy. He also bought her every issue of a monthly magazine, *Hong Kong 'Seventies*, critical of the Hong Kong establishment. Sworn Brother was not a union member, though, and he looked askance at the avowedly political Hong Kong unions.

In spite of her heavy schedule of work and family obligations, Wai-gun kept up an amazing roster of activities. One evening, while she and I were strolling in Victoria Park, Wai-gun showed me the rink where she and Shing-wa often roller-skated. Later, while we sipped tea on the terrace overlooking the park's 50-meter swimming pool, she mentioned that she was also learning to swim. "I attend lessons after work three times a week for an hour. We have to rush like mad to get to the pool at six-thirty, because traffic jams slow down our bus. I hope to pass the test with my class in two weeks, then go on to the next class. The program is run by the Urban Council, and it's free."

I asked Wai-gun about her other activities. Wai-gun ticked them off on her fingers: "English at night school, but I am stopping next month until the fall because I need the time to study Mandarin; folk dancing; singing; and theater. We write and perform our own plays. My sworn brother plays the Chinese flute, but he discourages me from learning because it's not 'feminine' " (she wrinkled her month to demonstrate how awkward it looked).

Wai-gun's parents did not overtly oppose her friendships, classes, and outings, but they harbored reservations, so she often kept her pursuits a secret. Their lukewarm receptivity to Wai-gun's keen pursuit of Chinese culture was obvious. They had objected to her purchase for HK$200 of a Chinese lute, the *p'i p'a*, and to lessons at HK$70 per month. For her parents, any outside activity had to be an investment, and learning the lute would not advance Wai-gun economically. Wai-gun borrowed money from her sworn brother and purchased the lute despite their objections. She stored it at his apartment and practiced it there. Wai-gun fetched the lute one day and brought it to her room to play for me. She sat on a straight chair, while her mother leaned out to watch from the lower bunk bed and her father squatted on a low stool. While Wai-gun demonstrated her lute, her mother provided a counterpoint of sarcastic comments, such as, "That little thing is so expensive, but if it broke, the wood in it would not even be sufficient to make a fire to cook a meal!"

She also defied her mother and went on an overnight camping trip with five friends in the New Territories, where they slept in a tent. "Boys and girls together, you don't know what will happen!" her mother exclaimed to me. Wai-gun went anyway, and eventually, after the fact, Mother resigned herself and gave Wai-gun permission to attend a camp outing sponsored by the YWCA. Wai-gun's parents grumbled whenever her social activities cost money or included contact with young men, although both were obviously beyond their control. Since this dutiful eldest child never reneged on her family obligations, I sensed that their protests were more for a dogged show of propriety than from the conviction that Wai-gun's behavior was unseeming.

Wai-gun also looked to the cinema for direction. Whereas other Hong Kong girls I knew preferred romantic, escapist Hollywood and Hong Kong films, Wai-gun sought out films with social commentary. Chaplin's *Modern Times* played to a full house in Hong Kong for weeks. This American classic, popular in the West for its trenchant condemnation of assembly line inhumanity, appealed to Hong Kong audiences for the cathartic relief it presented, through humor, of severe pressures in primarily Western-owned industry. When Wai-gun took me to see it, she remarked on the similarity of her own work environment to the one enacted by Chaplin, "My boss should get together with that one and compare notes on how to get more out of the workers!"

Wai-gun's visits to the People's Republic of China were another crucial step in her search for roots. On her first trip in 1974, she and her parents visited relatives, but much to her parents' discomfort, she was most interested in posing social questions, especially regarding the role of youth, to her village relations. At first, the fact that her parents were in flight from their Chinese roots gave Wai-gun pause, but she was magnetically attracted to China, like many Hong Kong youth, and in 1975 she and Shing-wa visited China alone. The main goal for Wai-gun, separate from the highly constrained structure of family obligations and work responsibilities, was her search with friends for her cultural roots. Wai-gun shared with other young working women in Hong Kong an attraction to a congenial peer group both as an end in itself and as support for the steps which could be taken toward adulthood. But for Wai-gun, the peer culture should be rooted in Chinese culture, not inspired by Western mass media.

Wai-gun's peers were her sole relief from family and economic restrictions. She considered her family structure constricting and had dreamed of moving away from home. She was straining for not only a physical space of her own but also her own psychological sphere. We had many conversations on this topic. One evening Wai-gun, her sworn sister Shing-wa, my Cantonese assistant (a sociology student at the Chinese University of Hong Kong), and I were strolling in Victoria Park. Wai-gun asked where my assistant lived. Upon hearing that my assistant shared quarters with friends, Wai-gun and Shing-wa said in one voice, "We wish we could do that, too. How wonderful!" Wai-gun went on wistfully about her wish to live alone. "We have so many people in our room. Do you have your own room at home? Your own bed? You have only two to a room! In a big family like ours, only when Eldest Daughter [herself], Eldest Son, and Second Daughter move out will my family's place be the right size!"

Single working-class girls as a rule did not live apart from their parents. Leaving home signified to Wai-gun and Shing-wa a break with the family rather than an approved search for independence. Most parents believed that their daughters' income belonged entirely to the family, and they looked askance at unnecessarily paying extra rent. In addition, the family system of control was associated with living under one roof. Young women who moved away from their families were unfilial. To my observation, daughters were able to obtain greater opportunities for peer activities and freedom in the home itself, as long as they agreed to remain there.

Some might think that under the circumstances of strong family demands and fledgling efforts to build a separate identity, Wai-gun and her friends might follow a desire for more independence and seek a marriage partner. However, taking the route of marriage was not a feasible option for Wai-gun until she fully discharged her economic obligation to her family. Furthermore, as Wai-gun and her contemporaries were aware, marriage, however desirable on other grounds, would entail even greater subordination to a new family unit—that of the husband.

Dating and Marriage

In principle, Mother wanted Wai-gun to marry someone from their home county in China, Taishan County in Kwangtung—someone who spoke the parents' form of dialect and practiced the same local traditions. Mother began arranging this when Wai-gun was only 17. Wai-gun complained, "Mother wants me to marry for money. She wanted to fix me up with a Taishanese who lives in America so I could bring over the rest of my brothers and sisters later to study. Mother would have arranged it through friends and relatives."

"What did you think of this arrangement?" I asked.

"There would be many practical difficulties. Maybe we'd have money, maybe not. Many Chinese in the United States are shopkeepers, and that means I'd be working in the shop all day long. That's a difficult life! Even though the man Mother found might claim that he had a high-paying job, he might not have a job at all! You can't really check up on his house and friends from here. I have a friend who entered an arranged marriage like that a few years back, but I don't know if it worked out. If she wasn't happy, she wouldn't dare admit that she made a bad choice! Anyway, money isn't everything."

In certain cases, the arrangements would involve finding a reliable relative or friend who knew many people or a professional matchmaker who could collect the names of eligible bachelors. Names, photographs, and qualifications, including testimonies from relatives, would be presented to Mother, who would select from among them and show the

candidates' material to Father and then Wai-gun. While such an arrangement might have had a chance of success in the village setting, or even in
Hong Kong, where reputations were well known or knowable, there was
less likelihood of success in an industrialized society that spanned the seas.
Wai-gun made it clear from the outset that she would not go along.

When she was 18, Wai-gun became enamored of Chen-kwok, the
roommate of her sworn brother, who was an active participant in the
magazine-reading and Chinese culture circle revolving around sworn
brother. Chen-kwok was a warehouseman of cloth and earned a modest
wage, a little more than Wai-gun. His work was steady, and he had a good
chance of promotion. Most important to Wai-gun were their common
experience and viewpoints. "Chen-kwok is my first boyfriend. Chen-
kwok is intelligent, thoughtful, and decisive and fits my marriage standards. While I know how to make up my mind, I do not want to have to
make all the crucial decisions. His salary is not too bad. Most important,
Chen-kwok is someone with whom I can have serious talks—someone
who is not Westernized and who likes things Chinese," she said, recalling
his participation in the Chinese cultural group. Chen-kwok was also four
or five years her senior, an age difference that accommodated their similar
peer interests but gave him an edge in maturity and experience.

There was one critical difference in their backgrounds. The young
man's family originated in southern Fukien Province; Wai-gun's
Taishanese roots are in southern Kwangtung Province. Their dialects and
traditional cultures were correspondingly different. Although this was no
obstacle to Wai-gun and Chen-kwok, who had both grown up in the
culture of Cantonese-speaking Hong Kong, Wai-gun's parents objected
to the match for this reason. Chen-kwok's father objected for similar
reasons.

Wai-gun and Chen-kwok disagreed over the type of wedding to hold.
Chen-kwok wanted to satisfy his family's wish for a lavish banquet with
friends and relatives, which runs to thousands of dollars, but Wai-gun
preferred a simple ceremony at the marriage registry, preceded by an
exchange of small cakes and followed by a honeymoon. For such a "travel
wedding," no banquet is required. Wai-gun faced opposition from everyone over this matter. "Mother doesn't want me to have the travel wedding. She prefers the feast because she's conservative. Without it, people
would gossip about us, saying that we are stingy and didn't want to invite
friends. A travel wedding is a bit like running away from home. They'd
say that Chen-kwok and I are avoiding social recognition of the marriage."

The most serious rift developed over the timing of the nuptials. As the
eldest child and only son, Chen-kwok was expected to marry quickly and
to present his mother with a grandson. In contrast, Wai-gun's family

might have swallowed their objections to a Fukien partner if the marriage could have been delayed several years. Their reasons were pecuniary—as long as she stayed engaged but unmarried, Wai-gun would have continued to swell the family purse. It is not uncommon in Hong Kong for couples in their early twenties to become engaged and then continue in the work force, thus contributing to their families for several more years. Wai-gun explained, "Mother wants me to marry later because of our household burden. Two or three years later would be just about right, but not longer, otherwise she might be stuck with an old maid!"

Chen-kwok's mother tried to settle the match by the end of the year by promising to pay for the banquet as well as the honeymoon for which Wai-gun pined. Both Wai-gun and Chen-kwok knew that this gesture was not without cost. "If any later conflict arises, she'll be able to say, 'You do as I say. After all, I paid for your wedding!'" However, while it pleased Wai-gun temporarily, this arrangement would not have upgraded the standard of living in Wai-gun's household. These sweeteners did not balance in the eyes of Wai-gun's parents the three years of continued support they would lose from their working daughter.

The bonds of love between Wai-gun and Chen-kwok were not strong enough to withstand the incessant disagreements of their families. In the end, Wai-gun dutifully obeyed her mother's strictures to delay marriage, and Chen-kwok acceded to his mother's plans for speeding it up. He returned to his home village in Fukien, and family members helped him contract a marriage with a woman from a neighboring village. After the ceremonies, he left his bride behind and returned alone to Hong Kong to his daily routine.

Mother said "I told you so" to anyone who would listen. Mother was self-righteously triumphant in her knowledge that a Fukienese was impatient and unreliable in family affairs. Wai-gun was crushed. She no longer visited her former friends, because Hong Kong youth consider engagements binding, and they ridiculed her unmercifully. As a consequence, she hesitated to visit her former haunts for fear of being embarrassed by running into Chen-kwok and even her sworn brother, who was inevitably identified with him. Shing-wa alone remained loyal, but she soon had her own budding romance and had little time to spend with her sworn sister. Most demoralizing to Wai-gun was the demise of her ideal of a chosen marriage.

New Stage in the Life Cycle

Wai-gun had to choose between her peers and her family over the issue of marriage versus maintenance of her family. If her family's economic position had gradually improved, as had been anticipated before the seriousness of her parents' illnesses became apparent, Wai-gun might not have had to choose so definitively between her fiancé and her family, but such was not the case. The necessity for maintaining the family wage economy posed the issue clearly, and the romantic impulses Wai-gun felt as an individual succumbed in the struggle.

When I revisited Hong Kong in the summer of 1976, I was stunned to learn from Wai-gun that Father had passed away from liver cancer in 1975. Mother's health steadily worsened until she, too, lay on her deathbed. Mother died later that year. The long-term illnesses of the parental bread-winners had severely taxed the family unit, which began to dissolve as a result. While the children were working and nursing their ill mother in shifts, they lacked the time and the will to keep the apartment in any semblance of order. Wai-gun adopted the leadership mantle in an effort to keep her brothers and sisters together. She organized a new household division of labor, in which each brother and sister received an assign-ment—to work or to attend school in day or night sessions. Each nursed Mother at other times.

Wai-gun arranged for Father's burial. Their relatives gave only the minimum assistance. Father's brother did the necessary paper work and visited various clan and other benevolent associations to raise the money for the coffin, but Wai-gun complained, "He asked for cab fare and money for lunch to do even that. None of our relatives helped us out financially at all." Father's brother did not attend the funeral, and only the small family saw him buried in their kinsmen's Chai Wan grave site. At Wai-gun's side, however, was none other than Chen-kwok, whom she still saw occa-sionally and who was able to give her moral support.

When Wai-gun took the leadership of the family, the other areas of her life were altered. She was forced to terminate her evening classes because she lacked the time and spirit to continue. Father's outspokenly negative views on political participation and trade union organizing had once dampened her ardor for entering the political arena. After his death, however, she transferred her commitment from schooling to a garment workers' union affiliated with the "patriotic" (pro-China) Federation of Trade Unions. In 1976, she found there a completely new set of friends who were ignorant of her engagement and shattered peer group. Wai-gun is thrilled that the union lionizes traditional Chinese folk culture, and she attends folk dances and songfests in the union hall. The union also ad-dresses the problem of industrial exploitation in Hong Kong more assert-ively than the individualistic and essentially defensive loosely organized cultural revival groups. Before she assumed family leadership, it is incon-ceivable that Wai-gun could have ever identified herself with such an activist organization.

Summary

Does the employment of young women on assembly lines at piecework tear apart long-standing family hierarchies? Have working daughters increased their power and influence in the family by their entrance into the industrial labor force? The stories of Rainbow and Wai-gun, women at work in service and factory industries in the industrial city of Hong Kong, provide a glimpse into still-restrictive family obligations and expectations, intricate patterns of obligation to co-workers and peer groups, and the rewards of being filial in the Hong Kong context.

The women's jobs provide little increase in their power to direct the course of the families in which they grew up. Both Chinese tradition and modern industrial-colonial structures accentuate the role of males as providers and protectors of the family, thereby limiting the status of working women and ensuring that employed daughters remain loyal to the demanding institutions that direct their lives. However, the daughters do earn the right to choose their own circle of friends. Satisfied with the influence they have gained in areas peripheral to family life, these young working women maintain filial piety in a new context.

Cambridge University Press has given permission to reprint "Wage Earners in Hong Kong" from Janet W. Salaff's *Working Daughters of Hong Kong*, 1981.

PART III
China

Part III returns to China, focusing on lives of
women in revolution and reconstruction. To begin
with, a methods chapter addresses the differences
between Western life history methods and the biographical methods used by Chinese authors in
China. This invites comparisons with chapters 2
and 6. The lives of model women in chapters 11
and 12 illustrate the Chinese biographical genre,
different from the life histories in the other chapters.
Finally, chapter 13 presents the rare perspective of
a Western scholar who shared the home and work
of a village woman in contemporary China. Thus
a continuity of experience brings us through contemporary generations to 1983.

10

The Chinese Biographical Method: A Moral and Didactic Tradition

By Jerome Ch'en

The contemporary Chinese biographical method stems from a non-psychological, didactic tradition. It was the job of the earliest Chinese historians, as employees of the princely court, to concern themselves chiefly with the glorification of morality and sagacity through didactic writings on the virtuous words and deeds of eminent men—philosophers, generals, and kings. These were recorded in official histories and later also in local gazetteers, epitaphs, obituary notices, jottings (*pi-chi*), and even in the freer style of short stories (*ch'uan-chi, hsiao-shuo*—small talks on things extraordinary).

Ssu-ma Ch'ien, the great historian of the Former Han dynasty (d. 85 B.C.), was not bound by these limitations when he created a new style of biography (*lieh-chuan*) in his *Chronicles*. He was most concerned with the role of individuals in history and how they influence or determine the development of society. He therefore included in his biographical writings some classes of people who had hitherto been excluded as being too lowly, such as physicians, assassins, and gang leaders. Ssu-ma Ch'ien's methodology was more liberal than that of either his predecessors or his successors. Yet even Ssu-ma Ch'ien excluded ordinary women from his records; only empresses and the loyal sister of one heroic assassin found their way into his records.

During and after the Sung dynasty (A.D. 960–1279), when Confucianism came to dominate the Chinese state philosophies, ethical formalism increasingly dominated biographical writing. In this ideological and institutional context, ordinary women began to appear in the records for the purpose of demonstrating the masculine strictures for impeccable feminine behavior. Thus side by side with the biographies of men of integrity (loyal ministers and learned gentlemen), biographies of chaste women and celibate girls began to appear. Even an occasional woman poet attracted gentlemanly interest. However, Confucian canons left no room in official records for licentious females, even as negative examples, although disloyal ministers and rebels (but not rakes) were granted a place.

175

The rise of commercial cities and the advent of movable-type printing after the tenth century brought forth a new ethos, new lifestyles, and a demand for pleasurable reading material. A wider range of experience was given a permanent record; consequently, for the first time, interesting women served as subject material for highly popular less formal literature. From Li'-wa, a prostitute with a golden heart, of the T'ang dynasty, to Golden Lotus of the late Ming, to Black Jade of the *Dream of the Red Chamber* of the high Ch'ing, new types of women appeared in poetry and prose. There were even sword-swinging warrior women. Strictly speaking, however, these were not biographies but fiction. Their popularity, however, was perhaps due to their suggestion to their female readers that life was far more varied and invigorating than that prescribed by Confucian tenets and that, like men, women could take action outside the confines of their chamber. Such fiction may have encouraged turn-of-the-century female political activists like Ch'iu Chin (1879?–1907), educators like Wu Yi-fang (1893–   ), physicians like Shih Mei-yü (Mary Stone) (1873–1954), and writers like Ting Ling (1902–   ) and Hsieh Ping-ying (1903–   ).

Chinese official biographies lack psychological dimension because they concentrate on very literal and condensed recording of highly selective exemplary words and deeds. It is left to the more entertaining literary writers to detail private lives and emotions. The introduction to China of European novels and biographies on the one hand and the increase in professional writers and translators on the other, both at the turn of the century, lent support to this new trend and prepared the ground for a drastic change in the methodology and art of biographical writing. For example, *Oliver Twist* was translated as *Tse-shih* (*The History of a Thief*), *The Old Curiosity Shop* as *Hsiao-nü Nai-erh Chuan* (*The Biography of the Filial Daughter, Nai-erh [Nell]*), and *Jane Eyre* as *Chien-ai Tzu-chuan* (*The Autobiography of Chien Ai*). Judging from the words used in the Chinese versions of titles, the translators evidently regarded these realistic novels as biographical or autobiographical. These works became popular in China on the eve of the May Fourth Movement of 1919, which stimulated many new intellectual and social concerns among writers of the 1920s and 1930s. For example, the autobiographical stories of the great writer Lu Hsün about the underprivileged in his native city, Shaohsing in Chekiang Province, led the way for the later publications of Hsü Chih-mo's *Tzu-p'o* (*Anatomy of Myself*) in 1928, Ting Ling's *Tzu-sha Jih-chi* (*Diary of a Suicide Attempt*) in 1937, and Hsieh Ping-ying's *I-ko Nü-ping Ti Tzu-chuan* (*Girl Rebel, The Autobiography of Hsieh Ping-ying, with Extracts from Her New War Diaries*) in 1936.

Despite marked changes in fiction between the May Fourth Movement and Liberation, biographies of political figures evinced very little change from their traditional function—to praise or to censure. In the period after World War I, published autobiographies took one of two forms—self-compiled chronological biography or a new form of candor. Inspired by Rousseau's *Confessions* and considerably more detailed and revealing, these biographies contained a great deal of psychological data but very little psychological analysis. The impact of the European tradition in China had awakened humanism and emboldened Chinese biographers. Although they lacked psychological method, these writers felt the urge to speak more personal truths. Their revelations constituted an assault on the constraints of Chinese social philosophy and its social institutions. Nevertheless, these were mainly protest biographies aimed at arousing sympathy, empathy, and similar personal and social defiance. In sociological terms, their authors came mainly from the declining lower middle class, which had compelling reasons to protest the social status quo and which was sensitive to the urgent need for social change.

These considerations did not fit into a Marxist frame of analysis. The Chinese Marxists, or, more precisely, the Communists, had a consensual plan for changing society, where collectives would take precedence over individuals, working people would lead the petit bourgeoisie, and the social infrastructure and superstructure were analyzed as the forces which shaped individuals. Individuals were not portrayed as shaping society.

How, then, should a Chinese Communist write a biography? Of the party leaders, only Ch'en Tu-hsiu, Ch'ü Ch'iu-pai, Chang Kuo-t'ao, Kung Ch'u, and a few others published their autobiographies or memoirs; all were written after the authors had left the party. The other leaders trusted only foreign biographers (Edgar Snow for Mao, Agnes Smedley for Chu Te, Nym Wales for several other leaders).[1] Biographical material on party leaders written originally in the Chinese language consists of only three main forms—official obituaries, memoirs that have appeared in unsystematized snippets, and an oral tradition which came from small group discussions. We know for certain that it is the practice for wayward leaders to write their autobiographical confessions as a form of self-criticism, but these have never been published.

The paucity of biographies of party leaders may stem from a theoretical ambivalence about the role of the individual in the development of state and society. Since Marxism rejects the "big man" theory of history, such theoretical ambivalence is not difficult to comprehend. An individual as great as Mao Tse-tung is a good example. His contribution is now depicted not as shaping China but as tempering and nurturing the social forces which did the shaping.[2] It is probably because of this theoretical formulation that Mao himself preferred to be remembered principally in his role as a teacher. As long as he or any other leader is serving the cause of the party, his media image is based upon public performance and social impact rather than psychological responses or private feelings. In the Chinese framework, performance and impact are more important than motivation, so there is no need to differentiate the public image and the private reality. (The recent revelation of Chiang Ch'ing's private life is therefore an extraordinary departure from the established tradition of avoiding discussion of private behavior in the public arena).[3]

The importance given by the party to the role of ordinary working people led to the growth of a new type of biographical writing beginning with the days of the Kiangsi Soviet in the early 1930s. The Yenan biographies in this book are typical of that period. These are an extremely rich collection of material about ordinary people whose political behavior was considered as important as that of the formal leadership. As the mass line approach became fully developed in the north Shensi border region, more and more biographies of this type appeared. The subjects of these life histories were invariably working people who excelled in their economic endeavors and soldiers who made an outstanding contribution to the revolutionary wars. These heroes were both inspired and guided by the accepted ideology and organized and led by the party. This trend has continued into the post-Liberation period.[4]

In these materials about ordinary people are found a set of values and norms indispensable for understanding the People's Republic today and in the recent past. The people themselves are considered the personification of the accepted ideology and the pacesetters of social and cultural change. They also embody those parts of the tradition which remain meaningful in the new social context.

For instance, in the pre-Liberation days, struggling young students were spurred on by their parents and teachers with stories of K'uang Heng, who, too poor to afford an oil lamp, read by the light from his neighbor's house through a crack in the wall. His industriousness paid off to the credit of his family in political power and high status. (K'uang was promoted to be chief minister of Emperor Yüan of the Former Han, 48–33 B.C.)

The norm of hard work continues today. K'uang's story is still taught to students in Hong Kong and Taiwan and is echoed in the industry and frugality of Ting Chih-hui, whose life is included in this book. Ting Chih-hui was working and contributing to people in need, not for personal glory and individual recognition but to further political goals. This motivation makes her more accessible to ordinary people. Her life history is presented for emulation by cadres today, just as the life history of K'uang Heng was presented during the dynasties for emulation by educated aspirants to imperial government office.

What these two life history styles share is their absolutely serious didactic intent.[5] The seriousness does not necessarily mean that Ting's life is written entirely without humor (e.g., her old comb smelled musty after years of use; her shirt was remade from another remade shirt), but the humor is never debunking, anti-hero, or self-debasing. For China, the old values have been destroyed, but the new values are still in the process of being established. It is not yet time for satire or for seeing values in shades of gray instead of sharply contrasting black and white. A Western reader may be repelled by the moralistic simplicity of this type of life history. But one must bear in mind that such simplicity is functional to this stage of socioeconomic development. This didactic style is neither exclusively Chinese nor purely Communist propaganda. One should read such Chinese life histories as we do Christian hagiographies of saints—in the spirit in which they were written—instead of with our modern cynicism.

For life histories to stimulate emulation, they must be attractively written. From the point of view of their Chinese readers, they are. As time passes, the taste of Chinese readers is developing further, and this genre of writing is becoming more complex in both content and style. This will be more satisfactory for social scientists outside China, who are anxious to analyze such life histories, and for biographers, who are anxious to accept them as literature.

11

Yenan Women in Revolution

Ch'en Min: In the Army and the Shoe Factory
Old Lady Liu: Heroine of Spinning and Weaving
Li Feng-lien: A Comrade in the Tunic Factory

By Mary Sheridan (translator and editor)

Introduction

To the remote northwestern corner of China–where cave dwellings burrow into the yellow loess hills and sparse rainfalls barely sustain a traditionally impoverished peasantry—the Red Army aimed its Long March. From 1936 to 1944, the Shensi-Kansu-Ninghsia Border Region, with headquarters in Yenan, became a mecca and a haven for young revolutionaries and an experimental crucible for policies and methods to be adopted in China after Liberation in 1949. Among the youth who came from the city were women with a strong commitment to feminism, which by 1942 brought them into confrontation with the Communist Party leadership. The feminists, headed by Ting Ling, advocated progressive ideas on marriage, divorce, and the emancipation of women from home and male dominion—ideas which the party was afraid would alienate the local peasantry on whom it depended for support.

The party therefore subordinated "emancipation" issues to the need for production self-sufficiency for survival behind the Kuomintang economic blockade. Revolutionary work was redefined for everyone in terms of production, a policy which sent women back to hearth and loom. The slogans were no longer "free choice and marriage" and "equality of the sexes" but "save the children," "a flourishing family," and "nurture health and prosperity."[1] Women activists became doubly accountable— responsible for all work in the home as well as a full quota of work in production and open to criticism if they failed in either. The lives of Ch'en Min and Li Feng-lien reflect these expectations but also indicate that they continued to strive for equality.

In spite of difficulties, the production drive offered many women positions of leadership and responsibility, socially approved activities

180

outside the home, and an independent income. For most women, these opportunities were unprecedented. The benefits reached women of all classes, from intellectuals and cadres (leaders and white-collar members of organizations) to peasants. The political importance of the production drive cannot be overestimated. It secured a safe base and supply area for the revolutionary forces without which the revolution would have collapsed.

Due to the shortage of trained cadres, peasants were encouraged to maximize their leadership abilities and to organize other peasants to increase their output in food, grain, salt, and cloth. Revival of the defunct cotton cloth craft enabled the Red Army to become self-sufficient in cloth and the peasants to become self-reliant. At a time of tremendous wartime inflation in China, the border region economy became relatively stable and prosperous.[2]

During the two years of the official Yenan production drive (1943–1944), extensive daily publicity on the lives, work methods, and innovations of labor models filled the pages of the *Liberation Daily*, the newspaper of the border region. Labor models were individuals who were evaluated and elected for others to emulate on the basis of their production work. Detailed biographies of models—peasants, soldiers, transport workers, weavers and dyers, and even child heroes—were published by the hundreds. They focused on skills in production, achievements in leadership, and mutual assistance among peasants and ordinary people.

After peasants had proved their personal reliability and organizational competence, the Yenan government channeled loans and material assistance directly through these individuals to the people they were assisting. The loans were repaid and produce sold back to the government through the same channel, with the labor models acting in cadre-like roles. The degree of responsibility given to a labor model depended on ability and experience. The responsibility and publicity given to the labor models raised them to an opinion leadership role and made them important examples for emulation for new social values as well as innovators of technical skills. Their organizational abilities were improved through nonformal education in meetings, evaluation sessions, and conferences.

The Labor Model Conference of 1944 brought together several hundred peasants, soldiers, and cadres to review their achievements, exchange experiences, and stir enthusiasm for wider participation in the coming year. News coverage included distribution of pamphlet biographies of models. Since most of the peasants were wholly illiterate and the cadres from rural backgrounds were only minimally literate, the written style was designed for reading aloud to catch the interest of an audience mainly concerned with daily survival. For example, the life of Old Lady Liu appealed to women on the basis of their desire to control food money.

Women in poor Chinese households often received the last share of food, after men and children had finished eating.[3] In such situations, women were usually undernourished. Hence Liu's economic success is reported in terms of improved women's diet.

The three lives translated here were originally intended to be read to people just like Old Lady Liu and Li Feng-lien.[4] The written style is spartan, without any attempt at emotional depth or psychological examination. The lives have the didactic purpose of describing desirable behavior, skills, and accomplishments. Occasionally it is difficult to produce verbatim translations which convey an adequate historical context for the reader in English, because the originals take such details for granted. I have therefore incorporated into the text minor social or historical data necessary to the understanding of certain sentences.

The cultivation of models as leaders among the masses, as a bridge between the masses and the party, and as a source of new leaders for recruitment into cadre roles continues as an important method of Chinese social, economic, and political development to the present day. Regardless of changing political lines (with new models publicized to represent the desirable characteristics of each line), the basic concept of model functions has been maintained with considerable consistency. The life of Ting Chih-hui, a model of the post-Cultural Revolution period (see chapter 12), continues this pattern.[5]

Ch'en Min: In the Army and the Shoe Factory

Shentse and the adjacent areas in central Hopei are fertile cotton-producing lands, where most of the women spin and weave. Comrade Ch'en Min was born there into an extremely old-fashioned family of declining wealth. Her father, who had the low status of an adopted son, had gone off to join a warlord's army in Szechuan. There he took another wife and seldom returned to Min's home in Hopei. Min's mother had three children—Min, her elder sister, and her younger brother—and all were dependents in the house of Second Grandfather.[6] Grandfather had a rigid feudal attitude toward women. He regarded girl children as "a money-losing proposition," to be used like beasts of burden. When Min was only eight, she was forced to spin, help her mother with needlework, and care for her aunt's children. In the autumn, she picked cotton in the fields. Thus she labored ceaselessly.

When Min was 11, her mother died. Her father returned from Szechuan, quarreled violently with Second Grandfather, and removed his three children to a boarding school in Paoting. Later, Min and her sister were admitted to Tung-jen Middle School, and their brother entered Yü-teh Middle School. In 1937, the guns of the Marco Polo Bridge incident opened the anti-Japanese war and shattered Min's dream of going to college to become "a man of a woman." In the wake of this event, the anti-Japanese patriotic sentiments of the period encouraged her. She was then 18 and in the eighth grade of the junior division of her school.[7]

Anti-Japanese patriotism was aflame across the Hopei plain. All red-blooded young men and women walked onto the battlefields. A cousin of Min's who had graduated from the Second Women's Teacher Training College gave up her teacher's position to become director of the county Women's Patriotic Association. In 1938, Min herself began to work in the village women's association. Once she invited the village women to her courtyard to sew and wash clothing for the local anti-Japanese guerrilla units. When Min's old Second Grandfather learned about this, he was so angry that his beard quivered and his eyes bulged. Abusing her with names like "madwoman," "slave," and "drudge," he accused her of violating family rules and the propriety of women. But with the threat of her country's enemy before her, Min would not listen to instructions from her grandfather.

By 1938, the walls of the household could no longer imprison the women's aspirations. Min's elder sister was the first to rebel against Second Grandfather's family instructions. She left home on the pretext of visiting her maternal grandmother but instead went to join the anti-Japanese War College in Chinchou, Shenhsien. When Second Grandfather heard this, he shouted, "This is the misfortune of our family—to have produced a traitor, a rebel like her." One day soon after this, when the old man went to market, Min and her younger brother Ch'en Yi ran away. Yi carried Min on his bicycle and pedaled over 100 *li* to join their sister at the War College. Thus the two sisters and brother took the bright path of revolution. The elder sister later joined the battlefront drama troupe and is still working in central Hopei. The younger brother is an instructor in a guerrilla unit.

Min's first uncle was even more reactionary than Second Grandfather. To protect his wealth and position and disassociate himself, he put out a public notice for the arrests of Min, her sister, and her brother. The uncle offered a reward of 700 *yüan* for their capture alive or 500 *yüan* for them dead. Later on, this heartless and crazy uncle became a traitor to his country.

After three months' study at the War College, Min was placed as a bookkeeper in the economic commission of central Hopei. Although her studies were demanding, she discharged them happily. From there she joined a work corps, where she met and married comrade T'an Wen-pang, a regimental commissar. Thus began Min's work in the Eighth Route Army beside her husband.

Their unit fought in North China, where comrade T'an was an organizer in the political department. The regiment fought day and night, their tactics requiring long marches. Sometimes they had nothing to eat, or had only gruel. Min carried her own pack, often shouldering additional rations. She sustained the same hardships as the men without moaning or slacking. Once, their unit stopped at Lingch'iu, where her husband led the main force to battle. Min, a teacher, and four younger cadres were left behind to guard 13 prisoners and the regimental baggage. At midnight, Min spotted the enemy approaching, but with only one small pistol to defend themselves, her group had to flee. They force-marched for three days before catching up to the main unit. Even under these critical conditions, Min did not panic. She was always brave and calm.

When Min was transferred from North China to the border region in 1940, she was pregnant. But she climbed the mountains with the men, marching 70, 80, or even 100 li a day without lagging behind. The leadership was concerned and tried to give her a horse, but she refused, saying, "According to our regulations, we cadres shouldn't ride. If I do, the ordinary soldiers will gossip that we are privileged or soft. That will be bad for the morale of the fighters." In the end, the horse was given to the medical team. When they crossed the Tat'ung-P'uchou railway in Shansi, they were ambushed by the enemy. Again she was completely calm under fire. She reached the border region in May, and her child was born in September. This child has since died.

In January 1941, Min went to work in Yenpei. At that time, the Kuomintang launched an annihilation campaign, and Min accompanied her unit in its mobile harassment of enemy outposts in Hsinhsien and Ningwu. It was an inconceivably difficult struggle. Once, the enemy completely encircled the lower slopes of the mountain where her unit was holding the peaks with a handful of soldiers. After nightfall, Min's group began to evacuate the summit. It was pitch-dark and snowing. Wind from the northern reaches beyond the Great Wall whipped down through the mountain passes, and the men trembled with hunger. No one knows how many times Min soundlessly slipped and fell. Later in the campaign, when her unit was crossing the enemy's lines along the Fen River at Hsinhsien, Min crossed two mountain ridges—a distance of more than 100 li—between three in the afternoon and nine the next morning. When they were climbing precipitous cliffs and many soldiers straggled timidly behind, Min kept up with the main body of the unit. Her determination inspired the soldiers to remark: "If the wife of the political commissar can make it, so can we." In every way, Min demonstrated her fine qualities of strength and toughness as a woman and a cadre.

At the end of 1941, Min left Yenpei and returned to the border region. After her second child was born, she was assigned the post of instructor in the shoe factory at Wayaopao. In 1943, she was transferred to a similar job in the shoe factory of Chinp'enwan, also within the border region. That March, she gave birth to her third child, but the children did not slow down either her studies or her production. The leadership praised her orderly methods and productivity regardless of circumstances. The best example of this is her management of the shoe factory at Wayaopao.

In 1942, everyone in the brigade was impressed that the men of the Wayaopao regiment had strong and durable shoes to wear, not merely sandals or leggings. At that time, Min was managing the shoe factory at Wayaopao singlehandedly. When she began, the factory had 8,000 *yüan* in cash, 300 *catties* of rags, 200 *catties* of jute, and some millet. The director was an uneducated man whose technical standard was high but who lacked experience in management. Therefore, apart from technical guidance, all the administrative responsibility fell on Min. Later, the director was transferred elsewhere, and Min undertook the whole responsibility.

Conditions were very difficult because of the war, and Min's shoe factory was often unable to get financial assistance from the government. Once Min walked several hundred *li* to the supply depot of the regiment to ask for money. After pleading for several days, she got only 400 *yüan* as her passage money back to the factory. Nevertheless, she did not lose heart when the leadership gave her the task of making the factory self-sufficient by finding her own raw materials and arranging her own finances. The leadership promised that apart from the shoes contracted for the army, she could freely sell any additional shoes produced. The factory was to pay for the millet it would get from the government, and, in turn, the army would pay for the shoes made by the factory. Because of her painstaking management, the factory achieved its target. It supplied the regiment with several thousand pairs of shoes, and at the end of the year it had a profit of 200,000 *yüan*.

Min took more care in running the factory than in her own affairs. She thought, "The party is the guardian of this property for the sake of the people. As I am a member of the party, the property is therefore also my concern." She took part in shoemaking herself, studying how to make shoes better and faster. She carefully calculated how many tops could be cut from one *chang* of cloth, how much rag was needed for a pair of shoes, and how much jute was needed for stitching. At that time, the cost of raw materials for a pair of shoes was 70 *yüan*, plus 15 *yüan* for wages, bringing the total cost to 85 *yüan* per pair. However, Min sold them at only 100 *yüan* a pair, far below the market price. For the army, she charged only 90 *yüan* a pair. Because the shoes were well designed and solidly made, many people bought them. The offices and army units sent orders to her, and business was thriving. Before long, she added a cloth loom and a toweling loom to expand the scale of production.

Under Min's management, close attention was paid to economizing.

She would not waste even a strand of jute, picking up shreds of fiber from the floor and mixing them with good jute to make string. Nor would she waste any rags. When she saw workers cut the tops of the shoes too wide, she corrected them. She took the scissors and cut away a ring from the soles. What was cut away was just enough to make a pair of ridges to hold the shape of the toepiece of a shoe. She often told the workers, "Don't ever neglect even a tiny piece of cloth. If you can save one *fen* each pair, you will save one *ch'ih* in a hundred."

The workers of the factory included 10 child apprentices—"little devils" from the army—two fully qualified workers, cooks, and buyers—28 people in all.[8] The children were rather naughty, and the hired workers were also difficult to control. Min, however, treated them all very well. She gave the workers simple literacy lessons and held meetings for them. She was concerned with general morale, including the meals of the workers, and often discussed good diet with the manager and cooks in the kitchen. By a shrewd exchange at the grain market, she improved their diet to include steamed buns and a gruel of millet and beans. Because of this, the workers were happy and at the same time did not consume more than their grain quota.

On the first of April in 1942, just after dinner, when Min was breast-feeding her child and chatting with a worker, she received a sudden message from the leadership saying that by the middle of June, the factory should complete 1,200 pairs of shoes. What a job! There were only two and a half months to go! Min began planning immediately. At a workers' meeting, it was decided to push ahead night and day, breaking only for Sunday afternoons. Even while Min was walking about managing the factory, she carried her sewing with her. In exactly two months, she dispatched the 1,200 pairs of shoes to the regiment. And do not forget that she still had to care for her infant!

Min confessed that she used to entertain an incorrect understanding of production. She thought that she had come to Yenan to do military and political work and did not understand that production was also part of the revolution. The meaningfulness of labor was clarified for her when she joined the factory, especially after the call for the production drive. She saw famous generals join their men to hoe the steep hills and reclaim land; she saw wounded soldiers who had barely recovered go out in the broiling sun to clear brush and plant their own grain. This deeply impressed her with the glory of labor. She thought, "I feel ashamed that my physical strength is limited and I cannot reclaim land like the men, but I will find a way to take part in production."

In 1943, Min moved with her two children to the shoe factory at Chinp'enwan to become its instructor. The workers there were all housewives or teen-agers. At the autumn harvest, Min carried her baby on her back and led the women comrades from the shoe factory up to the hills to cut millet, temporarily leaving their sewing behind. In October, Brigadier General Wang Chen[9] called on everyone at the women's production conference of the brigade to spin yarn. This made Min very happy. She said, "I have found a way to produce with my own hands." When she went back to the regiment, she bought a spinning wheel and began to spin. She also organized the other women comrades, teaching those who did not know how.[10]

Min's daily schedule begins at six. After rising and washing her face, she attends to her children's needs until ten o'clock—washing their diapers, making the fire, cooking for the older child, breast-feeding the infant, and taking her own meal. After ten, she begins to spin. One may ask how she manages this with two children beside her. The elder child can run and play about by himself. She puts the baby on the *kang* (the brick platform bed which is warmed by a fire within), knocks a wedge into its edge, and ties a long sash onto it. She fastens the other end of the sash around the infant, and he can crawl on the *kang* with no fear of falling. There is a mat on the kang, and when her infant does his small and big business there, she can easily wash and change the mat. Recently Brigadier Wang's wife gave Min a crib.[11] This provides a new world for her infant.

The baby has the bad habit of refusing to sleep when carried on his mother's back as usual, so Min cradles him in one arm and continues to spin with her free hand. Thus she tries everything to make time for her work. Apart from breast-feeding the baby, eating her own meal, and taking a stroll in the courtyard at dusk, she spins until ten o'clock at night. Then she cooks for the older boy, tending the fire while turning her wheel. On the average, she finds at least six hours a day for spinning. Even with this, she often helps her husband with other matters. From ten to eleven, she reads documents and newspapers for her studies. She goes to bed at eleven to get seven hours of sleep.

In the past, Min spun one *tael* of yarn every two hours. When the newspapers publicized her plan of 60 *catties* for this year, it was based on this average. But she has become more skilled through practice, so in six hours she can now spin four *taels* and has raised her goal to 75 *catties* for the year.

Min does not dress or eat extravagantly—habits of plain living fostered in childhood. She never complains about army rations, even when there is little to eat. At the time of her marriage, Min received a rather elegant dress as a wedding gift, but she has yet to unpack it, preferring the comfort of simple clothes. Last year, Min got a "milk money" subsidy (worth 20 *catties* of meat a year) because she was breast-feeding her baby. She was reluctant to use the subsidy and saved it instead. In one year, she saved 20,000 *yüan* for this year's spinning.[12] Min is thrifty even in small matters.

For example, when she spins at night, she turns down the wick of the kerosene lamp and doesn't use the glass chimney, because she doesn't need much light for spinning. This saves a lot of kerosene each month for the government. She doesn't even use a charcoal stove to heat her house. Instead, she puts three bricks in a triangle and makes her fire there.

Since the publication of comrade Ch'en Min's plans for production and economizing, the other women comrades and housewives in Yenan's offices and schools are learning from her to "get organized."[13] Even the wife of a bigwig like District Commissioner Ts'ao, a mother of three, has joined Min's spinning groups. The wife of comrade Kuo Feng, a section head in the political department of the garrison troops, has also responded to Min's challenge. Not being a mother, she spins four *taels* of yarn daily and has become self-sufficient with regard to her food and clothing, not depending on her husband. One wife of a staff officer, a mother of one, did not show enough productive fervor at the beginning. Min repeatedly advised her, painstakingly taught her, and helped her to repair her spinning wheel. Eventually she reformed this comrade, who now spins three *taels* of yarn every day and covers all her personal expenses.

Comrade Ch'en Min's two major tasks at present are productive work and the care of her children; both tasks are revolutionary, so both should be well done. She must take care not to damage her health or that of her children, and she must spare one hour a day for study. Now Min is very busy with daily meetings, discussions, and interviews on her work experience. Collective and individual challenges to production competitions include the anti-Japanese League of the border region, the First Nursery of the Construction Bureau of the border region government, and the women comrades and housewives in Yangchialing and Nanniwan. This mother of two is really like a boxer standing in the ring and taking on all comers.

Old Lady Liu: Heroine of Spinning and Weaving

Liu Kuei-ying is the organizer of the women's spinning campaign in the city of Suite, where this year's great progress has been largely due to her leadership. For her fine contribution, she was elected to attend the first Labor Model Conference in Yenan, and her name has become familiar to all in the border region.

Affectionately known as "Old Lady Liu," she is 50 and has always used her maiden name. She was born in Chiehkuping and moved to Hsüeh-chiakou after her marriage at 14 to Hsüeh Ping-hung. Her husband's family of seven lived comfortably on their 70 *hsiang* of land, which annually yielded 70 *piculs* of grain. But in 1936, the depredations of the warlord Ho Shao-nan caused the family great suffering, and Liu's husband

died not long after. Liu was forced to support herself by taking in sewing
and laundry. She labored under great hardship until the Eighth Route
Army drove the warlord away and the general situation improved. Liu
now lives in Hsialiuchiakou, in the first district of Suite.

Old Lady Liu is dexterous in spinning and weaving, and her experience
is precious in the border region, where this skill has been lost. She
stretches and twists the balls of raw cotton into long fluffy strips and spins
them quickly into yarn of an even thickness. Aiming to minimize waste
even if the cotton is inferior, she loses only one *tael*. In the summer, she
spins in the courtyard to keep cool, but she carefully covers the thin fluffy
strips with a slightly damp towel to prevent them from getting dirty or
from being blown too dry. She also saves on cords for the spinning wheel,
using only half as much as other women. She makes her own cord by
twising 12 threads together and polishing them with a wet towel. The
result is just as smooth and durable as if she had followed common practice
and polished with garlic and beeswax. Thus Liu carefully protects these
scarce supplies. She is paid in cotton, and due to her thriftiness, skill, and
high-quality work, the city co-op pays her 12 *taels* of cotton instead of the
usual 11 for each *catty* of yarn.

In 1943, Liu spun a total of 58 *catties* and 12 *taels* of yarn, from which she
made more than 70,000 *yüan*.[14] Her circumstances have steadily improved. Whereas in 1941 she could afford flour only once every 10 days, in
1942 she could afford flour every four or five days. In 1943, she had 11
catties of meat for the year and noodles or buns made of flour every single
day instead of her former diet of coarse grains like millet and sorghum. Liu
put on new clothes without patches, shook off poverty, and went on to
plentifulness.

Household spinning had almost died out in the last generation in Suite
due to the importation of machine-spun yarn. But last year in March, Liu
quietly helped three women from poor families to get cotton from the
textile factory and become the factory's basic spinners. The city government of Suite became aware of Liu's enthusiasm and ability and encouraged her to organize more women to spin at home. Guided by members of
the city government, Liu went from house to house, carrying the yarn she
had spun and the raw cotton she had earned, in order to spread the news.
First she asked the women, "What sort of food do you eat? What do you
drink? Women and children can afford to dress better, even if it is only
with pocket money." They examined the yarn she had spun: "Old Lady
Liu spins very neat yarn and earns pure white cotton." Liu continued,
"Now the border region is covered everywhere with a layer of money. All
you have to do is pick it up."

Liu set an example by her own work and then tried to influence those
women whose income was relatively low. She opened their eyes to the

benefits, and they came to join the work one by one. Seven women came on the first day, five more on the second, and another nine on the third. By May, 34 women had begun spinning and weaving inside the city alone. Under the direction of the city officials, Liu called a meeting and organized the women into three teams led by reliable people. She herself was the director and the instructor of spinning. She helped the women to obtain cotton and deliver their yarn, organized small meetings for them on technique, inspected their quality of output, and corrected such problems as delays in sending back the finished yarn. Last year alone, Liu taught nine women to spin and supplied spinning wheels to women who needed them. She did her utmost to solve all the women's problems.

Word spread rapidly to the surrounding villages that women could earn money by spinning, and scores went to Liu's house to ask for cotton. As more people flocked to her, she became so involved that she could hardly keep up her own output. Refugees who had fled the terrible drought in nearby Honan were resettled through government assistance and then helped by Liu to get cotton and spinning wheels. They were so happy about this that they gave her a dinner party to show their gratitude.

Old Lady Liu helped these women solve their economic difficulties and showed no fear of being taken advantage of. For example, in the women's teams there were three lazybones who tried to squeeze an extra *tael* from every deal. These rogues underweighed their raw cotton and claimed that their finished yarn tipped the scales. Liu used her own cotton to make up the difference they owed the government, thus shaming them, This, together with criticism from the other women, helped the troublesome three to reform.

Liu also uncovered some shady dealings by profiteers who wanted to buy the women's cheap government-issued raw cotton in order to resell it dearly. As the women's representative, Liu took part in the struggle meeting against these schemers and assisted the women they had victimized. Thereafter the spinning movement developed smoothly.

Last year, Liu helped more than 300 spinners in the city to produce 1,700 *catties* of yarn, worth 60 *piculs* of rice. The 67 women directly under Liu's leadership spun 430 *catties* of yarn, from which they earned 15 *piculs* of rice. Liu said, "Let's all make money, so that women and children have something to wear, pocket money to spend, and fruit, sweet melons, and dates to eat. These things need not be paid for by menfolk now, and the whole family—old and young—will be happy."

Suite elected Liu a labor hero in June, awarding her a spinning wheel and two *catties* of cotton. In October, she received as further prizes a towel, a pair of socks, a mirror, and two *catties* of cotton. She was invited to dinner by the district commissioner and the military headquarters. The women praised her by saying: "Without Old Ma Liu, we'd have nothing to spin."

Old Lady Liu was overjoyed by her participation in the Labor Model

Conference. She told everyone, "I went to Yenan as a labor hero. I rode in a bus and ate things I had never seen before. The party showed their respect for us as people who have suffered. They gave us better food and warmer clothes. Some of us ordinary folk even went up to the rostrum to speak and saw Chairman Mao. Next year I shall do what Chairman Mao says and organize more women and children."

Liu has confidently drawn up her plan for 1944, setting the following goals: first, to spin 80 *catties* of first-grade yarn and to weave 30 *chang* of cloth by herself and, second, to organize 19 spinning teams in the city, or about 180 people. The district directly under her leadership will add four more teams to these for a total of 113 people. They will spin 3,000 *catties* of yarn, of which 2,000 *catties* will be first grade. She also plans to mobilize women to support the army. The teams under her direct leadership will knit 100 pairs of socks and sew 100 shirts for the soldiers free of charge. She will inspect production within the households and expose and struggle against bad people; reform lazybones and counsel people to give up opium, especially the two addicted couples in the Chu and Kao families, so that they will work harder and be more productive; and call on immigrants and refugees to move south from Suite to Yenan, explaining to them that Yenan treats immigrants and refugees very well.[15]

Liu has also set out her methods for promoting the spinning movement. She herself will resume spinning early on the last day of the New Year's festival, using two-thirds of her time this year on spinning at the rate of one *catty* of first-grade yarn every three days. The rest of her time will be spent organizing women's spinning teams. At the beginning of the year, Liu will launch a competition among the experienced spinners, and those who achieve a rate of 10 *catties* of good yarn a month will be awarded and publicized in March at the International Women's Day celebration. This will encourage others. At midyear, there will be a second competition for assessment, and a year-end competition will determine the hero spinners.

Each spinning team will meet regularly once every 10 days for about two or three hours. The central task of these meetings is to study techniques for achieving good-quality yarn with as few knots as possible by ensuring that wheels are easy to handle and their cords durable. The factory and co-op will supply the raw materials, and the spinners will make their own tools or borrow them from the city government. Liu will personally inspect the team leader's work every fortnight, and wherever a problem arises, she will be there to solve it.

Li Feng-lien: A Comrade in the Tunic Factory

Comrade Li Feng-lien works in the border region tunic factory and has taken part in the revolution in north Shensi for nine years, although she is only 24. The following is a brief recollection of her childhood and youth.

"My maiden home was in Hsiachiakou, the second village of the fourth district in Chingpien county. My father was employed since boyhood as a laborer for wealthy families. Following each harvest, he went back into the hills to tend their flocks through the winter. He made only a few *yüan* a year, and although he had a bit of hilly land, it lay fallow because he had no fertilizer. His meager wages barely kept our family of seven (father, mother, two elder sisters, myself, a younger sister, and a younger brother) on bran and wild vegetables. We wore rags even in the bitter of winter. Finally, Father resorted to selling his daughters. When I was three, I was sold to a family slightly better off who lived 30 *li* away, but I still remained with my own mother and sisters. I picked wild vegetables, carried water, and gathered firewood with them. When I was 13, my mother became ill and died. Only then was I sent off to my new home as a child bride, because my father could not feed me any longer.

"When I arrived in my new home, I discovered that my fiancé was a paralytic, unable to work, and that my mother-in-law had a foul temper. Although I was very young, I had to carry water, cook, turn the millstone, and do all the other heavy work. I was often scolded and beaten by my mother-in-law, who intensely disliked my unbound feet. She often cursed me in the name of my father: 'Wretched devil! He didn't bring you up properly, leaving you with a pair of big feet!' She fed me leftover millet and dishwater and cursed me more: 'Go and die. When you are dead, I'll buy a better one.' The hardship was unbearable.

"But the revolution came to us in 1935. When the Red Army broke into the village, all the women were summoned to a meeting to listen to the reasons for the revolution. There I heard that women could join the Red Army, and I was overjoyed. With my second elder sister, Li-p'ing, I ran away and enlisted. This, of course, became known to my mother-in-law's family, but they did nothing to stop me. In the army, I put on a new uniform and ate well. I was deeply moved by the way men and women comrades welcomed us.

"At the beginning of our revolutionary work, my second sister, two other girls, and I were sent to Yungp'ing to work in the supply department. Soon after that, the enemy began an encirclement, and fighting broke out so close that we could hear the firing. We joined a women's factory which was moving from place to place to escape the enemy. We stopped at Yungp'ing, Wayaopao, Wuch'i, and Chihtan. I knew that the revolution would inevitably triumph, because there were so many poor people. So in spite of the constant relocation under war conditions, I was not fatigued or afraid but on the contrary felt very happy."

In the women's factory, Feng-lien spent her first month buying food and cooking for the 20 workers, which she did quickly and carefully, never wasting a cent. When the factory was enlarged, she was assigned to the job of weighing cotton from dawn to dusk for the more than 200 workers. She was both patient and fair. In 1936, she was sent to the tunic factory, because there was a shortage of women workers. There she stitched buttonholes, ironed, and padded tunics. Feng-lien also studied hard and managed to learn a few hundred characters. She liked current affairs discussions and political classes.

After the establishment of a united front in 1936, the tunic factory was moved to Ch'aerhkou in Yenan. Some women comrades wanted to enjoy the peace by going home or entering school. They felt dissatisfied with continuing in the factory. However, Feng-lien thought, "One must be thorough in whatever revolutionary work one does, since this depends on the party's assignments." This showed her determined spirit.

Early in 1937, Feng-lien married comrade Chao Yung-t'ai from the same factory. Although Chao was a tailor, he was also in charge of the trade union's education and entertainment. Feng-lien said, "I don't think one should try to marry someone of a higher social station or more money. One should marry a comrade with whom one can cooperate. I am marrying Chao because his cultural level is higher than mine. I want him to help me to improve myself." In February or March, the factory was moved to Yench'ang and then temporarily closed down. Feng-lien also went to Yenan, where she passed the entrance examination for an accountancy training course. Her husband went briefly to the battle front with the supply department and then returned to work in the central printing factory. In June or July, Feng-lien joined the same factory.

Feng-lien worked in the bookbinding department. Although other apprentices were required to take four courses to become qualified workers, she needed only two. Both the quantity and quality of her work were excellent. She could fold over 4,500 folios a day.[16] All were done neatly and evenly, with the pagination carefully checked. At that time, the other 18 workers in her department could fold no more than 2,000 folios a day. Feng-lien explained, "I do more work chiefly because I take my job seriously and don't waste time. I also get up very early, when the stars are still out, make a fire, and then fold a couple of hundred folios before the others arise." She also knew how to bind books and how to cut pages quickly and neatly with a sickle-shaped knife.

Early in 1938, Feng-lien joined the party. About her work in this period, she remarked, "I was still young and rather ignorant—all I understood was hard work and helping others! At every summing up of production results, I was always evaluated number one in the binding department. I often organized women to compete with each other. Early in 1939, when I was in the crack workers' team, I went up the hills to reclaim land on Sunday. The factory praised me for that. Once Kuo Feng-ying didn't receive any award and was despondent over it, but I encouraged her by saying: 'Your feet are bound, so you can't climb the hills, but you and I can have a race in binding and studying.' Her attitude became more positive, and her work improved. Another woman worker, Shen Kui-lan, secretly smoked opium. I don't remember how many times I talked with her or how many women I asked to keep an eye on her; in the end, she gave up her bad habit. Meanwhile, our studies in the factory were carried on energetically, and I learned to write simple letters. On International Women's Day in 1940, I was elected a model woman and received an award. On May Day, the great competition organized by the workers of the border region gave me a five-star badge from the general trade union for being a model of production and study. The factory also gave me various other awards which I don't remember clearly now."

Feng-lien continued, "At the mid-autumn festival in 1940, the child of the head of the central publication department had no milk, and no wet nurse could be found. I was asked if I could breast-feed this baby, and as I still had milk from my own infant, I thought there was no reason for another child to starve.[17] After three months, the baby grew sturdy and pudgy. At that time, the day nursery set up in the central printing factory had difficulty finding a nurse. I was transferred to work in this nursery, where I looked after more than 20 children, all of whom grew very healthy."

There were six women working in the nursery, five of whom had just come from the villages and were old-fashioned about hygiene and child care. Feng-lien introduced new ideas of training infants through patience and without spanking. The babies must be clean, bathed, and changed frequently. They must be fed at regular intervals. Those who can eat solids should have their food increased gradually. Feng-lien advised the other nurses, "These are revolutionary successors, and we should take care of them." Under her influence and encouragement, everyone acted responsibly, the children flourished, and Feng-lien was consequently decorated for her work. In order to make an even greater contribution to the revolution, Feng-lien has now placed her own children in a nursery to set an example for others.

Feng-lien's relationship with her husband also deserves mention. Although comrade Chao Yung-t'ai is able and quite well educated, his manner was too easygoing. He was fond of good food, drinking, and gambling and sometimes made Feng-lien the butt of his temper. However, she has always been calm and stern in her efforts to criticize and convince him. In this way, Chao's bad habits have been changed. Chao also works for the trade union but sometimes lacks enthusiasm, so Feng-lien has been encouraging and helping him with this as well.

In January 1942, Feng-lien and her husband were transferred back to the tunic factory, where she is now part of the women's team, stitching buttonholes. At the beginning of last year, she could stitch 30 sets a day—nine buttonholes to a set. This was the highest record in the factory. A year later, when the winter's output of uniforms was reviewed, her daily average had reached 44 sets. None of the other comrades exceeded 36 sets a day, and their average was 20 sets. Feng-lien's record results from her time-saving methods. She has surpassed the factory's stipulation that a big buttonhole have 24 stitches and a smaller one should have 18. Her buttonholes are all neatly done.

By linking the pieces of thread together, she does not waste an inch and has taught others the same method. She also takes care of the needles. Some comrades frequently lose needles or misplace scissors. Feng-lien has criticized them for this. She draws the factory's attention to any waste of small pieces of cloth, coal, or wood. The clothes she handles remain clean and are neatly folded.

After setting the overall work plan for the factory, Feng-lien has each woman discuss her individual tasks. Every fortnight, the workers meet to review their progress. She unites the activists around her and through this group influences the rest. She also uses the methods of challenge and competition to patiently teach her own sewing skills.

Among the buttonhole stitchers in the tunic factory, there were a couple of lazybones, both of whom were "fond of food, while disliking work." They played hooky and stitched only five or six sets a day. Last year, Feng-lien asked these two to sit beside her so she could converse and compete with them. By publicizing their progress as well as their faults, she encouraged them and helped them to change. Now each of them stitches over 20 sets a day. She explained that the reform of lazybones requires very close attention, giving them specific tasks, and constant supervision and concern. We must not look down on them or attack them but must combine individual persuasion and mass struggle, giving encouragement to the slightest sign of progress.

Feng-lien shows deep concern for the women workers. She explains points of hygiene and methods of child care, looking after those who become ill by carrying water, cooking, and washing clothes for them. The 20 workers in the factory unanimously regard her as their best labor hero. During the past two years, Feng-lien has simultaneously served as head of the administrative team, woman cadre in the party cell of the factory, and woman executive in the trade union.

At the Labor Model Conference, comrade Li Feng-lien put forward her new production plan, which included the following resolutions on education: "In the past year or two, I have not raised my cultural standard, and this is a great defeat. From now on, I will study harder. I will organize a

women's reading team with the specific goal of learning two new characters each day and give general encouragement to all women's studies.
Education will also strengthen the unity of the workers. It will help to
correct the bad habits of women workers who bicker among themselves
or quarrel with their husbands."

12

"On the Eve of Her Departure"[1]
Ting Chih-hui: Model Cadre

By Jerome Ch'en (translator and editor)

Introduction

This piece on the death of Ting Chih-hui, head of the general logistical department, Health Department, People's Liberation Army, was published in 1980, at a time when many people were under a shadow. During the Cultural Revolution, a common criticism leveled against cadres was an easy life and loss of revolutionary fervor. This commemorative piece with recollections by her family and colleagues stresses that, in contrast, Ting Chih-hui (and by implication other high-level cadres) remained worthy. The didactic goal of the piece is to show that the criticisms of the Cultural Revolution were stereotypical and wrong; this is presented as an example for the younger generation. Despite her earnings as a high-ranking cadre, Ting Chih-hui spent little and gave back much as dues to the Communist Party. Her industriousness, frugality, and dedication to the party and the people are exemplary virtues that other cadres should strive for. Hence this piece reestablishes her name, reassesses her work, and represents the genre of rehabilitation literature of 1979–1980.

Ting Chih-hui is extolled for several characteristics. She was a poorly educated woman who became a technical cadre skilled in first aid logistics after self-study as an adult. The technical cadre is "modern"; since 1977, the importance of cadres learning a specialty has been emphasized.

Ting Chih-hui is a successor to the women of Yenan in this volume, having shared many revolutionary hardships of their period (she appears to have joined the party about 1938) and their values of hard work, frugality, and service. Her life history shows the transition to the present of women in such roles.

Ting Chih-hui

She is going away to a far, far distant place. You see, she is not riding a horse or riding in a cart. Like 41 years ago, when she went to join the revolutionary columns, she is on foot. The footprints she leaves behind still show the same urgency and the same briskness.

There is a saying in her hometown: "Prepare well for a long stay; take your December clothes when you leave home in June." She leaves home in June but without even extra underwear—only a neat army uniform over a neatly patched and mended shirt and a pair of walking shoes, as if she were still pounding the mountain paths of years ago—those shoes seem to grow sturdier and stronger on mountain paths.

She is used to this outfit. When the years were crowded with battles and campaigns, when she participated in conferences, when she met with foreign guests on special occasions, or when she took her children to the park, she was always in the same outfit. She stitched it up when the shoulders came unstitched; she mended it when the collar was worn out; she washed it when the cuffs were dirty.

"No, she mustn't be dressed like this on her departure!" Her husband, Old Liu, rushed home and searched all the drawers—a shirt full of patches on its lapel, a sweater with a hole on its shoulder, an army uniform faded through washing. One by one, these clothes dropped from his hands— there were also the tattered slippers, a white vest altered from a short-sleeved blouse which in turn had been altered from a long-sleeved blouse, and a towel cut and trimmed through the middle and sewed together. He examined them with a lump in his throat. "You, as poor as this! Now you are going away, and yet you are still so shabby!" With tears in his eyes, he went to a store to buy a new shirt and took it to Papaoshan, the shrine of the martyrs. Choked with sobs, he murmured, "You'd probably blame me for wasting money. But this time, don't argue with me, OK?" Unbelieving that she was dead, he gently held her hand while the tears streamed down his face.

Who was she?

The name, Ting Chih-hui, may not be all that familiar to our younger comrades, but it is unforgettable to the older generation. It is the name of a well-known heroine in the New Fourth Army and the People's Liberation Army. She led a medical team in the south of the Yangtze, Liaoning and Shenyang, Peking and Tientsin, to save the lives of numerous soldiers. Her youth was spent in the flames of war to earn for herself four honored titles—"a model Communist," "a model cadre," "a model woman," and "a model medical worker." She was the pride of the Chinese people, of our women comrades. Her name was well remembered by even such a statesman as Premier Chou En-lai, a man constantly preoccupied by a myriad of things. The premier saw Ting Chih-hui after an interval of 20 years. He remembered not only her name but her hometown and also the sickness she had contracted in the war years. All of us remember you, Ting Chih-hui!

But today she went away so hurriedly that her daughter and daughter-in-law did not have time to come to her. There was not enough time for them to get together for a last reunion dinner; there was not even time for her to taste the delicious chicken broth her sister-in-law had prepared. She left while the bowl of broth was still steaming on the table, as if to show her sister-in-law's love or to blame the abruptness of her departure.

For years, she had suffered from schistosomiasis and cirrhosis of the liver. As a result, the count of the white corpuscles of her blood was only one-fifth normal. She was badly undernourished. However, she often thought twice before she took even an egg; in her 30 years of living in the city, she had never once been to a restaurant; she seldom ate a piece of fruit. When her children worried and urged an apple upon her, she was unwilling to eat by herself; she cut it into crescent sections for the whole family. Once, on a scorchingly hot midday, she saw some foreign visitors back to the Peking Hotel for a rest after their morning tour. Then she quietly slipped to the hotel store and bought a bun, which she washed down with a cup of boiled water. She enjoyed this simple meal instead of a lavish free lunch at the hotel to which she was fully entitled or the lunch at home of rice in hot soup which she could have relished had she rushed back in the small sedan. But she would waste neither gasoline nor the delicious food on herself. "A lavish meal like that can go on just as well without me. I am on strike," she said. Another time, her daughter-in-law went to see how she was recovering from a bout of illness and found a bowl of leftovers being preserved from the hot weather in a basin of cold water. "Throw it away, Mom. It's pointless to keep it. There will be plenty of food for dinner. Leftovers will make you feel worse!" the daughter-in-law reproached her. But Ting Chih-hui ignored her and consumed the leftovers.

Was she so poor that she had to be so frugal? Not at all. She was the head of the general logistics department, Health Department, People's Liberation Army, holding the rank of an army commander. Did she have a special dislike of good food? No, her taste was not in any way different from ordinary people's taste for food. The explanation lies in her way of life. "When we took part in the revolution, didn't we want all the poor people to have better food to eat and better clothes to wear, to free themselves from poverty? Now, since the general standard of living remains low, how can we cadres be fussy about the meat being too fat or too lean, the noodles too thick or too thin? The revolutionary fervor of a Communist shouldn't be like a film of oil on a bowl of water that shines but is icy-cold underneath." This unwritten rule of her life was like a red thread which tied together all the details of her daily conduct.

The comb on the table is a good example. It is an ordinary plastic comb which she brought back from abroad in the year the fatherland was liberated. Through the seasons of the years, it has been with her. For 30 years, it has combed her black hair, her gray hair, and recently her white hair. It has lost many of its teeth and much of its luster, but it was always in her bag or on her table—visiting other countries, traveling with medical teams, and working in night shifts. In the shops were combs of all descriptions, long and short, straight and folded, steel and electric, but she never gave a thought to buying a new one. "After all, it's old ginger which tastes hotter." Her daughter, Mao-mao, failed to understand her and threw the comb away. "Mom, let's put an end to its historical mission," the girl said. Ting Chih-hui cast a censorious glance at her daughter before retrieving it. Ting Chih-hui's sternness and extraordinary action caused Mao-mao to regret her rashness. She washed the comb and placed it on the table as before.

Tonight the comb continues to emit the endearing fragrance of its mistress's hair, but its mistress is gone. Her legs are so swollen that the flesh has lost its elasticity. Her footprints, deep and ponderous, bring back many memories.

As a young peasant girl, she tasted the bitterness of life on the shores of Lake Tai [near Suchow and Hangchow]. She gathered firewood, carried buckets of water, picked wild vegetables, and worked in paddy fields. She walked all the way to the revolution, not traveling by sedan chair or automobile. She walked from the lake to the revolutionary underground contact man in Shanghai, then to a new Fourth Army camp north of the Huai, to the frozen land of the northeast, and further to the soil of Korea covered under golden flowers. She had to walk hundreds of miles until her feet were full of blisters and corns, tenacious like a camel and persevering like an ox. Thus she developed from a peasant girl to a meritorious worker of the people, a high-ranking cadre of the party, and a member of the National People's Congress [she was at least a 38-rank cadre].

At her job in Peking, unless it was something urgent, she would not use her official car. Once on the Lunar New Year's holiday, she went to the Peking railway station to meet her daughter, coming home from her school in Shanghai for the family reunion. As soon as they left the station, the girl asked, "Mom, where is your car?" Ting Chih-hui pointed to the entrance to the subway: "There!" "So you came by subway." "Yes, and go home with you the same way. It's so convenient, taking us all the way to our doorstep."

Last fall, when he had his vacation, Old Liu came to see her at the Talien Hospital, but she was about to be transferred to Nanchang. The Ministry of Health planned to have someone escort her all the way. This she firmly declined: "My hubby's here. There's no need to send another man. It will cost too much money." Her husband accompanied her to Nanchang. Before he left for Peking, she told him again and again, "You've come here on private business to keep me company. When you get back, you mustn't report your expenses from Talien to Nanchang to the government for reimbursement."

She said once to her son, Ch'ao-p'ing, and her daughter-in-law, Li-sha, "You've been married a year now. At your wedding, I wouldn't let you buy this or buy that. I even returned the big wardrobe closet which your friends had bought for you. I didn't come to your wedding, and I wouldn't allow you to lay out a lavish wedding banquet. Did you feel unhappy about that?"

Ch'ao-p'ing nodded his head and spoke first, "Yes, Mom, we did for a while. Now, looking back on it, we were a little childish. Unlike other mothers, you didn't arrange a comfortable home for us or a ladder to special privileges. However, you've given us a priceless revolutionary spirit. You *are* a good mother."

Then Ting Chih-hui turned to Li-sha: "Li-sha, you are the daughter of a martyr. For many years, you have been like a daughter to me, too. You wanted to get into a university by the back door and asked me to have you transferred to Peking. I refused both because the people didn't give me the power to do what you asked. Nor did the party allow me to look after our private interests."

"Mom, there is no need for you to say any more. I understand."

A few days ago, her son would not leave her sickbed, and she, too, at the point of her eternal departure, naturally wanted to see more of him. A loving and kind mother, she needed her children then more than ever. But she stifled her feelings and ordered Ch'ao-p'ing to go—"Away, go away. I am sorry that I can't work for the party now. It would be even worse if I kept you from your work. You must realize that your mother's life continues in yours." Her son slowly withdrew from the room fighting back tears.

A month or so ago, her daughter came to see her. "Mom, you've got to take care of yourself and get more rest." The mother only shook her head. She was hooked up to a glucose transfusion tube in one arm; with her other hand she was busy writing a report on first aid techniques for the battlefield. Now her daughter wanted to come home from her Shanghai school to be with her, but she would not allow the girl to leave her studies. There was her daughter-in-law, who rushed home from a great distance but too late.

Once, in days gone by, her colleagues remember that she walked through the forests, across the rivers, the snow-capped mountains, and the vast stretches of sand in the northeast. Near one of the rivers, she recovered a box of anesthetics under heavy enemy machine gun fire. At the foot of mountains, she worked nonstop for days and nights, saving the lives of several hundred soldiers. On snowbound plains, she wrapped the frostbitten feet of soldiers with her padded gown. Where Mongols and

Han lived as neighbors, she led a contingent of wounded soldiers across the desert. Plunging into the revolution, she never counted the footprints behind her or stretched out her hand to beg for higher pay from the party and the people.

Another memory of her colleagues was of the summer of 1965, when Ting Chih-hui, deputy director of the hospital, took a bank savings book to the party secretary and solemnly handed it to him. "These are my party dues. Please take them." The amount was 10,000 *yüan* plus 617 *yüan* of interest. The secretary smiled, "Old Ting, you are really thorough—not only the dues but also the interest. The party committee will accept your goodwill but not the money. It's too much."[2] Afterward, a comrade was sent to suggest again that she should keep part of the money for her own needs in case of an emergency. Ting stubbornly refused. "The money was paid to me by the party and the people; it is to them that I must return it."

Another act of her personal generosity is recalled by an old peasant in the Hsingtai earthquake area. When Premier Chou En-lai came to the disaster area, he brought Ting's personal donation of 700 *yüan* together with many messages and contributions. Ting's letter said briefly, "Please accept the regards of a Communist; overcome the catastrophe; rebuild your homes."

Ting's husband, comrade Liu Teh-mou, remembers that in the Cultural Revolution the whole family was persecuted by Lin Piao and the Gang of Four. Ting Chih-hui was then going through labor reform under supervision,[3] away from Peking, while he was imprisoned. All communications between the couple were cut. When Ting was released and they were reunited in Peking, they did not dwell upon the physical or mental agony they had endured; they discussed only the disposal of their reparations of 5,200 *yüan* back pay. Liu thought that it should be handed to the party as their dues in arrears, and Ting readily agreed to this. "The harder the times, the greater the need for us to take practical action to demonstrate unshakable faith in the party. Both of us are old comrades now. What's a little suffering to us?"

Some well-meaning people went to see them, "Haven't you had enough in the Cultural Revolution? Some said you bought your political capital—bought your way into being labor models. Why are you still asking for punishment by donating money to the party?" Farsighted as always, Ting smiled, "The mouth is round, and the tongue is flat. Let them wag, but I won't change my mind. Without the party we are nothing!"

The people of Changke in Honan remember that in the extraordinarily severe flood and drought of the summer of 1975, Ting came to the affected areas as deputy director of the central government's relief team. She went from home to home, village to village, asking how people were and conveying the party's concerns to each household. In the evening, as she left, she quietly handed a money order of 10,000 *yüan* to the relief command. Afterward she neither reported this donation to the leadership nor announced it to the people. It became known only when the representative from Changke openly thanked her at the fifth National People's Congress in Peking.

Altogether, these donations totaling 25,000 *yüan* can easily be checked. As to her help to comrades and people on numerous occasions when they were in dire need of money, it is impossible to check. No one knows how many in the north and south, in the army and among the people, have received assistance from her.

She is on her way home. Contrary to what people believe, it is not a lonely, sad, and ghostly way. People have come from all over the country to bid her farewell. The one with white in her hair is a comrade-in-arms who fought with her in the same trench many years ago; the one with tears in his eyes is a soldier she saved from death; the one yelling, "Sister, sister!" is a "little red devil" (an orphan) she brought up; the one who threw herself over the body is a baby she delivered. Among the crowd is a family of three who came from far off at their own expense. Others did not have time to pack before they came. A cadre whose legs were disabled by the cruelty of the Gang of Four has come out of his house for the first time in years with the help of a pair of crutches, hobbling inch by inch in the funeral procession.

She is leaving, really leaving, for a far, far away place. But neither her family nor her comrades believe that she is. Is this because her clothes still retain her warmth? Is this because the ink of her 60,000-word manuscript is still fresh? No, it is because, like coal, she is "dead in bed but alive in the furnace of the revolution."

On the path of the new Long March, she is not deserting us; she is walking ahead.

13

Contemporary Generations
Zhao Xiuyin: Lady of the Sties

By Mary Sheridan

Introduction: The Village in 1981

Jingang Brigade—my village—is composed of scattered hamlets which nestle among the bristly pine ridges and stepped paddy valleys of Gele Mountain. A few hours from Chongqing, one of the largest cities in China and the industrial center of the southwestern province of Sichuan, the village maintains its rural charm in relative obscurity. This mountain retreat is blessed with gentle winds to sweep its air clean and springwaters to nourish its unpolluted soils; it does not suffer from industrial sprawl like other villages on the lowlands. One can still find villagers here who in their lifetime have never been to the city.

But things are changing. Those women in the younger generation feel the city's influence and make self-conscious comparisons between urban life-styles and their own. From the mountain, the village women see the world from many windows—through visits to the city and especially the markets, through movies and the news on television, through the young men who come home from many parts of China after serving in the army, and through the few of their own people who have been sent by the district to meetings in Canton, Chengdu, and Beijing. Observing this wider world, three generations of women alike raise the question: "What, really, will China's drive for modernization mean here, in our village, in my lifetime, to me?"

My first visits to Jingang Brigade were made in 1973 and 1978 during trips around China to study methods of agricultural modernization. I was immensely impressed by the innovativeness of this village, by the progress it was making, and by its natural beauty. So it was my first choice for a village in which to live and study farming systems. During 1979–1981, I lived in Jingang and made a study of Jingang's vegetable polycropping methods. I left at the end of October 1981 but returned again in March

204

1983 for the Spring Festival holidays, after I had begun teaching at Beijing Agricultural University.

Jingang is one of five brigades which constitute the commune on Gele Mountain—altogether a population of some 22,000. Jingang's 5,000 people live in homesteads and hamlets scattered up and down its hills and valleys. Under the brigade's central management, land and households are divided into 17 production teams (centered on the main hamlets), which plan the day-to-day farming. In 1981, the teams' labor was organized into small work groups as the basis for production responsibility and accounting. When I returned in 1983, the small groups had been disbanded, and farming production was assigned to households.

During the years when I lived in Jingang, I was adopted as a "family member" in several different households scattered throughout the hamlets of the village. I shared in farm work, household tasks, and daily life. As time passed, I found among these families some of the closest friendships of my life, and when it came time to depart in 1981, I left my heart in the village and knew that I must go back. This indeed came to pass. In March 1983, when I went "home" to Jingang for Spring Festival, I was assured that these friendships are a secure part of my life and my future.

I collected no formal life histories of women in this village and did no formal interviews. Living and working together through the seasons while I concentrated on my agricultural studies in the village, my understanding of family situations deepened naturally. Later in Beijing, I was asked to write articles about these experiences for Chinese newspapers and journals in English. This chapter expands on those publications. In order to preserve continuity and facilitate cross-reference, *pinyin* is used here for Chinese spellings.

The people I describe here are very special to me, but they are quite representative of the best qualities to be found in any Chinese village. I have changed names and altered some details to protect privacy, but all the people are real, and events are told as they happened. The Li family members are Old Li (father, age 52); Zhao Xiuyin (Li's wife, 48); Popo (Li's mother, 73); an eldest son and daughter, both married and living away from the house; Second Son (25) and his wife, Yin (Xiuyin's daughter-in-law, 22); Simei (daughter, the fourth child, 22) and her fiancé, Xiao Hao (25); and the youngest son (17).

The father, Li Dazhi, is an admirable man of complex character. He is one of the production leaders of the village—intelligent and bold and sensitive, reflective yet decisive in action, full of anger and sweetness and humor, a talker and a thinker and a late-night reader, completely modern in his attitudes toward science and the wider world yet self-professedly old-fashioned in some (but not all) of his attitudes toward women. Other people say that he is good to his wife and family.

Old Li's character dominates the household—provoking it while fiercely but gently holding it together. The women move in counterpoint to him and to one another. His sons strive one by one to find their own orbits. Because the father loves his own independence, he has gradually let the sons find theirs. The case of the women is somewhat different. I have taken up their stories as I learned them in 1981.

A Day in July

Zhao Xiuyin pauses in her narrative and goes into the kitchen to get a bowl of pickled ginger. Popo, Simei, and I continue eating our rice porridge slowly at the round table. It is only eight-thirty in the morning, but already the air is heavy with moisture and warmth. Through the open doorway, purple and orange flowers shoot sparks of fiery color into the courtyard hedge, still glistening from last night's heavy rain. Below the hill, tiers of green paddies slide gradually out from under the lifting mist. The men went out to work before eight, and we women are dawdling. Although I've been coming to live in this home and others on and off for over a year, this is the first time Xiuyin has talked about the past. Usually we are too interested in discussing our work and life in the present.

Xiuyin returns to the table and continues her story: "Our mountain was liberated on my eighteenth birthday. My family killed a pig to celebrate, then a lot of relatives came over to our house because the Guomindang soldiers were fleeing. As the soldiers ran, they dropped their bedrolls in our fields, and many rifles were flung down too—just over there [pointing across the hill]. That was the day the Liberation Army arrived in our village.

"Before Liberation, we suffered through so many bitter experiences, One time my sister-in-law and I went with my father to sell our basket-loads of *digua* [a kind of sweet root vegetable]. Suddenly, a bunch of Guomindang soldiers came along and grabbed my father to make him carry their things. We were terrified. Maybe our father would be taken away forever. We clung to his jacket, wailing, and trailed him all the way to the place now called Neisemao. Those Guomindang soldiers hit me and beat my father to the ground, even though he was over 50. Finally, they let him go, but we didn't dare return by the same road. So we took the long way around the moutain, by all the small steep trails. My sister fainted, and finally we stumbled home long after dark. In those days, you know, nobody went outside at night. The forests on the moutain were much wilder, and there were still large animals in them, even leopards—not like today.

"At the time of Liberation, we didn't know who was good and who was bad. But afterward, when we formed our mutual aid teams and cooperatives, we knew that the party and Chairman Mao were good. My mother-in-law [nodding at Popo] was one of the first to join the party branch in the village, and when we carried out mutual aid, I was work point recorder for our team.

"I got married at the time of Spring Festival in 1950, just after Liberation. If there had been no Liberation, I probably couldn't have married Li, because my family was better off than his. But we had been classmates, and because of Liberation, we could decide the matter ourselves. Of course, in those days, young people were very shy and proper. So we asked a matchmaker to do all the talking and to go around to settle with our parents, who agreed. Even today, it is often done that way." (Xiuyin glances at Simei, whose schoolteacher-fiancé has been "introduced" by the village school's headmistress. Simei blushes.)

Xiuyin continues: "When I was young, I went to elementary school. To go to school, we paid in unhusked rice [because of the worthlessness of money during high wartime inflation]. I went to elementary school for five years, then for another two years to a school which tutored us in the Confucian classics. Compared to my seven years of schooling, my husband had only five. Of my age group, I had the most schooling on the mountain, and my marks were not bad [actually very good]. I am better at writing and the abacus than my children.

"After I finished those seven years, I took the examination for three middle schools and did well on all of them. But my family opposed my going to middle school—it cost a lot, and they were uneasy about my being so far away. [The school was only about an hour's walk to the foot of the mountain, and many village boys and girls study there today. In the old days, however, families were reluctant to let a young girl out of their sight.] Before Liberation, few people had any book learning. In our hamlet, there was only one who had ever been to middle school. Because I loved school so much, I'd hoped my children would go on to a university. But they all made a poor showing on the difficult entrance exams. In our village, few have ever passed.

"Just after Liberation, the village was quite feudal. At that time—about 1950—everyone elected me to be the leader of the women's work. But my husband didn't want me to go the women's meetings and scolded me about it all the time. He didn't understand as much as I did. Just after Liberation, it was possible to take a literacy examination to become a cadre. I could have become a cadre even without the examination, because I had high marks in school and had a graduation diploma. If I had presented these to the leadership, I would have been given work immediately. But my husband opposed it. He scolded me and scolded me. I cried and cried—for years."

Popo goes into the kitchen to wash dishes. Simei is off to her job across the hill in the brigade noodle factory. Xiuyin pauses for a while, and I pause too, thinking of the old framed photos on the wall of the next room. One shows Xiuyin as a young girl just after her marriage; she is hoeing, towel around her neck over her flower print jacket, with a glowing smile—the most beautiful girl in the village then, still robust and lovely now. A snapshot shows her husband as a stocky youth, and a formal portrait poses the young family—Popo, Xiuyin, and Li, together with their first baby. In this household, Popo is an exceptionally independent, energetic character, and Xiuyin's husband Li is a brilliant farmer, perhaps the most intellectually enlightened man in the village. A talented, strong-willed older generation, they are united by genuine admiration and affection. Yet each has confided to me a private sorrow or a failed ambition that is partly the result of conflicts between character and sentiment insoluble within the family structure. I mull this over silently until Xiuyin picks up the thread of her thought and goes on.

"In those days, things were just too feudal. Now things have gotten much better. At that time, though, I couldn't do anything about the situation; I couldn't go to work as a cadre. Even now, when I think of it, it still makes me unhappy. I'm not stupid. It's just that my husband interferes so much—always trying to control me. In 1954, the brigade leadership asked me to study the new methods of midwifery. But by then I already had two children. I studied for a month, but because of the children, it was very troublesome. The brigade said just to forget it.

"The next year, the brigade leadership again sent me to study, this time at a special training school for nursery teachers. [This school is at the foot of the mountain—about an hour away by bus.] But I was pregnant with Simei. I had to carry this burden while I was trying to study. After a year, I had to come home without finishing the two-year program. Back in the village, I worked in the brigade kindergarten.

"At that time, my husband's mother was running the kindergarten. In those days, the kindergarten had both half-day and full-day charges, but all ate lunch in the school whether they came from near or far [to ensure proper nourishment]. I worked there for a year, but my husband thought it was inconvenient, so I had to give it up and just do agricultural labor in our team. That way I was always near our house to cook for him and mind our children.

"It wasn't long before the brigade leadership called me for another training program, but my husband was still opposed. I remember one time after he had been berating me, I thought I must certainly leave home. I got up very early and made breakfast. Then I told his younger sister: 'I can't stand it. I'm going.' But his mother heard me and ran out to block my way. She did not want me to go and told me to be a good daughter-in-law—that a family should not quarrel.

"Nowadays it's different. If my husband tried to control me that way now, I could run away. But then it wasn't in my character to fight him. I just cried. He's a good man, but he didn't understand. Men are more feudal than women. Before Liberation and just afterward, women were terribly oppressed. Of course, at that time, there were some women who did run away. One woman whose child had died did not want to stay in her mother-in-law's household. Because she had milk, she ran away to work for other people as a wet nurse. Her husband's household went out to search for her and dragged her back. There were also some who did not return and some married ones who ran away and later married another man.

"Now I don't think about the past so much. But even though life is better, things do not go well in my heart. Every day I go to work and then come home to do housework. I can't study, and I don't know much about important things in our country. If my husband hadn't controlled me, then I'd probably be working in a different place today—"

Xiuyin stops abruptly in mid-sentence, because Popo comes into the room and exclaims: "What? You haven't gone to work yet? It's already past nine o'clock!" Jumping up, Xiuyin grabs her broad-brimmed straw hat from the hook on the wall and runs out. I gather up my notebook, straw hat, and towel and rush out to catch up with her.

She is 48 and I am 43, but we go off together like girls—slipping and sliding down the steep path, sloshing and laughing through puddles in our plastic sandals. The moist gray haze has lifted, and the paddies are spotted with dabbling white ducks which scold us as we pass. We turn off the road at a long building of packed earth with a small center courtyard. It stands slightly apart from a cluster of family houses. Xiuyin unlocks the doors, and we enter. This is the pigsty of her production team, and she is the keeper.

She checks the pens and starts a fire in the huge stove which fills one corner of the sty's kitchen. The fire is fueled with straw and pine branches which she has carried in towering bundles on her back from the forest slopes an hour away, then stacked along the outside walls of the sty under the eaves. The fire begins to heat the water in the giant iron *guo* (also called a *wok*, a curved iron cauldron shaped like the smaller Chinese frying pans in my own kitchen at home). Xiuyin puts chopped leaves and vines into the water to simmer, adding mash from rice bran and a few sweet potatoes. We go back to sweep out the pens, talking as we work. When the watery swill is hot, we ladle it into large wooden buckets to carry to the pens.

The pigs are a white variety—long and lean at the moment. It is the custom here to raise pigs lean and full size "so their bones will grow strong." This is why they get the watery diet of cooked greens, with bran added for nourishment. Only in the last few weeks before sale are the pigs fattened up quickly, mostly on sweet potatoes.

The animals in this sty are very clean—no sores on their backs, no nervous rubbing against the stones of the pens. Every day, following their afternoon meal, Xiuyin hoses them down (there is piped-in running water), and the pens are washed out morning and evening. The stone floors of the pens slope outward and drain into fertilizer pits, the grounds of the sty are swept up twice a day, and lime is used so that there is no odor. I comment to Xiuyin: "Your sty is so clean. I've been around to the sties of other production teams, and yours is the cleanest one!"

She replies: "Ah, Mali [her pronunciation of my name], pigs are like people. They don't like dirt. Right now we have 26 pigs in this sty. In the winter, we had over 50, and last year there were many more than that. Because of my work, the brigade elected me to go as a representative to the district meeting of advanced producers."

"Why aren't you raising so many pigs now?"

"It's too tiring for one person to do so much. Last year, I took care of the sty alone, but this year the production team appointed a half-time person to help me. Last year, the jobs were undertaken by contract, and I earned over 8,000 work points, which are distributed according to the profits made for the team. But afterward people said I got too many work points. So now I'm just paid according to the hours I spend at work. It comes to eight work points each day."

I say, "But I met a man in the Tingzishan production team who earns 20 points a day just for looking after four plow oxen. When I saw him, he was just sitting around on the grass smoking comfortably, while the oxen cooled off in the reservoir. Surely your work is as heavy as his."

"It's very hard to look after oxen."

"So—just because it's a bit harder physically, which seems doubtful anyway, he gets more than twice as much as you do for raising over 50 pigs? How can that be?"

"Ahh—his work points are set by job contract."

Silently I contemplate Xiuyin's modesty and understatement in accounting for her tasks. From other quarters in the village, I've heard that she is considered outstanding in pig-raising. When she took over the work of the sty, it had been losing money, but she turned it around and made a huge profit for the team. In spite of these profits, from which everyone benefited, the large number of work points she earned aroused jealousy. Some people felt it unfair that one person could earn so much. So she was cut back to an hourly pay rate. Now she will be paid the same whether she raises 20 pigs or 50. Under her present pay scheme, even if she shirks on the job, she will still earn her hourly wage. But she continues as conscientiously as before.

To spread income opportunities (there is hidden underemployment on this overpopulated mountain), another woman was assigned to help Xiuyin for half a day each day. Throughout China, it has been more or less standard to assign women a maximum of six to eight work points per day, according to individual strength and skill. For men, the work point range has been seven to ten. The ox herder therefore does well at 20 work points a day.

At this point in our morning tasks, a young woman of about 35 comes to join us. This is Xiuyin's *tangmei* (female cousin on her paternal side). She is the additional half-day laborer assigned to the sty. Xiuyin comments that having a helper from the family makes work a little more convenient. The two women can sometimes swap tasks or working hours to help each other when illness or special occasions like weddings call them away, without having to make troublesome arrangements through the team leaders. This doesn't affect their efficiency or output. In some work groups which are based on family relationships, the kinship ties seem to have a negative effect on reporting and accounting. For this reason, teams have tried not to allow kinship to be the basis of work groupings. Of one work group whose members were all relatives, other people said, "That group is unmanageable. You can't tell them a thing. They stick together against everyone else, but among themselves it's nothing but constant squabbling."

I ask the cousin about the crumbly reddish-brown granular feed piled in a *guo* in the corner of the kitchen: "What kind of feed is this?"

"It's the roughage left over from making soy sauce. We buy it from Ciqikou, the peasant free market at the foot of this mountain. It's good because it has some salt in it."

Xiuyin adds, "Every pig gets three or four *liang* of fodder a day—corn or sweet potatoes, depending on the season. If we feed them wheat bran or rice bran, then we figure that two *jin* of these are equal to one *jin* of grain. Fresh green fodder or fermented greens are used just to fill up the pigs [to assuage their appetites without actually fattening them] and are not figured at any certain amount per day. When the production team members harvest vegetables in the team's fields, they strip off the outer waste leaves in the fields before bringing the vegetables to the loading platform for weighing and trucking into the city. If there is a lot of waste left in the fields, we ask the team to send it over; if not, the two of us just collect it ourselves. The fermenting greens here in the courtyard are cabbage leaves. We pile them up, water then, and trample them down with our feet. Ten days later, they are ready to use as fodder. It takes a year to raise a pig until it is fat enough to sell."

While Xiuyin is talking, she has started to make a long-handled broom from a large dried plant. She wraps the springy branches tight with a long supple strip of bamboo and ties them to form a suitable sweeping shape. I ask her about this.

"I'm making a broom from a kind of wild plant called *tiesiaoba*—iron broom plant. When I took over this job in the sty, I went up the mountain slopes and brought back some seedlings to plant here in front of the sty—these bushes in front here. They are easy to use. I just pull up a bush, let it dry out in the storeroom, then bind it up with bamboo this way. The other teams haven't thought of this method—just us. So we don't waste money on bamboo brooms."

Xiuyin thus saves money for her team by her ingenuity and thrifty management. It takes her extra effort yet brings no additional remuneration for her. I begin to understand the difference in work attitudes and how difficult it is to arrive at fair remuneration for any effort in a farming village, because individual character, production skill, and physical strength are inevitably uneven, and social relationships further influence such complex factors. Our tasks are done by eleven o'clock, and Xiuyin locks up the sty. The cousin takes my hand, and we three walk home in the light drizzle which has started to cool off the day. It is peaceful and pleasant, like many such days which Xiuyin and I have shared together.

Between 1979 and 1981, when I lived in the village, there were no women on Gele Mountain who did not work. Whoever wanted to work could do so, and suitable jobs were found for women and old or handicapped people. Many men over 70 still like to earn work points in the fields whenever the weather is not too formidable. (Extremes of summer heat and winter cold, intensified by high humidity in both seasons, keep most older folk indoors.) Some young women have husbands with salaries as rural factory workers, truck drivers, or small cadres, so often they go to the fields less than others, but they don't stop altogether. The women say that their situation is better here than in some other parts of China. Some villages have sent their women back to the hearth because of overpopulation and hidden underemployment, saving the jobs that earn work points for the men. When this happens, the women lose their economic independence.

The women's relative equality of work opportunities in this village sometimes has its negative side. Sturdy girls vie with men for jobs at the gravel works, where they lift, haul, and breathe the harmful dust. They choose these jobs because they get equal pay for equal work (unlike the work point system in the fields). On the other hand, chemical spraying of crops (done with small backpack hand pump sprayers) is done mostly by women, because they themselves demand it as "light" labor. Pregnant women especially want this task. The leaders of the village strenuously and continuously warn against such hazardous practices. But at the level of the small work groups, where tasks are actually assigned, the women get their way. Neglecting safety instructions, they spray without masks, even on windy days. (One sees the same thing in Japan and throughout Asia—farm women walking the fields in a halo of chemicals.)

In this village, the use of the work point system contributes to the women's choice of spraying as a "light" task. The task is considered an eight-point day, the same eight points which Xiuyin receives for the much greater labor and management skill she puts into running her team's pigsty. These inequities are very difficult to adjust, and no one method is satisfactory for all situations. This is one reason why a variety of forms of work accounting are now being tried. Of these, the most important are work points set per person per day, set tasks for set points, productivity and profit incentives, and responsibility systems.

Work points are a labor value per person per day assigned on the basis of the individual's strength. The work points have no intrinsic monetary equivalent, because their value is determined at the end of the year when the production team's total profits are divided between its membership. If the team's entire profit has increased over the previous year, then each work point is worth more, and vice versa. Thus Xiuyin's sty may earn a huge profit, but if other team enterprises lose money, the value of her work points decreases according to the final average.

Set tasks may be assigned a set work point value. Whether the task is done quickly or slowly, by a woman or a man, the pay is the same. Sometimes this leads to hasty or sloppy work, so it provides an incentive for some tasks and is inappropriate to others. The ox herder who earns 20 work points per day is paid in this way.

Productivity and profit incentives may be fixed so that work points are earned according to the profits made by an enterprise. This is how Xiuyin earned over 8,000 work points in 1980, arousing the envy which brought about a change in the method by which she is paid. If she had done a poor job and had lost money on the sty, her team might have kept her pay tied to profits and losses. If she were a less conscientious person, she might have slacked on the job when her pay was reduced to eight work points per day. But because of her strong character and her own fairness, she worked as hard under one system as the other.

Responsibility systems include a variety of new methods for contracting tasks. Intended to reward higher productivity and penalize lower productivity, these were being introduced gradually but did not affect Xiuyin's work in 1981.

Between eleven and two o'clock, most of the family members are home for lunch as usual. Li is back from inspecting some fields across the hill, Xiuyin is home from the sty, Second Son is back from his job in the brigade's small iron foundry, Simei has returned from the brigade noodle factory with her fiancé from the village elementary school, and youngest son is in from the fields. All walk at least 20 minutes to reach home—to wash, eat, and rest at the noonday break. In this summer season, the morning fieldwork starts earlier than in winter to allow a longer midday rest from the sweltering heat and humidity—temperatures average over 90°F and sometimes climb above 105°F.

During these past few days, Simei's fiancé, Xiao Hao, has been a guest in the house, sharing the father's bed at night and the family table for his meals—a custom in the village during the year before a marriage. The young man is expected to help his future father-in-law with wedding arrangements, but this shy young teacher—so handsome, gentle, and suitable for lovely Simei—is hopelessly inept at practical things. Li tolerates the young man's uselessness in making furniture and planning for guests only because he knows the boy will make a kind husband for his favorite child. The father himself is 10 times more capable and lets me know in private that he thinks the boy slow—schoolteacher or not.

Simei spends every spare minute in her bedroom, embroidering pillowcases and bed hangings for her wedding. For this she has even given up her beloved short story romance and movie magazines, the new rage among village youth. She embroiders before breakfast, before lunch, and after dinner; this is now enhanced by discreet whisperings with her young teacher. Sometimes she closets herself with her young sister-in-law, Yin, to discuss the price and quality of sheets and quilt covers she will buy for her trousseau. They are planning a shopping expedition into the city one day next month. Yin has been keeping to herself lately in her separate wing of the house. She says that she isn't feeling well, but really it is because of tensions between herself and the parents.

Lunch is served at one o'clock by Popo, who prepared it. The central delicacy is *doufer*, a kind of soft white bean powder custard or pudding which is different and lighter than the more familiar bean curd *doufu*. Side dishes are steaming squash (towel gourd), fat pork slices fried with green chili peppers, sliced lean pork fried with green chili (the two pork dishes have quite different tastes), boiled sliced pumpkin, and pickled long green beans called *jiangdou*. Large bowls of each dish are set out in the center of the table. We help ourselves to rice as often as we like from a large wooden tub on the sideboard. The older generation does most of the talking. I feel drowsy and look forward to my nap. After lunch, we clear the table. Then Simei and I go into her bedroom, one of four in this large farmhouse, and I fall asleep at once.

At three o'clock, I awake with a start. It must have been the sound of Xiuyin going back to work which startled me. Oppressed by the humidity and with a headache throbbing in the waves of heat, I cringe in a low armchair and labor over notes until dinnertime.

By seven o'clock, I've finished writing my notes. Most of the family is home, and Popo has dinner on the table. We eat quickly in order to catch the start of the sports on TV. Six families in this hamlet have TV, which is regarded as a mixed blessing. Neighbors invite themselves in for favorite programs, and the schoolteachers complain that the children neglect their homework. Tonight it is women's volleyball—a hot match between Cuba and China. The family knows by name all the women on the Chinese team. Popo takes a lively interest, but Xiuyin's eyes are poor. She won't bother to buy glasses, saying she doesn't watch TV or read. Before the program is over, she has gone to bed.

I leave the room and go outside to the garden. The sky has cleared, and the moon is sailing on a light wind which rustles the bamboo. Li is doing his knee bends. I stretch my arms out to the mountain and fold over to touch my toes. As we go in, Li bolts the outer Dutch doors and the thick double wooden inner doors. The house is secure for the night.

A Day in August

This morning, I am back early from the fields and find Yin alone, sewing in the bedroom. She is finishing a new nylon blouse by hand. I settle down in the armchair next to her. No one else is home except Popo, who is in the back courtyard, washing the vegetables for lunch.

My eyes travel over the room, noting its now familiar furniture—the sewing machine piled with Yin's flower print fabrics, the solid wooden wardrobe with its full-length mirror, and the two huge fourposter beds draped with cotton mosquito netting, their bamboo mats clean and shining for cool sleeping in the sweltering heat. Ensconced in the two deep-seated "modern" armchairs, we are quiet and private here. This is really the women's room, shared only by Popo, Simei, and me. Xiuyin and Li have the large bedroom at the other end of the house. The unmarried son and male guests sleep in a separate room at the back. Second Son and Yin have two rooms, built with a separate entrance from the courtyard, but they still take meals with the family. Lately, however, Yin has been eating in her room by herself.

Yin leans back and sighs, "I always feel so tired. I don't know why. In the morning, when I sit over my sewing machine in our workshop, I feel drowsy and long to come home for the lunch break. In the evening, I just don't feel like doing anything. Everyone else in this family is always running around, but I haven't their kind of energy. I guess you'd say I'm a lazy one."

She gives me a shy, apologetic smile, and for the first time I feel a liking for her. She's being so honest about herself. I've watched her for months, and she rarely helps around the house or in the family vegetable plot; she leaves all the heavy, dirty chores to Xiuyin and Popo. Her full squarish face, downcast expression, and mute presence at the dinner table had struck me as unattractive. Couldn't this woman say anything? But those in the younger generation consider her pretty, and her demeanor is considered suitable by the menfolk in this particular house. (Village families differ vastly with regard to the liveliness they prefer in their female members, and I know one woman whose fireworks-and-flowers gaity is adored by her new father-in-law. He openly brags of it, saying, "It's because she's an only child! Everyone should have just one child like this!")

I suddenly feel like Yin—tired by the heat and oppressed by the thought of endlessly repetitious household chores. In the silence, the scrubbing and chopping noises that Popo is making sound like a rebuke. After a long pause, Yin begins in her diffident way to tell me about her job in the production team sewing workshop: how she practiced so long at home before taking her examination, how nervous she was taking the practical test under the sharp eyes of the village master tailor. Leaving me for a minute, she fetches some sample orders of children's clothes she has made. Holding up the pretty things, she explains them to me.

"This little boy's jacket—it takes very little material to make. The trim is what is difficult." The small tan jacket is cut with a complicated collar, bib, and tucking and is elaborately edged with bias-cut blue and white striped cotton around the cuffs, collar, center panel, and bottom. The bias itself is pieced together from many miniscule scraps of waste material. Tiny appliqué flowers of colored fabric embellish the pockets. A pair of little trousers displays similar appliquéd bunnies on the knees.

Yin explains, "Our workshop gets commissions from the large clothing factories in the city. They send us material left over from making adult clothes as well as the patterns we must use. Sometimes they send one of their people here to demonstrate the patterns—how to do the stitching and so forth. We don't design anything ourselves; we just follow their orders. It's very hard work, because the scraps of material are so small and must be fitted together carefully. Sometimes we have trouble with the factory. Once we finished an order and the factory refused our work; they said it wasn't good enough. They made us take off all the collars and restitch them. Recently, we haven't been getting enough orders to keep us busy—not just our workshop but the other two in our brigade as well. We don't know what will happen."

I admire her handiwork, remembering what one city friend has told me—that some urban craftsmen do not like to pass on their skills to the village workshops. They thus maintain a dependent relationship between villagers and urban "masters," who earn a small supplementary income this way. All of the workshops and small factories in this brigade have at least one such urban "master worker" to advise them. The relationships are helpful to upgrading village skills, but rural workmanship still lags behind that in the city. The garments Yin made are examples of extremely labor-intensive production. Materials and labor are cheap, and profits for the city factory which subcontracts to the village, collects the finished products, and markets them are considerable, because such goods bring a high price. People spend lavishly for cuteness in children's clothes while skimping on quality for themselves.

Yin knows her wages are low, kept down by the huge surplus in the rural labor pool but relatively favorable compared to other village incomes. She considers herself lucky, compared to her friends who must work under the blazing sun, wielding their iron hoes against the lumpy earth, slopping the manure buckets, scratching their arms in the rice straw as they scythe the harvest. The boredom she describes indoors, in the shade, in relative inactivity, seems preferable to her. Yin, like Simei, whose job keeps her indoors in the brigade noodle factory, feels that she has escaped the fate of Xiuyin and Popo (even though they do their outside work with enthusiasm). But still—she is bored.

At this moment Xiuyin comes in. For a greeting I say, "It's very hot today—you must be really tired." She laughs curtly: "I don't know what it is to be tired, or to be cold, or to be hot—I just know what it is to be hungry! I'm happiest when I have work to do." She grins at me and goes to the kitchen to help Popo. Yin silently rises and disappears into her part of the house. She does not reappear for lunch.

After dinner, Xiuyin and I go into the courtyard to drink hot tea and enjoy the cooler air and flowery scent of nightfall. Leaning back in our comfortable wicker armchairs, fanning ourselves, and whispering together in the dark, we can unburden our hearts of much that seems immodest or incautious by day. Confidences between friends, like the love between husband and wife, are saved for the nighttime.

I tell Xiuyin that I've rarely seen her children help her with the heavy work. She nods regretfully, "Well, Mali—I guess my husband and I—we'd say our children are lazy. The younger generation just doesn't have the strength and energy we do. Why, when I was 30, I could still carry 100 *jin* of vegetables in my baskets, just like my husband. We'd walk an hour over the mountain to market without resting on the way. None of my young sons will do that. One time I got so angry—I had a lot of extra vegetables left from our family plot, so I told my youngest boy to sell them in Geleshan and keep whatever he made. It's only a half-hour's walk, but he refused. He said the bit of money wasn't worth his bother—just to let the vegetables rot. I hit him! It hurt me too much. We've known hunger, and we've labored all our lives. How can the young ones just waste things?"

I point out that she worked hard because she *wanted* to give her children things she didn't have herself. Yes, she agrees, it is a contradiction: "Mali, you know I'd wanted to go on for more education myself, and I didn't get to, so I'd hoped my children might—" But as we both know, no young people from this brigade have succeeded in passing the increasingly difficult university extrance exams in the last few years. Many of the village youth are very bright, but they just can't compete with the advantaged urban generation. I reflect on the differences in character between generations—any generations—my own generations, remembering my grandmother's complaints to my mother: "Your child is so lazy—why don't you bring her up right!" Poor mother, poor me. Like Popo and Xiuyin. Like Xiuyin and Yin.

Yet Popo and Xiuyin never seem bored. They take a joyful pride in their own physical strength, a vigorous pleasure in outdoor work, a mischievous delight in their economic cunning. Nor do all the young women want to escape from agriculture—the neighboring brigades have some women as production team leaders. Many boys as well relish the chance to show off their physical and mental prowess through farming, and the more serious ones develop leadership roles.

Since 1979, when the nation began reorganizing its economic life, a wave of consumerism has swept the countryside; televisions, tape recorders, fashions, movie magazines, and romantic love have become synonymous with modernization in the minds of many youth. Purchasing power of the village youth has greatly increased in farming areas surrounding the cities, and girls wear wristwatches and imported nylon socks to hoe in the fields. But not all feel at ease with this. When rural youth contemplate their prospects, they find that regulations restrict their movement into the already overcrowded cities, that nonagricultural jobs in some villages are less numerous now than previously, and that few seem to be getting beyond high school. Many wonder if there should be something more to village life.

As for this village, part of its problem lies in the nature of its prosperity, which it owes to its role as a vegetable supply brigade for the city. Its complex and intensive agriculture requires a continuous turnover of planting and harvesting of more than 60 types of intercropped vegetables, wheat, and rice. Unlike the farmers in grain supply brigades, Jingang farmers have no slack seasons and rest only when it rains. There's work every day and no days off. The living standard has gone up, but they haven't caught up culturally. Except for four days at Spring Festival, no one has time to plan any kind of festival, play, opera, sports competition. The village in 1979–1981 had few movies, no library, no painting classes, no sports, no acting groups. In families with hardships, the young people continue their parents' struggle for basics. But in more prosperous households like Xiuyin's, girls ask: "Marriage and a baby and then what?"

This is one of Yin's problems. She wants a baby to alleviate her boredom, and she will have to wait. A recent regulation stipulates that women here must be 23 before they can receive a childbearing permit. This is an attempt to simplify previous procedures, which limited child-birth more strictly to three per 1,000 according to a complicated age-preference list. (Thus a woman who married at 25 and got to the top of the list at 27 could be set back again if a newly married woman of 30 asked for preference.)

Xiuyin and I discuss the new marriage law of 1980, which raised the legal marriage age for girls from 18 to 20 and for boys from 20 to 22. This new legal age, however, is actually lower than the previous political guidelines of the 1970s for marriage of girls to be delayed until 25 and boys until 27. Thus in 1980, the baby-boom population of the 1950s rushed into wedlock, and a new baby boom threatened. China's population as a whole has more than doubled since 1949, and Jingang's population has increased faster than the national average. The whole village is acutely aware that its land must now sustain more than twice the population it supported 30 years ago. Family planning work has taken on a great urgency.

Xiuyin is adamant about the importance of family planning. She refers to Yin: "Why is she in such a hurry? She has her whole life ahead. Look at my life! If I'd had only one child, think of the schooling and other interesting work I could have done. But in those days, the policy encour-aged us to have more children. What a mistake! How prosperous we'd be today if we'd begun controlling population back then. I should have had just one child. Then I'd be doing some kind of interesting work like you, Mali! Of course, you don't have any children, and you should have one. Every woman should have *one* child! You have a baby and bring it here to the village. I'll raise it for you, so you can go on doing your work."

I say, "Oh, that would be splendid. I only wish—well, I don't think every woman needs a child, but I do think the whole world needs a policy of just one child per woman. It would solve all the other problems—hunger, war—"

Xiuyin agrees, "The limitation to one child is right. The trouble with the new regulation is that it separates the childbearing age from the marriage age, and that makes it sticky to enforce. If the policy has to be adjusted from time to time, that's all right, as long as it becomes stricter. If the regulations were relaxed in the future to allow one child at *any* time after marriage, the women who had had abortions would go back to curse the family planning workers, making their job even more difficult. They already have a really rough time of it."

"Yes—what a terrific bunch of outspoken women that lot is! Fighters, eh?"

Most of the family planning workers are women in their thirties. Most have only one or two children (from before the present limit of one child). I repeat to Xiuyin what the family planning women's group told me: "We are trying now to get the women who have started first pregnancies too young and without permission to go to the hospital for an abortion. When the woman agrees, we pay her full work points for the hospital time and rest period afterward, just the same as for childbirth. Hospitalization is paid by the government. We try to persuade them by talking about the benefits to their own lives of having fewer children and how our village living standard will just get lower and lower with too many people—"

Xiuyin interrupts me to explain: "Look how dangerous this is for all of us! Look how hard my husband works to raise production. We've had a lot of success with our farming, but it won't do any good if there are too many people. At Liberation, in 1949, we had 2,000 people in this village; now we have 5,000. At Liberation, we had one *mou* of land per person— that's what it should be today for the most efficient vegetable production; now we average only four-tenths *mou* per person."

She continues, "It wasn't just births that raised our population. When our brigade became more prosperous, both men and women refused to move out when they married. [The more traditional pattern was for women to move to their husband's village. This stalemate was already a recognized problem when I first visited Jingang in 1973.] Village women can't move into the city, even if they marry a city man. And since August of this year, our district has a new regulation that county people can't move into our village when they marry, although our people can move to the county. This should help us, but now a lot of engagements with county people have been broken off. Our living standard is higher, so our young ones all want to marry others from our mountain."

Xiuyin recollects, "When I was a girl, we children on the mountain didn't have shoes and went around in tatters. The fields were small and stony, not broad terraces like you see today, and there weren't any irrigation pipes or reservoirs. We ate potatoes and beans if we had anything. In those days, people wore homespun. Just a shirt and pants of factory-made blue cotton, like I am wearing now, cost three *dan* of rice in those days. That's 1,350 *jin* of husked white rice, equal to two years' rice ration for me today—a fortune then. Ordinary peasants couldn't afford it."

I know this. I've seen old pictures. I recall to myself the pictures I've seen of China in the days before Liberation—of the desperate poverty of so much of the countryside. Then I think of the soft pile of cotton and nylon print fabric on the sewing machine this morning—the new blouses that Simei and Yin are making. They have studied the fashion magazines from Shanghai, and when they hold up the garments, they ask if I think they are as pretty as city girls.

I bring my attention back to Xiuyin and continue telling her what the family planning workers said to me: "Every production team has a woman who does women's work. They report to us. Of course, there are some wives who try to hide their pregnancy. Some of the small work groups are mostly relatives, and then even if they know, they don't tell us. One got pregnant and ran away to hide in her mother-in-law's home in Ba County. Because it's her first child, the fine is not so high. [The fine for a firstborn without permission is 20 percent of the mother's annual work points for seven years, a total of about 1,000 *yuan*.] We must make her wait until she is 23 years and nine months old before giving her a registration book for her child to get its rations of grains, oil, cloth, and so on. Moreover, she won't get the work points we normally give women for their rest period before and after pregnancy nor any medical expenses for the baby if it is ill. She can still manage by paying for these things herself; it just makes things harder for her."

The women had warmed to their subject: "Every house has its own circumstances, and some families raise all sorts of confusing side issues to complicate their arguments and try to put us off. This morning, we had to argue really fiercely—a bad business. This one fellow planted more land for his private plot than he was entitled to, so our production leader went over and hoed out the extra rows of vegetables. But now he says to us, 'You'll have to pay me compensation for my vegetables, or I won't take my wife to the hospital for the abortion.' It's two unrelated things, but he pulls them together and tries to tie us up until it's too late.

"Anyway, we agreed to pay, but we forgot to agree on an amount. Imagine—we'd hoed up 200 vegetables, worth not more than 10 *yuan*. He wanted 80 *yuan*! We fought—all of us against the one of him. Finally he agreed to 20 *yuan*. But then he said that the brigade leaders would have to sign, too. We've been after this fellow since our tomatoes were planted, and now the tomatoes are being picked, and it's still not done. We run around every day this way.

"When we have a tough case, we go in a group. Sometimes we go to a house, and they lock the door in our faces. We sit on the doorstep and don't budge. The family sends their small children, who don't understand, out to cry and fuss and beg us to go, but we don't. If one day isn't enough, we go back for two, or three, or four until the adults will talk to us."

Xiuyin laughs when I get to this point, and it is clear that she doesn't want such trouble on her own doorstep. This is part of the tension in the family—Yin wants to break the rules and have an early baby, and the older ones in the family are against it. I repeat the words of the women's group: "The men are the most difficult to deal with—they get quite belligerent because they are the household managers. In our group of women, we all have earning power and get work points like our husbands, so we can manage some family affairs—but you still can't call that being the head of the house. If it comes to a fight, we're not as strong as the men. [laughter from all of us]."

Xiuyin laughs, too. She picks up the thread of my story: "Household heads! That's like my husband. All of us have earning power; even Popo gets 15 *yuan* a month for minding the neighbor's baby. But Li controls all of it. He does it well, but still—"

As it is quite dark by then and we have moved our chairs closer, Xiuyin leans over to me and chuckles, "Mali, do you still share the bed with your husband sometimes? My old man and I—sometimes, well, it's good to let go of the past, eh? One has to let go of the pain and try to forget. People should still be good to each other, eh?"

A Day in September

Popo is up at five o'clock to get breakfast. Simei follows her out at five-thirty. I hear their movements in the dark, but I want to sleep. I drowse until seven o'clock and get up reluctantly. I was up until two this morning working on my notes, but I'm ashamed to sleep late. While I comb my hair, Xiuyin comes in: "Mali—today is something special! It's the mid-autumn festival—the night of the full moon. We all go into the garden to eat and drink some wine, and there's *ciba*, sticky rice. So don't be late coming home, eh?" I promise, and we join Popo for breakfast. The men are already gone.

While we are eating, I ask, "Popo was an activist, wasn't she?" Xiuyin answers, "Yes, she entered the party in 1956. That was the second batch from our village to join."

Popo explains, "Originally I was from Ba County. That's just over the mountain. When I was 16, I married into my husband's family in this village, because we had a bit of relationship with them through in-laws. My son's father liked to smoke opium and play around—gambling, cards, things like that. Before Liberation, he took me into the city to live with a relative. We lived with our two children for eight years there."

Xiuyin interrupts: "That was a clan relationship. Popo's family were peasants; they worked as servants." Popo nods and goes on, "That relative was a butcher. He had a bit of money and a house, because he was a small chief in the Green Gang [one of the old nonpolitical secret societies of Chongqing]. While I lived there, I did washing and mending chores. Then my son's father became very ill. His opium smoking made it worse, and he was selling all our things to support his habit. We got so poor that in order to live, we moved back to this village, where we still had a little land to keep us. Three years after that, my son's father died."

Mental arithmetic showed me that Popo was widowed when she was still young, about 30. I began to understand her independent character. Popo said: "At that time, my son was only 13 and my daughter six. Because my children were still so young, I couldn't leave the house to work in the fields, so I had to have someone farm our land for us."

Xiuyin says, "The person who worked the land took the profits, paid the high taxes, and just gave Popo a bit of grain as the rent. In those days, it was hard to be a widow or the son of a widow. When my husband was a boy, the children chased him and taunted him, calling him a *guawazi*, boy with no father. He became a real fighter. He could beat any man on the mountain—he was that strong. When he was 16, he took over the farming and supported the family. Of course, Popo always worked, too. After Liberation, she ran the brigade nursery for years. I told you that I helped her for a while."

I comment to both of them: "Popo's hearing is still good, and she speaks very clearly. Is she still active?" Xiuyin says, "She is a party branch representative. During the Cultural Revolution, some leftists dug up the old business of her land before Liberation—that other people had worked it for her. But she was a widow! Of course, at Land Reform, long ago, that was all settled legally—she was never a landlord. But this leftist bunch brought it up again and tried to call her a 'black party person.' They tried to make her wear a tall hat. That was quickly stopped. All that bad business of digging up things over and over again—everyone knows Popo's circumstances and how hard she has always worked. Nowadays she still goes to party meetings and study sessions. On rainy days, we don't want her to go out, because we are afraid she might slip and fall. Otherwise, she just stays at home and does housework."

Xiuyin hops up and goes to the sty; I help Popo clear the table. I think about Popo's day. She's over 70, but she's up before anyone else in the morning, rarely naps at noon, and stays up late for TV, which she loves. She prepares three meals a day for the family of seven and their frequent houseguests with only a little help from Xiuyin and Simei and none from Yin. By herself, she raises the four to six family pigs—a major task requiring chopping greens, cooking and slopping swill in heavy buckets, and cleaning pens. This is a substantial economic contribution, as each pig sells for 130 to 150 *yuan*. She also raises a few chickens for "a small bank of eggs," as the people call pocket money. She does all the laundry, cleans the whole seven-room house and the yard, helps Xiuyin with the family vegetable garden, and minds the neighbor's baby for 15 *yuan* a month. It seems that she does more than any of the women in the house.

Popo is something special, too. She takes relish in her work. She is small, lean, and quick on her feet. She is very independent-minded, keeps to herself when she pleases, and often takes her rice to the garden to enjoy alone. But when she feels sociable, her conversation is sharp and her laughter infectious. Li still seeks her counsel on family matters. I remember how he bragged once about her strength: "You know, Mali, when they work in the collective fields, some people are lazy but still want full work points. Me—in one morning I can plant three-tenths *mou* of cornfield. My mother also used to be very able. She could hoe seven-tenths *mou* in one day. Nowadays, if the collective wants to hoe that much, they must pay 40 work points. That is four full *man* labor days!" That staggered me. I said, "Surely the goal of modernization is not to have everyone slave as hard as your mother has done but to gain more comfortable working conditions." I got a decidedly mixed reaction.

When I think about Popo, the words of another friend come to mind: "We Chinese are always saying we take such good care of our old parents. But no household wants the bother of old people who don't have their own money. I don't know a single family which does not have arguments and quarrels over who should take care of its old parents and how the responsibility should be divided." All the older people in the village face this. The most important concern in family planning is the prospect of old age. A marriage between two only children burdens the young couple with four old folk. Imagine a young couple with four old ones and one baby to nurse! If a female only child marries away from home, who will succor her parents? Who will carry their water and manure, garden for them, and do all the heavy tasks upon which a village household depends? Until the community can guarantee security for its aged, villagers dread the risk of an only child, especially a girl. Yet the mountain has its brave couples. In this commune, more than 1,000 couples have guaranteed only one child by an operation for either the father or the mother. Gele Mountain has an old age home, and Jingang is talking about some form of retirement assistance plan. It's on everyone's mind, on everyone's tongue.

Dinner is served indoors because it's raining, so we'll have to do without the romance of the full moon. But everyone is in a cheerful mood, and we have 10 at the table—Li, Xiuyin, Popo, Second Son, Simei, her fiancé, the youngest son, two carpenters, and me. Yin is missing. Several pork and vegetable dishes cover the center of the round table. Popo ladles out the sticky *ciba* into our rice bowls, and Li pours wine into thimble-size porcelain cups for the men, who start drinking games. I struggle to disengage my chopsticks from the gooey rice, and Xiuyin sympathetically assures me that table manners are informal. "We're not like other families who fuss if you don't eat. Not all of us really like to eat *ciba* either."

Table talk turns to the subject of furniture prices, workmanship, and weddings—the reason the carpenters are here. For several weeks, the living room has been full of lumber, wood shavings, and the smell of hot glue, as wardrobes, beds, and tables take shape for the wedding trousseau.

They are making two of everything—one for Simei, one for Second Son. Traditionally, only the daughter would have received a set.

Li declares proudly: "Not bad, eh? I'm that kind of father—I give each of my children the same—the boys and the girls." Simei blushes. Second Son glowers into his rice bowl. He has been trying to squeeze his father for another piece of furniture. Everything Simei gets, he jealously fingers, appraises, and measures to see if his is the same. I ask whose wedding feast will take place first, and Second Son snaps: "Mine, of course—it goes from the elder to the younger!"

Li says, "It was the same for my eldest son and eldest daughter [both of whom now live elsewhere]. It's not the furniture that's most troublesome; it's the wedding feast. Leaving aside the money, it's just not easy to prepare all the food. There's either too little or too much, and we've had to buy so many dishes [pointing to stacks of chinaware under the bed] and spoons. I had to buy over 100 spoons! And then there's the bother about invitations. If you invite these relatives and not those, this friend and not that one, it's no good. There's also the kind of relative who doesn't want to come. You invite him, he shows up, and everyone feels uncomfortable."

Xiuyin says, "I'm not afraid of hard work, but I can't work at night. When my eldest son married, I was running back and forth for two nights. Afterward, I couldn't stand up." I suggest, "Maybe it's better just to give the kids the money and let them plan how to use it?" Xiuyin answers, "That was our idea—to let the young ones have some solid benefit."

Li looks at Simei and her fiancé and says, "You could travel and see something—open your eyes a bit. I've read how some couples nowadays do that instead of inviting people." Simei and her young teacher look confused, as though even the effort of buying the train tickets would be too much. Li warms to his subject: "Originally I thought I wouldn't bother with guests, but [nodding at Second Son] *her* relatives—let's not put it *too* strongly—they don't leave me any alternative." Second Son slams his rice bowl down and leaves the table. Xiuyin's eyes meet mine, and we silently begin to clear. She explains to me in the kitchen, "Yin's relatives have been gossiping about Li because there's been no wedding feast. They want a big display, and he doesn't. Village marriage customs are all mixed up these days!"

I ponder what I know of weddings in this village. I've attended several. During the Cultural Revolution, feasting was censured as wasteful consumption, and only intimate friends came for tea and candy. Brides got only necessities and no trousseau, which certainly helped their parents, especially in families with many daughters. In the more relaxed atmosphere of 1979–1981, celebrating resumed, although still on a rather modest scale. The 2,000 *yuan* Li was giving is typical of more prosperous rural families, but it is not lavish, considering that it provides the couple with their household and furniture necessities for a lifetime. Guests come from long distances and deserve a good meal.

Most important, marriages are the only social event in this village. There is no other occasion to bring together all one's friends and relations. In this sense, wedding celebrations are a sign of vitality in rural life. In the countryside today, the parents' approval of an engagement still constitutes the most important step of the marriage. This significance derives from the traditional concept of the engagement as a contract between families. According to the new marriage law, a couple can marry even if their parents object, but parental opposition creates almost insurmountable economic and social hardships. It is difficult to survive in a village if one is cut off, so social pressure is brought to bear on parents to give formal consent.

In Jingang, the bride-to-be often comes to stay as a houseguest of the groom's family for a month or more before the marriage contract is signed. The groom-to-be also visits the bride's family. Signatures on the marriage certificate constitute the only legal recognition of marriage, but a couple may then live together for a year or more, as in the case of Second Son and Yin, before guests are invited. The invitation of guests is still regarded by many as the necessary social consummation.

Thus it may be unclear to many couples at what stage they are "partly" or "completely" married—in the family sense (engagement), the legal sense (marriage contract), and the social sense (inviting guests). However, engagement, the first step, remains the most important in the moral sense. It defines an obligation. Even in the cities, a girl or boy who breaks off an engagement may be considered fickle, untrustworthy, and a poor marriage prospect for anyone else. Public opinion can be even harsher in the villages. Yet no one in this village criticizes their children for breaking off an engagement to a county family when the new regulations would cause them to move. No one wants to lose a son from a household or blames a daughter for not wanting to move to a poorer place. This is considered an economic issue, not a moral one.

The dishes done, Xiuyin and I join the others in the family room. Li brings in some small tables with cakes, candies, and tea. Xiuyin and I hunch down comfortably on the sofa and watch as the men take turns with jokes and card tricks. Li tells stories and then does some sleight of hand. Standing in the middle of the room, upstage, so to speak, he takes a paper-wrapped candy between his long square fingers. Waving it like a magician, he begins to make it disappear and reappear from different parts of his clothing. Finally he pops it into his mouth. His eyes wrinkle, his broad forehead smooths out, and his throat muscles contract with herculean swallowing. Xiuyin and I giggle and flop against each other in convulsions, the boys are falling off their stools howling, and Popo has tears running down her face. Xiuyin's tiger of a husband is killing us with a comic act.

Suddenly, Li reaches to the back of his jacket collar and brings his hand forward in a long graceful stage gesture, revealing the "swallowed" candy in his palm. Xiuyin and I sputter and clutch each other with delight. She sits up sharply and wants to know how he does it. Li pulls up a stool, places himself squarely before her, and demonstrates gently—the hand passes thus to the collar, the candy is tucked in, the empty hand moves to the mouth and pretends to put the candy in, the hands moves back, then forward—

Xiuyin can't follow it; she shakes her head. Li slowly repeats. Xiuyin becomes tense beside me. She still can't understand. Li's patience is breaking: "See—like this—and this—and this—" Xiuyin's eyes have clouded, and there are tears on her lids. She slides off the sofa and excuses herself for bed. I reflect on their two kinds of intelligence, abrading.

Late October

First Day

It's evening when I reach the path to the house. A tawny copper luminescence shimmers in the bare wet paddies. I pause beside Xiuyin's vegetable plot to check what's likely to cross our table this week. Suddenly a screech and a yell announce the hot pursuit of a neighbor's chicken by a stick-wielding Popo. There is one hen that won't trespass again among Popo's vegetable sprouts! Popo sees me, flourishes a final joyous curse at her enemy, and comes over to welcome me: "*Xike, Xike*—Mali, we haven't seen you for so long! Welcome, welcome—come in quickly; you haven't eaten yet, have you?"

It's been a two-hour walk. I come in shivering, tired, and damp. I'm feeling scared. This is my last week in the village, and I don't think I'll make it. What if I start crying? I've already started in the fields walking over here. I've spent two years in this village and don't know when I can return—

I sit down, and Popo brings me a mug of hot water. Li comes in and puts his sheepskin jacket around my shoulders. Night on the mountain is colder than on the flatlands, and this October is especially chilly because of the unduly heavy rains. Xiuyin sits close to me, rubbing and thumping my back to warm me. We're all laughing. Actually, I think I'm going to cry again. Li sees that I'm still shivering and tells Popo, "Show Mali how to use a towel to warm up."

Popo takes me into the bedroom and teaches me an old peasant trick. When you're perspiring from work or whatever and don't have a change of dry clothes, slide a dry towel down your back, inside your undershirt, flat against your skin. Leave it there to absorb the evaporating moisture. Popo helps me pull a small towel inside my shirt. Ah—comfort. It works! I begin to stop trembling and feel warm. I won't catch a cold after all.

The family has already eaten, but they heat up some rice and vegetables for me. While I eat, they pore over the photographs I've brought. We've all been taking pictures of each other, and I gloat over our successes: "Look at Popo—in that one she's laughing! Li's smiling in this one—I've never seen him smile in a picture before!" Xiuyin stiffens her arms and marches to the center of the room like a little soldier: "Yes, he never laughs; he always pulls a long face!" She presses her arms tight to her sides and tips her body slightly forward, jutting her small chin and drawing down her mouth in an imitation of Li's dour formal portraits. The rest of us break up. Her mimicry a success, she repeats the performance. We break up again. Li looks sheepish, but he is pleased too and comments, "When people look natural in a photo, it's better, ah!"

For the rest of the evening, Li and I check over my drawings of vegetable cropping systems and arrange a study schedule for these last few days. It will be a hard time for all of us. The guests for Second Son's wedding have been invited for next week, and the household is over-worked with preparations. I cannot stay for the wedding, because there are many other families for me to visit in other parts of the village. We agree to carry on our chores as though I were not going away after all—business as usual. Late to bed and early to rise.

Second Day

Early this morning, Xiuyin and Li go off to market. Happily figuring what to buy for the wedding, their quick steps set the large baskets dancing from their shoulder poles. They are a handsome couple, and, for all their protestations about the bother of the wedding, clearly they are enjoying the excitement. At lunchtime, when we are already at the table, they reappear. Their baskets are still partly empty, but some goodies are buried inside. Having gone to buy things for Second Son's event, Li returns with his main purchase something for Simei instead—a beautiful soft red and tan wool blanket. Popo gets up to feel it and grins: "Ahh—" Simei feels it and blushes. Second Son feels it, then mutters to Yin, "It's thicker than the one he gave us!"

This afternoon I've come to the sty to help Xiuyin. She must carry on here as usual until the wedding feast, then someone will take over for her for three days. I help her fork piles of green fodder into a square pit at the front of the sty. We pack it in by stomping around on top. We bounce up and down on the springy stuff, laughing at each other, until my knees are wobbly. Then we cover the greens with black plastic sheeting, and I shovel manure on top to raise the temperature for composting. Pit storage of fodder by fermentation is important for preserving winter supplies. It takes me the afternoon to finish this, while Xiuyin does the other chores.

Xiuyin has told me an old Chinese saying: "When you are poor, you can't live without pigs; when you prosper, you can't live without books." Nowadays, this saying has been amended to stress the general importance throughout China of pigs for providing high-quality organic fertilizer for the whole agricultural cycle: "In agriculture we can't live without pigs." Because Jingang's main crops are vegetables, all the surplus or waste leaves, vines, and sweet potatoes are fed to the pigs, which thus do not compete for grain consumed by people. Pigs are valued first as "fertilizer factories," only secondarily for their meat.

In Jingang, pig manure (including a very small amount of cow manure) provides fully 40 percent of the fertilizer for the collective vegetable fields, human wastes provide 10 percent, and chemical fertilizers make up the other 50 percent. Of the pig manure used on the collective fields, fully three-fourths comes from family pig-raising. For example, in Xiuyin's production team, only 60 pigs were raised collectively in 1981 (including the 30 in Xiuyin's sty), compared to 140 pigs raised in families.

The standard for collective pig-raising in Jingang is 30 head in the care of one keeper, as in Xiuyin's sty this year. After calculating the cost of fuel for heating the feed in the sty kitchen, high-quality grain supplement supplied by the government, and medicine and not counting silage or labor, only a few hundred *yuan* profit is possible from the sale of the animals for meat. Vegetable silage is "free" because it would otherwise be wasted. In other words, labor is exchanged for the production of fertilizer.

Xiuyin's sty in 1980, when she was responsible for raising 60 pigs by herself, was actually quite exceptional. The team wanted to try out a new contract system, fixing the amount of fodder, fuel, number of pigs to sell, costs, and labor. No one else wanted to take on the heavy task, so Xiuyin volunteered. She got up at four every morning, prepared the family breakfast, and went to the pigsty at six. After lunch, she went back to the sty until seven and still had the housework and family vegetable garden to look after. It is not customary to work outdoors after dark, so people quipped that she had "night eyes." She did all the heavy work by herself—cleaning the pens, carrying waste vegetable leaves back from the fields, and gathering firewood on the mountain and toting it on her back. After 10 months of such labor, she had fulfilled the task of raising 60 pigs and had earned over 8,000 work points. The value of one workday in her production team that year was 1.59, so she earned 1,367 *yuan* for 10 months' work and made a profit for the meat sold of 600 *yuan* for her team in addition to the pigs' production of 250,000 *jin* of manure.

Family pig-raising depends mainly on women and old people, not on the main labor force. In Jingang, the average household has four to five pigs; some families raise only one or two, others as many as eight or nine. Only 2 to 3 percent of the families raise no pigs; these are usually cadres' or workers' households with a salaried income. It takes one person about one and a half to two hours of work per day to raise three family pigs. As for consumption, in 1981, Jingang households averaged two pigs for meat, of which they raised 1.2 head by themselves and bought the balance from the market. The average annual pork consumption per person in Jingang is 60 *jin* per year. Thus the situation in Xiuyin's home is typical—Popo is raising five pigs, and the family plans to kill one pig each for the wedding feasts of Second Son and Simei and to sell the other three to the state. The contribution of women and old people (mostly the grandmothers), to the agricultural cycle, through pig-raising, is enormous.

At the evening meal, everyone seems exhausted and subdued; no one talks. I am feeling sorry for myself, thinking how I love these people and doubting that they understand. There is a peasant phrase, "a chicken who can't even lay eggs," which refers to a woman who doesn't have a child. I've no child, only my work. What must my village friends think of me? I help Xiuyin do the dishes, then prepare for bed by washing my feet in a wooden tub of hot water. I move my small stool next to hers in front of the kitchen stove. After a long silence, staring at the flames together, she nudges me and says in her small husky whisper, "Mali—you have a good heart. If you didn't, I wouldn't pay attention to you. I wouldn't even bother to speak to you." She adds wood shavings to the fire and stokes it. Then she leans against me and says: "Mali, I understand about your studies and your work. *Ni di gongzuo shi ni de jia*—your work is your family." I feel ashamed that I should think she does not understand. I am amazed. None of my friends abroad has understood, or comforted, as well.

Third Day

This morning, Popo began pulling chinaware dishes out from under the beds—stacks and stacks of large white rice bowls covered with dust, piles and piles of porcelain spoons. She will spend the whole morning washing them.

Xiuyin and I go to the sty, where she sets me to work chopping greens with a huge cleaver. She shows me how to hold tight the bunch of sweet potato vines so that leaves and stems can be shredded without mincing my fingers. I cut stiffly at first—not enough wrist action. By the end of the morning, I've speeded up, and two-thirds of the vines are done. I've cut 50 *jin* in two hours. But my elation is short-lived; I am quickly humbled when I learn that Xiuyin can do this much in 10 minutes. Working steadily, she and other expert women can chop up 2,000 *jin* in a day. My admiration grows. There are more skills to raising pigs than first meet the eye—more skills, more strength, more management acumen. We wash out the fodder buckets and hose down the pigs and the pens. Hanging up our work aprons, we slip into our jackets, and Xiuyin locks the wooden doors. We head back across the fields to lunch. My eyes follow the curve of the bronze-hued paddies to the vegetable terraces and the farmhouses under clumps of bamboo. Above them, the crown of pines on the rim of the mountain stretches away. I reflect that but for an accident of birth, I could be doing Xiuyin's work and she mine.

Liferoads—after dinner, I think more about this and write it in my notes. Xiuyin would have liked more education. She was capable of it, and for a short time after Liberation, it seemed that she would have a chance when the brigade sent her to study. The chance to be a cadre and to do something beyond farming and family roles came and went. She told me it wasn't in her character to fight, to run; she couldn't oppose Li. She dissolved in tears. It was her nature, she said. For years and years, she cried. Now she goes to the sty and comes home again; she rarely goes to the other hamlets, not even to visit her old mother across the hill. Her mother comes here. Xiuyin goes back and forth from the house to the pigsty. She is 48 and finds the work getting hard now. Her children are moving out, and in a year or so she will come back to the house and take over Popo's role. Popo will rest. She could never stand to be idle, but the heavy chores will fall from her shoulders onto Xiuyin's.

Popo too had her active years outside the house in the peasant association and running the brigade nursery. Popo's marriage was arranged and brought her sorrow; thanks to Liberation, she enjoys a greater independence in her widowhood. Xiuyin's match was self-made—a love match, thanks to Liberation—and she still has good moments with Li, although the marriage has its constraints. The new society brought change and promises of social and economic betterment for women. Many have been fulfilled. Popo, Xiuyin, Simei, and Yin, at one time or another, have all had economic roles which are nontraditional, have all held jobs outside agriculture. Yet all except Simei have now been drawn back into the labor of farming. Even Yin. Yin's sewing workshop has no orders, and it has closed down. Next month, she will go back to the fields. The brigade must absorb 80 of its youth back into agricultural jobs after the shutdown of their small village industries. The city youth will get Yin's work. She is told that peasants must farm. Yin's path will follow that of Xiuyin and Popo now.

From the view of other peasants in the village, Popo, Xiuyin, Simei, and Yin have a good life—they live in a comfortable, prosperous home, blessed by good health. An old woman whose son wants to ease her last days counts herself lucky. Popo works so that she won't feel unwanted and also because she really enjoys being active. No one in the older generation would consider this a hard life.

Xiuyin talks to me about the disappointments and sorrows in her life, and I feel that they are very real and painful. They've eaten at her heart for years; when she talks to me, I hear them as something new. But if Xiuyin tried to tell other village women that she suffered because she couldn't become a cadre when she was young, they would never understand. Her life appears more comfortable (TV, nice furniture, very good food, beautiful healthy children, strong clever husband) than theirs. Peasants observe to me that people whose social position is lower than theirs have some suffering, but they can't see this for people whose position is above them. How can Xiuyin say she suffered from not becoming a cadre? Few village women in her generation became cadres. Why should anyone sympathize with her? Raising pigs is not a bad job by village standards. If she did it badly, she'd be criticized. But whatever she does, she does well, so some neighbors are jealous, some praise her, and the brigade presents her with merit awards.

Xiuyin appears to stay the same. From day to day, she nourishes her large family with the patience and compassion needed to balance their many temperaments and characters. But underneath her lovely smile remains the small sharp kernel of everlasting pain—her secret feeling that she had other abilities which she could not use to the utmost. Altogether, her life has been fuller and more complex than most in the village.

When I finish my notes, I put my head down on my arms. This is my last night—the end of whatever I can learn. My understanding falters. The so-called objectivity of the fieldworker dissolves. Her road? My road? Xiuyin comes in and finds me. She pulls Li's sheepskin coat tighter around my shoulders and lays her hand on my head: "Mali, you will come back, eh? This is your home. Your work clothes are waiting for you, folded in my cupboard. I have the pictures of us together—I can look at them when you're gone. When people separate, their hearts are all like this, eh—the same."

Epilogue: March 1983

Just after Spring Festival—the Chinese new year by the traditional lunar calendar—I leave Beijing and go back to Chongqing to visit Jingang. I take the local rural bus up Gele Mountain and walk alone across the fields from the bus stop on the highway. As soon as I step onto the small paths and wind my way between the velveteen greenery of fresh spring wheat, I am back in a world I feel I have never left. But although the landscape remains constant and unspoiled, some things have changed in the village.

The green wheat which used to grow in even stands, uniformly healthy and thick across the broad fields, now grows in small, uneven patches. Farming responsibility has been given to families instead of teams and groups, and families still have uneven degrees of skill in cultivation. The vegetable fields show the same irregularities. Instead of groups working, gossiping, and sharing the tasks in the fields, people work alone—one here, one there. Women especially seem more isolated, struggling with tasks too heavy for them or requiring skills and techniques beyond their capacity. The whole of China is now farmed by families again, a change which affects all of my friends' households. Families who are prospering show it openly. A crowd of new two-story stone houses, complete with stone-walled flower beds and potted plants adorning their balconies, give some hamlets a faint resemblance to southern Italian villages. Compared to the new standards, Li's house can no longer be considered special.

After my joyous reunion with friends at the village office, Li takes me to his house for lunch. On the way, he tells me: "My wife has lost the use of one eye. Part of it had to be cut out—it was some kind of disease, and they couldn't cure it. They've saved the other eye, and they say the disease is halted. It began shortly after you left, Mali, and she suffered a lot of pain. At that time, I did a lot of thinking—about all these years together—and I tried to be more patient. I guess I used to be quick-tempered with her sometimes. When she was ill, I regretted all that—"

We reach the house and go to the back courtyard, where Xiuyin is preparing vegetables for lunch. Li tells her I am here and gently brushes the hair from her face on the side of the injured eye. Part of the pupil is cut or scraped away. The injury is somewhat hidden behind a pair of glasses she wears now, and with the other eye she can still see fairly well. But she shows a tiredness of spirit now, and as we go in to sit together, this comes through. Some of her outer glow has disappeared, although there is still the inner glow. As Xiuyin says, "The pain was so bad, Mali, that they gave me many drugs. Now, my memory for details is not as good as before. I forget things. But, you know, when all this happened, Li was very good to me. When I was young, I used to cry a lot—you know, that old business—but, well, I've got to say, he was really good through this bad time."

In fact, Xiuyin is working harder than ever these days because all farming responsibility including land and animals, has been assigned on a household basis. The collective pigsty where she used to work has been closed down, and the pigs have been divided between families. Like other women in the village, Xiuyin is now fully occupied on the land allotted to her household. This is a heavy task, because, like many other women, she is the mainstay of the family's labor. Li's duties keep him fully occupied elsewhere in the village, so he can help her only occasionally with the tasks that require strength, such as hoeing the heavy clay soils after rain. To help her, she has only the youngest son and occasionally Simei's husband, Xiao Hao, who comes over to hoe or harvest. The young couple married last year and moved in with his parents in a nearby hamlet. Because Simei works in the noodle factory and Xiao Hao is a salaried schoolteacher, they receive no land allotment.

Xiuyin's household is smaller because of Simei's marriage, although the young couple visit several times a week and remain very close. Popo is also away these days, living across the hill in another hamlet where she is nanny and full-time baby sitter for the little girl of Xiuyin's oldest daughter and for two other relatives' children. In the new-style single-child families, grandmothers are at a premium. Popo is having a wonderful time—every day visiting here and running there, undaunted by the baby in tow, now free from the constraints of housework. One day, I meet her going to buy milk in the morning, minding three children at noon, and gossiping with a roomful of girls at the dressmaker's in the afternoon. Popo's share of housework now also falls on Xiuyin.

But the biggest change in the household is with Yin. She is transformed and radiant, animatedly joining the talk at the family table and constantly popping in and out of the main house from her separate wing, completed with a new kitchen. The source of her transformation appears in the arms of her husband—a bubbly little boy of three months. She must have had the baby immediately upon reaching the acceptable age, now raised to 24. Yet even she is not as doting as her husband.

Second Son is absolutely besotted by fatherhood. For hours, he pulls his infant's little bamboo walking crib up and down the courtyard, cooing and wriggling his fingers at its contented occupant. The child is roly-poly and utterly good natured. Second Son carries the baby everywhere in the house, bouncing it, cuddling it, kissing it, cradling it. The child never cries and basks in the adoration of its grandfather and many uncles even when an all-male company passes the bundle from hand to hand like a patchwork-quilted football. Truly, the "only children" in the village today will bring a new kind of Chinese personality and with it momentous change in the family system.

Xiuyin and I consider this—her young daughter-in-law now in the limelight, the family cycle turning and changing. Future generations will never again experience the kind of large household in which Xiuyin raised her family. The family planning regulations of Jingang are stricter now—a woman can marry at 20 but must wait until 24 to bear her child. With only one child to dote upon, the young fathers now take on a bigger share of responsibility—minding the baby, helping with housework, cleaning, and cooking. Among young couples, as with Simei and Yin, the partners are now more equal in their decision-making and spend more leisure time together. For these young ones, the village is now starting up some cultural activities.

On the last day of my homecoming, I work outdoors for a while with Xiuyin, tamping down the plastic sheeting over a hot house seedling bed and preparing seedling cups—a silent time to share together. We have reviewed the past and are content with the prospect of other visits in the future. It is a kind of pause—a suspension in our effort to see ahead down the road and, perhaps, an unwillingness, for the moment, to do so.

CONCLUSION

By Mary Sheridan and Janet W. Salaff

Work

Work creates and sustains social life, but there abounds in the West a popular image of passive Chinese women who do not work, hence we emphasized work roles in this volume. Since work and family roles for women are intimately connected, the study of one involves consideration of the other.

The main types of work represented in these lives were sericulture and textiles, domestic service, porterage, agricultural occupations, factory assembly, shopkeeping, trading, waitressing, haircutting, and other service occupations. It is no surprise that many of the women in these lives were engaged in the garment and textile industries, because these were the first to introduce mass factory production in China.

In China today, women engage in a wide range of occupations, including a few in almost all jobs open to men. In both Hong Kong and Taiwan, women form a distinct majority in light industrial production, where their opportunities for promotion are apparently limited. In the factory and modern service settings, minimal value is placed on the accumulation of skills or abilities that would enhance the opportunities for older women. Consequently, older and younger women compete for the same jobs, and as younger women enter the labor force, older women are compelled to leave. In contrast, in the preindustrialized environment of Sifu, Great-Aunt Yeung, and Old Lady Liu, older women were able to accumulate skills that enhanced their value as workers. More information on the accumulation of skills at work needs to be gathered on women in different occupations.

Acceptable jobs for women have changed over time. Jobs which Sifu and Great-Aunt Yeung held are no longer available; women now enter white-collar, factory assembly, or waitressing positions. From the accounts of Hong Kong and Taiwan, it seems that the range of acceptable jobs for women has narrowed over the generations, whereas in China, it has greatly expanded. More information must be obtained on this possibility. Certainly, the best-paying working-class position in our accounts was sericulture; no other position approached its relative stature for our women.[1]

In addition to historical change, political process affects women's opportunities for promotion. Political work for women greatly affects their social roles. Women appear to gain new opportunities for promotion during political campaigns. The political work for women in China in our account has an integrative function involving not only leadership but also morale-boosting. Women leaders in Yenan and in China were expected to pay special attention to the family problems of their co-workers. They had a wide-ranging, legitimate concern for their teammates that was defined as nurturing a new socialist family. Perhaps the nurtural qualities of the cadres are expected to replace those of the uterine family. Thus political activities may be sex-specific in some contexts but not in others—another area for further research.

The lives in this volume range across varied historical settings. In war-torn societies, women in families without men must work particularly hard, and even where husbands are present, as in Yenan, women are discouraged from being financially dependent. In Hong Kong and Taiwan, the younger generation of wage earners matured in peacetime, but their families lived in a society lacking social insurance or a minimum wage and were quite poor. The women portrayed here contributed faithfully to the family economy—they peeled seeds, picked bean sprouts, worked in family stores, and did housework and child care to enable their mothers' entry into the labor force. When factories opened their doors, our respondents were among the first wave of participants in the new industrial labor force, taking wage jobs to aid their families. Today the factory work of women makes a considerable contribution to the family economy in Hong Kong and Taiwan as well as in China.[2]

The wages of men and women appear to differ in all three societies, although the data do not permit full comparison. In Hong Kong and Taiwan, most women are still considered economically dependent on their family. The jobs of most working-class women apparently pay less and have fewer routes to advancement than the jobs held by men in the same class. In China, women have greater economic self-sufficiency, but the family economy seems to remain controlled by the men. Although more comparative data are needed on wage levels by sex, we can safely assume for the present that their lower wages make it difficult for women to survive outside the family in Taiwan and Hong Kong. Sifu was an exception. In China, social sanctions and precepts of political morality keep women tied to the family.

Since it is highly important in all three Chinese culture areas for people to form families and since family life is considered the natural state for women and men, the lower wages of women most hinder their health and happiness when families fail. The lives of the adopted, divorced, deserted, and aged women poignantly depict the interrelationships of income and family issues.

Family

All the women in our volume matured in the patrilineal family system. Despite the important changes brought about by modern family law codes, the women in this volume live in an environment closely shaped by expectations and obligations rooted in the patrilineal family system. Their struggle to obtain resources—control over the family budget, purchased and inherited property, education, and wages—must be understood in the context of the patrilineal culture and the ways that communities and families interpret the law.

Daughters in our account did not receive an equal share of family property. In Hong Kong, Rainbow's brother was considered the likely inheritor of the family trade, and Rainbow became a waitress. Part of the contention over the adopted daughter's position in the family was her right to property. The life of A-suat in Taiwan indicates the informal arrangements that are accepted in order to deny an adopted daughter a dowry. Primary and secondary wives were often treated differently by husbands, in-laws, and sons. They had modest wedding celebrations, less of a dowry, and possibly a smaller share of household funds. These differences in treatment are hinted at in the life of Great-Aunt Yeung.

Sympathetic family ties may elevate individual women above the position predicted by their family role. Teng Hsiu-ling reported that the adopted daughter received better treatment than she—the natural daughter—because her mother, herself an adopted daughter, sympathized with her plight. Great-Aunt Yeung helped raise the children of the senior wife, thereby cementing a uterine, or sympathetic, family bond. The social support provided through the uterine connection was short-lived, however, and her daughter-in-law treated Great-Aunt Yeung relatively poorly.

When poverty limits the resources that men control, competition surfaces over such assets as pigs, bags of rice, wood, wages, and tips. Women gain greatest control over family funds when they head the *chia*—when they take charge of the family economy of the household. When women live in all-female families because of the outmigration or death of the male wage earners, the male's right to head the family and control property is maintained in principle. Women do not translate their sizable economic power into legitimate authority in the family.

Nevertheless, in this century, the ability of women to work hard and earn funds appears to have strengthened their authority in the economic family. In this book, women engaged in porterage, raised pigs, spun, barbered, and waitressed to enlarge the share of personal funds under their control. Great-Aunt Yeung was able to purchase a house with her private earnings. Rainbow and Wai-gun used their tips and overtime pay for recreation and clothing. Unsupported by a legal right to their earnings, they struggle to keep their share by bargaining, stealth, and subterfuge. Moreover, under certain circumstances, such as the absence of men, earning power could be translated into decision-making power in the family. Great-Aunt Yeung benefited from her recognized ability when she assumed management of the family economy.

All Chinese women are expected to marry. In the past, religious beliefs made spinsterhood taboo. Sifu stretched the pattern of the traditional family system to its widest extent, but her ability to do so was supported by her extraordinary earning power. In order to escape the bondage of marriage, Sifu joined with other silk weavers to create a surrogate family—a sisterhood sanctioned by social rituals equivalent to marriage. Sifu's choice of spinsterhood represented an historical option, but in Hong Kong, Taiwan, and the People's Republic of China today, there are few alternatives to marriage for working-class women. Granny Cheung's life as a peasant describes the family pattern Sifu might have followed had she married—unremitting hard work well into old age.

Historical changes in family structure represented here include the decline of legitimate spinsterhood because of changes in the form of silk production and the apparent end of community boys' and girls' houses in China. Respondents also report the end of minor marriages in Taiwan, and it is likely that adoption of daughters will continue to decline. The decline in fertility in East Asia and the increase in life expectancy mean fewer orphans and other girls available for adoption. The status of daughters will probably soon be related as much to their earning power as to their prescribed role.

The women described here worked hard. The poorer women found that as they matured, especially with the burdens of age, fatigue, and ill health, they had to justify the economic strain they placed upon their families. All the old women in this book worked to support themselves, and some were the mainstay of others. Sifu had to say 10,000 sutras and manage the finances of the vegetarian hall in order to protect the aging women for whom she has accepted responsibility. Old Lady Liu led a spinning and weaving movement to provide herself with a living and contribute to the livelihood of the needy women in her surrogate socialist family. Great-Aunt Yeung, who toiled in Hong Kong industry, represents another combination of women's work and family roles in middle age. Granny Cheung's mother lies dying with sacks of accumulated rice tucked under her bed to ensure her proper burial. These examples belie the cultural myth of an easy old age.

Nevertheless, middle age and old age find many women with increasing control over their own funds. Older women take charge of the household budget and invest in loan societies, whereas younger women appear to lack such opportunities.

Existential Anchors and Other Themes

People in all societies establish structures, relationships, and self-conceptions that give them support and security. These supports have been called existential anchors.[3] The life histories and biographies here have proved an excellent source for understanding the existential anchors for women of different ages and settings. We have seen how different women strive for self-determination and fulfillment. A desire for a measure of self-determination manifests itself in their choice of economic strategy, life-style, and alternative family structure and in the tension the women feel between personal freedom and family demands. Despite the strictures of the patrilineal family, self-determination is also sought within it, especially by the women who define their achievement in terms of their ability to contribute financially to their family rather than by other accomplishments.

However, many women felt they must change the family structure. The pre-1949 revolutionary women reviewed by McElderry (see Chapter 2) all found their family to be an obstacle to their own improvement and sought to change family and social structures to achieve a nontraditional role. In contrast, under the current cultural ethos of Taiwan and Hong Kong, the women portrayed by Kung, Arrigo, and Salaff accepted as a given the family structure idealized in their society and interpreted obstacles to their self-determination as personal, not general, problems.[4]

Other women sought fulfillment outside the family and took small steps to express themselves through their work. When Sifu the spinster says, "We were bold and free!" she echoes many women. Even the filial daughter Wang Su-lan in Taiwan perceives her minute initiatives in gaining employment as small rebellions.

Another existential anchor is sought in support groups of other women and peers and in a variety of work, study, and political groups outside the family. However, hierarchial political and social structures limit their ability to create a strong alternative support system. Wai-gun's friends reject her because she fails to live up to their ideal of entering a romantic marriage. Similarly, Rainbow's peer sorority in the café culture can support her only during a short-lived unmarried career. Tsai Chen-hwei is better received by other formerly married women than by unmarried women. Life experiences and marital status thus interfere with support networks. Somewhat greater support is provided by political groups, such as Wai-gun's union solidarity and the revolutionary organizations that provided refuge for Ch'en Min. Compared to these, it appears that rural women have fewer support groups external to their family.

A third existential anchor is found in the search for meaningful work. The dialogue of the women in this book is brimming with details about their occupations. Whether reeling silk, nurturing pigs, or shouldering steel, the women are experts. As Great-Aunt Yeung stated firmly, "No work was impossible for a woman to do; we could do anything!" When society places a high value on manual labor, then physical strength and personal endurance become an expression of pride. Great-Aunt Yeung and Ch'en Min articulate this pride, Granny Cheung commends her daughter's muscle, and Zhao Xiuyin comments on her daughter-in-law's lack of it. Under different circumstances, similar work becomes meaningless drudgery. Ch'en Min regards spinning as servile when performed in her grandfather's house but noble when done for the Red Army.

Many of the older women achieved a high personal standard in crafts or industrial skills, while the younger wage earners are deterred from self-improvement by management's disincentives. Examples are Wai-gun, the factory women in Taiwan, and Rainbow in the Hong Kong café. The extent to which their work experience is gratifying clearly affects women's self-confidence. It appears that in Hong Kong and Taiwan, a process of degradation of labor has occurred.[5] Further study of this process would be an important crosscultural contribution on women's roles.

Women's efforts to find wider options for themselves and their search for personal effectiveness extend from struggles at the social and psychological level to those of social action. This theme is identified in Chapter 1 as one of private dilemmas and public issues. It is clear that work can become an existential anchor to a much greater extent if the society accepts some responsibility for resolving the role conflicts that originate from simultaneously demanding work and family spheres, as in Yenan.

The public issue/private dilemma has been defined differently in Taiwan, Hong Kong, and China. Our Taiwanese and Hong Kong women believed that many of their problems were personal, and they attempted to find personal solutions. When they found their life dilemmas belittled, they could not see such criticism as part of a general social pattern.

In contrast, women in the People's Republic of China are encouraged to resolve many of the same conflicts in the public arena. Conditions in the Yenan revolutionary base area presented women with many contradictory demands. There they were encouraged to place national goals before family ones, which required stretching to the limit their contribution to family obligations. The problems faced by Ch'en Min and Li Feng-lien of being responsible for all household chores in addition to proving themselves equal to men in public roles continue in China today but are more publicly discussed.

In addition to these major themes, other motifs can be traced through the lives in this book. Recurrent issues are the pangs of adoption; the responsibilities of eldest daughters; violence in the family; sibling affection and rivalry; religious expression; dreams and premonitions; the importance of food and diet; the delights and hazards of gossip; power struggles in personal relationships; loyalty, self-interest, and sacrifice; and the reflection on the meaning of life.

The lives in our volume depict great rootedness and strength. Although the structures and philosophical precepts of Chinese society give primacy to men in public and private realms, women are not necessarily subordinate or passive figures. On the contrary, the women depicted here are pillars and foundations of their communities.

We believe that the life history method helps capture the spirit of ordinary women in a vivid fashion. This approach presents organic or holistic material that reveals the complex rationales and motivations of each subject. The life history method provides a format that contributes to our recognition of women as strong and able members of society. Finally, these biographical records remain a tribute to their subjects—a memorial crafted with the affection of their biographers in the best tradition of the literature.

NOTES

INTRODUCTION

1. John A. Clausen, "The Life Course of Individuals," in M. W. Riley, M. Johnson, and A. Foner (eds.), *Aging and Society* (New York: Russell Sage Foundation, 1972), vol. 3, pp. 457–514; Glen H. Elder, Jr., *Children of the Great Depression* (Chicago: University of Chicago Press, 1974); Tamara K. Hareven (ed.), *Transitions: The Family and the Life Course in Historical Perspective* (New York: Academic Press, 1973); David G. Mandelbaum, "The Study of Life History: Gandhi," *Current Anthropology* 14/3 (June 1973):177–206; and Erik Erikson, *Gandhi's Truth: On the Origin of Militant Non-Violence* (New York: Norton, 1969).

2. For a general overview of modern and contemporary Chinese history to supplement our brief introduction, the reader can consult Frederic Wakeman, Jr., *The Fall of Imperial China* (New York: Free Press, 1975); James E. Sheridan, *China in Disintegration: The Republican Era in Chinese History, 1912–1949* (New York: Free Press, 1975); and Maurice Meisner, *Mao's China: A History of the People's Republic* (New York: Free Press, 1977).

3. See Agnes Smedley, *Portraits of Chinese Women in Revolution* (Old Westbury, New York: Feminist Press, 1976); and Andrea McElderry (chapter 2 of this book).

4. Mandarin. Henceforth the Wade-Giles romanization for Mandarin is used, with the exception of chapter 13, which uses *pinyin*.

5. Among the many fine analytic studies of the Chinese family, the reader can consult Arthur P. Wolf and Chieh-shan Huang, *Marriage and Adoption in China, 1845–1945* (Stanford: Stanford University Press, 1980), especially pp. 57–69, from which this classification was drawn; Margery Wolf, *Women and the Family in Rural Taiwan* (Stanford: Stanford Press, 1972); Maurice Freedman, *Lineage Organization in Southeastern China* (London: Athlone, 1958) and *Chinese Lineage and Society* (London: Athlone, 1966); Myron L. Cohen, *House United, House Divided: The Chinese Family in Taiwan* (New York: Columbia University Press, 1976); David C. Buxbaum (ed.), *Chinese Family Law and Social Change in Historical and Comparative Perspective* (Seattle: University of Washington Press, 1978); and Hugh D. R. Baker, *Chinese Family and Kinship* (New York: Columbia University Press, 1979).

6. See Emily M. Ahern, *The Cult of the Dead in a Chinese Village* (Stanford: Stanford University Press, 1973).

7. Freedman, *Lineage Organization*.

8. Kay Ann Johnson, *Women, the Family, and Peasant Revolution in China* (Chicago: University of Chicago Press, 1983); M. J. Meijer, *Marriage Law and Policy in the Chinese People's Republic* (Hong Kong: Hong Kong University Press, 1971); and Judith Stacey, *Patriarchy and Socialist Revolution in China* (Berkeley: University of California Press, 1983).

9. Stephen Andors, *China's Industrial Revolution* (New York: Pantheon, 1971), especially p. 215; Phyllis Andors, "Politics of Chinese Development: The Case of Women 1960–66," *Signs* 2/1 (Autumn 1976): 89–119, and "Social Revolution and Women's Emancipation: China during the Great Leap Forward," *Bulletin of*

Concerned Asian Scholars 7 (January–March, 1975):33–42; and Janet W. Salaff and Judith Merkle, "Women and Revolution: The Lessons of the Soviet Union and China," in Marilyn B. Young (ed.), *Women in China* (Ann Arbor: Center for Chinese Studies, University of Michigan, 1973), pp. 145–178.

10. The early economic experiences of the island are summarized in C. S. Chen, *Taiwan: An Economic and Social Geography* (Taipei: Fu-Min Geographical Institute of Economic Development, 1963). More recent change is summarized in Hollis Burnley Chenery et al., *Redistribution with Growth* (London: Oxford University Press, 1974).

11. For a study of management practices in an indigenous capitalized factory in Taiwan, see Robert H. Silin, *Leadership and Values* (Cambridge: Harvard University Press, 1975).

12. Vermier Y. Chiu, *Marriage Laws and Customs of China* (Hong Kong: New Asia College, 1966), pp. 108–190. Field studies describe the continued power of the lineage over property; see Bernard Gallin, *Hsin Hsing, Taiwan: A Chinese Village in Change* (Berkeley: University of California Press, 1966); and Cohen, *House United.* Wolf and Huang, *Marriage and Adoption,* traces the decline of minor marriage.

13. Joe England and John Rear, *Chinese Labour under British Rule* (London and Hong Kong: Oxford University Press, 1975); and Angela Wei Djau, "Social Control in a Colonial Society: A Case Study of Working Class Consciousness in Hong Kong" (Ph.D. dissertation, University of Toronto, 1976).

14. Janet W. Salaff, *Working Daughters of Hong Kong* (Cambridge: Cambridge University Press, 1981); for local associations, see also Henry Lethbridge, *Hong Kong: Stability and Change: A Collection of Essays* (Hong Kong and Oxford: Oxford University Press, 1978); and Aline K. Wong, *The Kaifong Associations and the Society of Hong Kong* (Taipei: Orient Cultural Service, 1972).

15. D. M. Emyrs Evans, "The New Law of Succession in Hong Kong," *Hong Kong Law Journal* 3 (1973):5–50.

1. THE LIFE HISTORY METHOD

1. Tamara K. Hareven and R. Langenbach, *Amoskeag: Life and Work in an American Factory City* (New York: Pantheon Books, 1978), and the Southern Oral History Project, Department of History, University of North Carolina, study early factory towns and utilize interviews to reconstruct historical detail. The generation of theory from an immersion in fieldwork is discussed more generally by Barney G. Glaser and Anselm L. Strauss, *The Discovery of Grounded Theory: Strategies for Qualitative Research* (New York: Aldine, 1967). See also Charles E. Frazier, "The Use of Life-Histories in Testing Theories of Criminal Behavior: Toward Reviving a Method," *Qualitative Sociology* 1/1 (May 1978):122–142.

2. Robert Redfield, the University of Chicago anthropologist, trained the eminent economic anthropologist Fei Hsiao-t'ung, author of important field studies of village life in China. Fei and his colleague Chow Yung-teh collected a fine set of lives, published in *China's Gentry* (Chicago: University of Chicago Press, 1968).

Among the numerous life histories collected by Oscar Lewis are those in Oscar Lewis, Ruth M. Lewis, and Susan M. Rigdon, *Four Women: Living the Revolution, An Oral History of Contemporary Cuba* (Urbana: University of Illinois, 1977). See also Eric Erikson, *Gandhi's Truth: On the Origin of Militant Non-Violence* (New York: Norton, 1969).

We are indebted to the work of L. L. Langness for many of the themes in this chapter. See L. L. Langness, *The Life History in Anthropological Science* (New York: Holt, Rinehart and Winston, 1965).

3. Hans H. Gerth and C. Wright Mills, *Character and Social Structure* (New York: Harcourt, Brace and World, 1953), p. 114.

4. C. Wright Mills, *The Sociological Imagination* (New York: Oxford University Press, 1959), pp. 8–13.

5. Robert K. Merton, "Insiders and Outsiders: A Chapter in the Sociology of Knowledge," *American Journal of Sociology* 78/1 (1972):9–47.

6. Langness, *The Life History*, p. 21.

7. This is ably portrayed in Jean L. Briggs, *Never in Anger* (Cambridge: Harvard University Press, 1970).

8. Edwin Ardener, "Belief and the Problem of Women," in Shirley Ardener (ed.), *Perceiving Women* (Toronto: J. M. Dent and Son, 1977), pp. 1–17.

9. Briggs, *Never*; E. S. Bowen, *Return to Laughter* (Garden City, New York: Natural History Press, 1964); and Rosalie H. Wax, *Doing Field Work* (Chicago: University of Chicago, 1971), pp. 15–20.

10. Langness, *The Life History*, p. 35; and Rosalie Hankey Wax, "Field Methods and Techniques: Reciprocity As A Field Technique," *Human Organization* (Fall, 1952):34–37.

11. William J. Filstead, *Qualitative Methodology* (Chicago: Markham Publishing Company, 1970), p. 2; Frazier, "The Use of Life Histories," p. 128.

12. Howard S. Becker and Blanche Geer, "Participant Observation and Interviewing: A Comparison," *Human Organization* 16/3 (1957):28–32.

13. Jack D. Douglas, *Investigative Social Research: Individual and Team Field Research* (Beverly Hills, California: Sage, 1976). Douglas devotes several chapters to the crosschecking of respondent's information and recall. We do not share Douglas's suspicion that it is impossible to obtain the "truth" from individuals in a "conflict-ridden, secretive society" (p. 56). For example, Normal Denzin, *The Research Act* (New York: McGraw Hill, 1978), pp. 214–255, emphasizes the importance of "triangulation," a multi-pronged research strategy that balances a life history with other accounts, perspectives, or data.

14. Howard Becker, "Introduction," in Clifford R. Shaw, *The Jackroller* (Chicago: University of Chicago Press, 1966), pp. v–xviii; and David G. Mandelbaum, "The Study of Life History: Gandhi," *Current Anthropology* 14/3 (June, 1973):177–206.

15. William S. Goode and Paul K. Hatt, *Methods in Social Research* (New York: McGraw Hill, 1952), pp. 230–231.

16. Raymond L. Gordon, *Interviewing: Strategy, Techniques, and Tactics* (Homewood, Illinois: Dorsey Press, 1966); Frazier, "Life Histories"; and Denzin, *The Research Act*, review methodological issues in life history gathering.

17. Langness, *The Life History*, p. 48.

18. Mandelbaum, "The Study," p. 181.

19. Eric Erikson, *Childhood and Society* (New York: Norton, 1959).

20. An analysis of how to read Chinese documents is found in Franz Schurmann, *Ideology and Organization in Communist China* (Berkeley: University of California Press, 1968), pp. 17–104.

21. Mary Sheridan, "The Emulation of Heroes," *China Quarterly* 33 (January–March, 1968):47–72.

22. Irene Eber, "Images of Women in Recent Chinese Fiction: Do Women Hold up Half the Sky?", *Signs*, 2/1 (Autumn 1976):24–34; and Al-li S. Chin, "Family Relations in Modern Chinese Fiction," in Maurice Freedman (ed.), *Family and Kinship in Chinese Society* (Stanford: Stanford University Press, 1970), pp. 87–120.

This genre of model lives bears close resemblance to the "four histories" (*ssu shih*). These histories of the family, the village, the commune, and the factory or the mine were gathered by students in 1963 under the impetus of the political movement known as the Socialist Education Campaign. These didactic histories were intended to provide a systematic understanding and chronicle of social change. The students who collected the four histories also broadened their political consciousness when they learned of the sufferings under the old society. The sociologist S. L. Wong notes that the four histories are significant as documents on social morality. They are explicitly didactic and are comparable to the traditional literary devices of moral approval and censure. Sui-lun Wong, *Sociology and Socialism in Contemporary China* (London: Routledge and Kegan Paul, 1979), pp. 93–105. A translation of several family histories is given in Sidney L. Greenblatt (ed.), *The People of Taihang: An Anthology of Family Histories* (White Plains, New York: IASP, 1976).

23. Ardener, "Belief."

24. Ida Pruitt, *A Daughter of Han, The Autobiography of a Chinese Working Woman* (reprint, Stanford: Stanford University Press, 1967), and *Old Madam Yin: A Memoir of Peking Life* (Stanford: Stanford University Press, 1979); and Margery Wolf, *The House of Lim: A Study of a Chinese Farm Family* (New York: Appleton Century Crofts, 1968).

25. Carol Smith-Rosenberg, "The Female World of Love and Ritual," *Signs* 1 (1975):1–29; Nancy F. Cott, *The Bonds of Womanhood: "Women's Sphere" in New England, 1789–1835* (New Haven: Yale University Press, 1977); and Ann Douglas, *The Feminization of American Culture* (New York: Alfred A. Knopf, 1977).

26. Carol Stack, *All Our Kin* (New York: Harper and Row, 1974); Barbara Garson, *All the Livelong Day* (Garden City, New York: Doubleday, 1975); Kathy Kahn, *Hillbilly Women* (New York: Avon, 1974); Louise Kapp Howe, *Pink Collar Workers* (New York: Putnam, 1977); Mimi Conway, *Rise, Gonna Rise: A Portrait of Southern Textile Workers* (Garden City, New York: Doubleday, 1979); Akemi Kikimura, *Through Harsh Winters: The Life of a Japanese Immigrant Woman* (Novato, California: Chandler and Sharp, 1981); Ann Cornelisen, *Women of the Shadows* (Boston: Little, Brown, 1976); Jean McCrindle and Sheila Rowbotham (eds.) *Dutiful Daughters* (Harmondsworth: Penguin, 1979); and Jane Holden Kelley, *Yaqui Women: Contemporary Life Histories* (Lincoln: University of Nebraska Press, 1978).

2. HISTORICAL BACKGROUND ON CHINESE WOMEN

1. Ida Pruitt, *A Daughter of Han, The Autobiography of a Chinese Working Woman*, reprint (Stanford: Stanford University Press, 1967).

2. One of the earliest such accounts is Eliza Jane (Gillet) Budgeman, *Daughters of China: Or Sketches of Domestic Life in the Celestial Empire* (New York, 1856). One day, she received a visit from a 40-year-old widow who taught a dozen pupils near Shanghai, who was the first Chinese woman Budgeman had met who was able to read and write. She notes, "Women among the working poor cook the rice and take care of the children, but very few know how to sew" (pp. 158, 198).

3. Alicia Helen Neva Bewicke Little, *The Land of the Blue Gown* (London: T. Fisher Unwin, 1902).

4. *Ibid.*, pp. 151, 172, 178, 184, 182.

5. Grace Thompson Seton, *Chinese Lanterns* (New York: Dodd Mead and Company, 1924).

6. *Ibid.*, pp. 281, 282.

7. Nora Waln, *The House of Exile* (Boston: Little Brown and Company, 1934). (Waln also wrote *The Street of Precious Pearls* (New York: Woman's Press, 1921),

the life of Kuei Ping, who, after many family difficulties, converted to Christianity, founded a school to support herself and her kin, and eventually became a teacher for Waln and other foreigners.)

8. *Ibid.,* pp. 19, 23.

9. *Ibid.,* p. 55.

10. *Ibid.,* pp. 62, 112, 51, 113, 42.

11. *Ibid.,* p. 113.

12. Chao Yang Bu-wei, *Autobiography of a Chinese Woman,* trans. by Chao Yuenren, reprint (Westport, Connecticut: Greenwood Press, 1970; originally published, New York: John Day Company, 1947). The Chinese title is *I-ko Nü-jen Ti Tzu-chuan.*

In addition to the autobiographies and biographies by and about Chinese women discussed in this chapter, the reader might wish to examine Su-ling Wong (pseud.) and Earl Herbert Cressey, *Daughter of Confucius* (New York: Farrar, Strauss and Young, 1952); and Irene Cheng, *Clare Ho Tung: A Hong Kong Lady, Her Family and Her Times* (Hong Kong: Chinese University of Hong Kong, 1976).

13. Chow Chung-cheng, *The Lotus Pool,* trans. by Joyce Emerson (New York: Appleton Century Crofts, 1961). The book was published in England as *The Lotus Pool of Memory.* Chung-cheng never gives her exact birthdate, but she notes that she was influenced by the ideas of the May Fourth Movement of 1919. Thus I have assumed she was around 15 in 1920.

14. *Ibid.,* p. 130.

15. *Ibid.,* p. 170.

16. See the chapter entitled "Wang Su Chun Dies for Freedom," in Anna Louise Strong, *China's Millions* (Peking: New World Press, 1965) pp. 138–154.

17. Mary Backus Rankin, "The Emergence of Women at the End of the Ch'ing: The Case of Ch'iu Chin," in Margery Wolf and Roxanne Witke, *Women in Chinese Society* (Stanford: Stanford University Press, 1975), pp. 39–66. Other English sources on Ch'iu Chin include a sketch of her life in Helen Snow, *Women in Modern China* (The Hague and Paris: Mouton, 1967), pp. 93 ff.

Two English-language periodicals published in the People's Republic of China contain articles about her: Fan Wen-lan, "Ch'iu Chin—A Woman Revolutionary," *Women of China* (October-December 1956); and Wei Chin-chin, "An Early Woman Revolutionary," *China Reconstructs* (June 1962). Writings in Chinese are Ch'iu Chin, *Ch'iu Chin Chi (Collected Writings of Ch'iu Chin)* (Peking, 1961); Chung-hua Shu-chü (ed.), *Ch'iu Chin Shih-chi (Memorabilia of Ch'iu Chin)* (Peking, 1958); Ch'iu Ts'an-chin, *Ch'iu Chin Ko-ming Chuan (Ch'iu Chin, A Revolutionary Record)* (Taipei, 1954); *Ch'iu Chin Nü-hsia I-chi (Legacy of a Heroine, Ch'iu Chin)* (Taipei, 1958); and Yü Chao-i, *Ch'iu Chin* (Hong Kong, 1968).

18. Wei Yu-hsiu (Madame Wei Tao-ming), *My Revolutionary Years* (New York: Charles Scribner's Sons, 1943).

Another woman active in the 1911 Revolution was Huang Shen Yi-yun (Madame Huang Fu). Her memoirs are housed at Columbia University in the Special Collection, Butler Library. See Huang Shen Yi-yun, "My Husband and I: Personal Reminiscences of an Eminent Woman," trans. by T. K. Tang. Only the early chapters deal with her personal life; the remainder concern the political career of her husband.

19. Wei, *My Revolutionary Years,* p. 9.

20. *Ibid.,* pp. 24, 27.

21. *Ibid.,* pp. 99–100.

22. See, for example, Agnes Smedley, *Portraits of Chinese Women in Revolution* (Old Westbury, New York: Feminist Press, 1976), who writes, "Every girl with

bobbed hair who was caught was stripped naked, raped by as many men as were present, then her body was slit in two, from below upwards" (p. 22).

23. Hsieh Ping-ying, *Autobiography of a Chinese Girl*, trans. by Tsui Chi (London: George Allen and Unwin, Ltd., 1943). See also Hsieh Ping-ying, *Girl Rebel*, trans. by Adet and Anor Lin (New York: The John Day Company, 1940). In Chinese, see Hsieh Ping-ying, *I-ko Nü-ping Ti Tzu-chuan* (Taipei, 1969; Hong Kong, 1954; Shanghai, 1936) and *Wo-ti Shao-nien Shih-tai* (Taipei, 1955).

24. Hsieh, *Autobiography*, p. 33.

25. *Ibid.*, p. 39.

26. *Ibid.*, pp. 92, 106, 132.

27. The vignettes of Agnes Smedley that depicted Chinese women during this era were originally published in *Chinese Destinies, Sketches of Present-Day China* (New York: Vanguard Press, 1933) and have been reprinted in *Portraits of Chinese Women in Revolution*. *Portraits* also includes material from three other books by Smedley: *China's Red Army Marches* (New York: Vanguard Press, 1934), *China Fights Back*, reprint (Westbury, Connecticut: Hyperion Press, Inc., 1977; originally published, Vanguard Press, 1938), and *Battle Hymn of China* (New York: Alfred A. Knopf, 1943). Smedley also left a fine autobiographical novel, *Daughter of Earth* (Westbury, New York: Feminist Press, 1973).

28. *Chinese Destinies*, pp. 69–89; *Portraits*, pp. 4–26.

29. *Chinese Destinies*, pp. 9–13; *Portraits*, pp. 34–39.

30. *Chinese Destinies*, pp. 237–253; *Portraits*, pp. 67–84.

31. Anna Louise Strong's account of China in the late 1920s is contained in *China's Millions* (New York: Knight Publishing Company, 1935). She also wrote an autobiography, *I Change Worlds*, reprint (Seattle: Madrona Publishers, Inc., 1980; originally published, New York: Garden City Publishing Company, Inc., 1937).

32. Dymphna Cusack, *Chinese Women Speak* (Sydney: Angus and Robertson, 1958), pp. 104–106.

33. Seton, *Chinese Lanterns*.

34. Jen-min Ch'u-pan She (ed.), *Chi-nien Hsiang Ching-yü T'ung-chih Yin-yung Chiu-yi Wu-shih Chou-nien* (Commemoration of the Fiftieth Anniversary of Comrade Hsiang Ching-yü's Heroic Death) (Peking, 1978); and Chung-kuo Fu-nü Tsa-chih She (ed.), *Lieh-shih Hsiang Ching-yü* (Martyr Hsiang Ching-yü) (Peking, 1958). See also Snow, *Women in Modern China*, pp. 236–249; Wang Yi-chih, "A Great Woman Revolutionary," *China Reconstructs* 14 (March 1965):22–24.

35. Biographical data on Ting Ling include Shen Ts'ung-wen, *Chi Ting Ling* (*About Ting Ling*) (Shanghai, 1933) and *Chi Ting Ling Hsüan-chi* (*More about Ting Ling*) (Shanghai, 1935). Ting Ling gave Helen Snow an account of her early life, published in *Women in Modern China*.

In addition, see Yi-tsi Feuerwerker, "Women as Writers in the 1920s and 1930s," in Wolf and Witke, *Women in Chinese Society*, pp. 143–168, which contains information on and sources for Ting Ling's literary works. References to Ting Ling's activities in Yenan are mentioned in Smedley, *China Fights Back* and *Battle Hymn of China*. Merle Goldman chronicles Ting Ling's political fortunes in *Literary Dissent in Communist China* (Cambridge: Harvard University Press, 1967).

36. Smedley, *China Fights Back*, p. 6.

37. *Lieh-shih Hsiang Ching-yü*, p. 15.

38. Goldman, *Literary Dissent*, p. 223.

39. Feuerwerker, "Women as Writers," pp. 157–59; 162.
40. Margaret Yang Briggs (Liang Yen, pseud.), *Daughter of the Khans* (New York: W. W. Norton and Company, 1955). Liang Yen does not give her birthdate, but textual references place it around 1920. Roxanne Witke, *Comrade Chiang Ch'ing* (Boston and Toronto: Little, Brown and Company, 1977).
41. Briggs, *Daughter*, p. 57.
42. *Ibid.*, p. 76.
43. *Ibid.*, p. 283.
44. Witke, *Comrade Chiang Ch'ing*, p. 47.
45. *Ibid.*, p. 68.
46. *Ibid.*, p. 74.
47. Tang Sheng, *The Long Journey Home* (London: Hutchinson and Company, Ltd., n.d., introduction dated 1949).
48. *Ibid.*, p. 129.
49. *Ibid.*, pp. 24–25.
50. *Ibid.*, pp. 120, 126.
51. *Ibid.*, pp. 100–101.
52. *Ibid.*, pp. 153–154, 155.
53. Han Su-yin, *Birdless Summer* (New York: Bantam, 1972). The other two volumes are *The Crippled Tree* (Bantam, 1972) and *A Mortal Flower* (Originally published, Putnam, 1968, 1965, 1966).
54. Han, *Birdless Summer*, pp. 133, 82.
55. *Ibid.*, pp. 47–48, 82.
56. *Ibid.*, p. 180.
57. *Ibid.*, p. 179.
58. Cusack, *Chinese Women Speak*, pp. 224–234.
59. *Ibid.*, pp. 230, 231.
60. *Ibid.*, pp. 232–233.
61. *Ibid.*, pp. 183–202; Helen Snow, *Women in Modern China*, pp. 254–259.
62. Cusack, p. 190.
63. *Ibid.*, pp. 197–198.
64. Jack Belden, *China Shakes the World* (New York: Monthly Review Press, 1970), pp. 275–318.
65. Claude Roy, *Into China*, trans. by Mervyn Savill (London: Sidgwick and Jackson, 1955), pp. 99–125.
66. Jan Myrdal, *Report from a Chinese Village* (New York: Signet Books, 1966). See especially pp. 234–271, 332–334, and 344–351. Jan Myrdal and Gun Kessle, *China: The Revolution Continued* (New York: Random House, 1970), describes the couple's return in 1969 to the same village.
67. Myrdal, *Report*, p. 244.
68. Cusack, *Chinese Women Speak*, p. 239.
69. *Ibid.*, p. 247.
70. *Ibid.*, p. 248.

3. SPINSTER SISTERHOODS

1. See the studies by Marjorie Topley summarized in "Marriage Resistance in Rural Kwangtung," in Margery Wolf and Roxanne Witke (eds.), *Women in Chinese Society* (Stanford: Stanford University Press, 1975), pp. 67–88.
2. Agnes Smedley interviewed silk weavers in the 1920s and reported that they

earned wages well above the level for most working-class Chinese women at the time. See "Silk Workers," in Agnes Smedley, *Portraits of Chinese Women in Revolution* (Old Westbury, New York: Feminist Press, 1976), pp. 103–110.

3. Unofficial Hong Kong government estimates placed the number of Buddhist and Taoist vegetarian halls at around 220 in 1975–1976, with membership ranging from three to 250 people. In addition to the halls which the government listed for tax or deed registration purposes, there are many small unofficial vegetarian halls. Ignorant of possible financial benefits of registration, women informally declare their abode a vegetarian hall and live quietly, following a vegetarian diet and conducting religious worship. There may be as many as 15 or 20 such informally established halls in Shatin alone.

4. *Shih-fu*, Mandarin. *Si-fu* (Cantonese) means "teacher" or "master." Henceforth Cantonese is used in this chapter.

5. A *seh* is a single-surname division in a village. In some villages, there were separate buildings for sleeping for teenage boys and girls from each *seh*. In some houses, girls learned the rudiments of housekeeping from a married woman, often a widow.

6. Obviously the narrator's memory was playing tricks on her. Hong Kong did not fall to the Japanese until 1941, and she went there in 1946. Her sojourn in Kwangsi could not have been longer than four years.

7. King Guh is a 76-year-old spinster amah. A native of Nanhai district, Kwangtung Province, she is a member of Sifu's vegetarian hall. She worked in silk production as a young girl; when her parents died, she joined her brothers in Malaysia. After a short time working as a laborer on a rubber plantation, she made contact with some spinster amahs in Kuala Lumpur, who secured her a position with a wealthy Cantonese family. King Guh remained with them until she retired at the age of 55. She accompanied the family in their moves to Canton, Nanking, India, Kuala Lumpur, and Hong Kong. When they moved to the United States, King Guh remained in Hong Kong and retired. During her stay in Nanking, King Guh became part of the sisterhood that forms the core membership of the vegetarian hall to which Sifu now belongs. It was King Guh who first introduced Sifu to this sisterhood.

8. The Seven Sisters Clubs take their name from the important festival celebrated on the seventh day of the seventh moon of the lunar calendar. In other areas of China, the primary focus of this festival is to emphasize the wifely arts of embroidery and spinning and to pray for a good husband. In the spinsterhood area, however, the festival celebrates the sisterhood and its important role in the economy and culture.

The club at Wong Tai Sin was formed by 40 sisters and organized by Ah Saam. In the late 1940s, they purchased two stone houses; the larger one was rented out and the money used to finance the festivals celebrated in the smaller house. The women observed many religious and secular holidays, although it was rare that they could all obtain permission to leave work on the same day and have the full association membership present for each celebration. The houses initially cost each member HK $100; five years ago, when they were sold, each member received HK $1,000. The shares of those who had died in the meantime were used to purchase ancestor tablets in the vegetarian hall that Ah Saam was then forming.

9. Man Kai is one of the nuns living at the neighboring monastery, Ling Faht Jih. She and Ling Yeung are said to be lovers. Ling Yeung is a member of the Chungking sisterhood. She is from Panyü county, Kwangtung Province, and decided at the age of 13 to become a spinster. To indicate this to her parents, Ling Yeung went to work in the silk factories. But she soon ran off to find a servant's job

in Canton because it was more "exciting." She returned when she was 16 to have her *sou hei* ceremony. In Canton she became the personal maid of a wealthy young woman, to whom she was completely devoted. The death of her mistress in Chungking during the war left Ling Yeung disconsolate. The family of her mistress paid for Ling Yeung's entrance to the Ling Faht Jih monastery. Because Ling Yeung ceased working in the factories at a young age, however, she does not have the savings the other members have. Thus she is unable to finance her own vegetarian hall. She dislikes the noise of the constant stream of visitors at Ling Faht Jih and often seeks the solitude of Yan Gap. Ling Yeung is able to seek refuge at Yan Gap because she was a religious "brother" of the founder (Buddhist religious kinship uses male terms of address). This makes her a religious "uncle" to the members of Yan Gap, and according to the rules of religious kinship, she is able to call on their hospitality.

10. The alleged plotters apparently hoped to make use of ambiguities resulting from discrepancies between Buddhist ecclesiastical law and British civil law. According to British law, in the absence of a will, the next of kin inherits property. Thus Man Man Guh could legally claim the vegetarian hall. But members of the religious community would have fought such a usurpation. To strengthen her claim, Man Man Guh decided to become a nun, which would have made her a legitimate inheritor.

11. The *gwai yih* ceremony marks a person's entry into Buddhism. The candidate takes the Three Jewels of Buddha, the Sangha, and the Dharma as the faith and the person who performs the ceremony as a teacher. The initiate is then given a religious name by the teacher. A person can go through the ceremony several times with different teachers.

4. VILLAGE WIVES

1. The case study was drawn from materials collected for my monograph, *Long Lives: Chinese Elderly and the Communist Revolution* (Cambridge: Harvard University Press, 1983). I relied on a variety of sources—official documents from the People's Republic of China, contemporary Chinese fiction and drama, and interviews with both old and young Chinese respondents. The interviews were conducted in two phases, the first during a nine-month stay in Hong Kong in 1976, and second during a three-month stay in China in the summer of 1979. The Hong Kong sample included 29 former residents of China, 10 of whom were women, and all but one of whom were under 55 years old. The sample from China included 87 individuals; 44 were women, of whom 35 were over 55 years old. All but six of the women from China came from working-class or peasant households; all but three of the Hong Kong female respondents came from educated, urban families. In short, the two sets of interviews do not represent a cross section of the female Chinese population. My primary research strategy was therefore to concentrate on probes for internal consistency and to seek repeated, lengthy interviews whenever possible.

Granny Cheung's education, work history, and family background resemble the typical case outlined in the Chinese press and in reports of other interviewees. She was exceptionally personable and recounted her past with vivid detail. If I had succeeded in drawing a random sample, I might have chosen someone else to speak for the women of her generation. But these conditions were not met, and Lam Mei-ying gave the most representative, personal statement I found. (See *Long Lives* for a further discussion of interview strategies.)

5. HAKKA WOMEN

1. Myron Cohen, "The Hakka or 'Guest People': Dialect as a Sociocultural Variable in Southeastern China," _Ethnohistory_ (Summer 1968):247.
2. Goran Aijmer, "Expansion and Extension in Hakka Society," _Journal of the Royal Asiatic Society, Hong Kong Branch_ 7 (1967):42–79.
3. Cohen, "The Hakka," p. 253.
4. Delia Davin, _Woman-Work_ (Oxford: Clarendon Press, 1976), pp. 115–124.
5. Myron Cohen, _House United, House Divided_ (New York: Columbia University Press, 1976). Additional references on the Hakka include the following: Jean Pratt, "Emigration and Unilineal Descent Groups: A Study of Marriage in a Hakka Village in the New Territories, Hong Kong," _Eastern Anthropologist_ 13/4 (June–August 1960):148–158; Myron Cohen: "A Case Study of Chinese Family Economy and Development," _Journal of Asian and African Studies_, 3 (1968):161–180, and "Developmental Process in the Chinese Domestic Group," in Maurice Freedman (ed.), _Family and Kinship in Chinese Society_ (Stanford: Stanford University Press, 1970), pp. 21–36; and Fred Blake, "Death and Abuse in Marriage Laments," _Asian Folklore Studies_ 37/1 (1978):13–33.
6. I lived in the village of Kwan Mun Hau for 18 months during 1968–1970 and interviewed members of 19 households for my doctoral dissertation, Elizabeth L. Johnson, "Households and Lineages in a Chinese Urban Village" (Ph.D. dissertation, Cornell University, 1976). I interviewed 25 women. The research reported in this chapter was conducted in Kwan Mun Hau in 1975 and 1976, when I interviewed five of the 18 women aged over 60. I interviewed two in great depth; Great-Aunt Yeung was one of them. We developed a close rapport, and I consider her representative of the women of her cohort in many respects. I am indebted to Jennifer Wun Chi-yee for very able assistance in this research.
7. The effects of rapid urbanization in Tsuen Wan upon kin groups in Kwan Mun Hau are discussed in Johnson, "Households and Lineages."
8. There are 460 villagers in Kwan Mun Hau, of whom at least nine couples are polygynous.
9. I have heard individuals refer to "my first mother" or "my second mother" without linguistic indication as to who is the biological mother. Blood ties are made clear only by use of the phrase "the mother who gave birth to me." Formal terms of address do make this distinction; a man's natural mother is addressed as "Mother," while his father's other wife is called "Father's older brother's wife" (_a leung_) if she is the senior wife or "Father's younger brother's wife" (_a sam_) if she is the junior wife. The terms are in Cantonese; henceforth Cantonese will be used unless otherwise indicated.
10. I prepared in advance a schedule of questions to be covered in the interviews. The questions were not posed in any particular order, which allowed the natural development of the conversation. We attempted to ask all questions of each informant. Some of the material was recorded on tape. The interview material in the text is presented in a translation as literal as possible without sacrificing meaning in English. The order of the statements has been altered so that related topics are grouped and in general chronological order.
11. A brief interview with the older wife contradicts this point. This form of marriage was common in Kwan Mun Hau only until the 1930s, when young men began to rebel against minor (little sister) marriage. Their destined brides then either ran away or were married to another person. Such arrangements were no longer contracted after that time. Arthur P. Wolf and Chieh-shan Huang, _Marriage and Adoption in China, 1845–1945_ (Stanford: Stanford University Press, 1980), analyze this practice in Taiwan.

12. Child mortality levels at that time were about 50 percent, according to my sample of 19 households. Mortality rates fell rapidly with the advent of modern medical care after World War II.

13. Villagers held the common belief that a woman was polluted after childbirth. During the first month after childbirth, women were forbidden to worship gods and ancestors and stayed in the house if possible. Sexual intercourse was forbidden for 100 days following childbirth because of the fear of pollution. See Emily Ahern, "The Power and Pollution of Chinese Women," in Margery Wolf and Roxanne Witke (eds.), *Women in Chinese Society* (Standford: Stanford University Press, 1975), pp. 143–214.

14. This arrangement may have been devised because the men were often working overseas. The belief was also prevalent that women were more cautious and trustworthy with money.

15. See James Hayes, "Itinerant Hakka Weavers," *Journal of the Royal Asiatic Society, Hong Kong Branch* 8 (1968):162–165.

16. This situation was reported by many informants. Safety for women may have been common because Tsuen Wan was a Hakka enclave in a largely Cantonese-speaking area. It is likely that strong norms developed in order to prevent conflict within the relatively small and potentially threatened group.

17. Other informants reported to me that the position of household manager carried with it the possibility of siphoning off some funds for personal benefit; this may have given Great-Aunt Yeung the resources to purchase a house.

18. Family division is a formal process adjudicated by persons outside the family. The members are divided into their constituent branches, and property is allocated among them. The branches also move into separate households and begin to eat separately. In Kwan Mun Hau, these stages sometimes precede the formal division of property.

19. According to another informant, the marriage of the son of Great-Aunt Yeung was actually more complicated: A small daughter-in-law was apparently taken to be a junior wife for Yeung's son. When he became of marriageable age, however, he refused to marry the girl unless another bride was also found for him. When another woman was found, he was married to both of them in the unusual form of marriage called "equal marriage" (*p'ing-ch'ai*, Mandarin). He also allegedly refused to sleep with the junior wife. She eventually found the situation untenable and ran away, much to the distress of Great-Aunt Yeung, who was very fond of her. The son then took an additional wife of his own choosing and divided his time between the two women. Each bore him several children.

20. This complaint was common among older women; they attributed it to the hard work they had done when they were younger.

21. See Cohen, *House United*, pp. 178–191.

22. See Olga Lang, *Chinese Family and Society* (New Haven: Yale University Press, 1946), pp. 17, 164; and Cohen, *House United*, pp. 91–97, 134–148.

23. Blake, "Death and Abuse," reports other laments.

24. The songs were recorded by Elizabeth L. Johnson and translated by Jennifer Wun Chi-yee.

6. DOING FIELDWORK

1. See Michael H. Agar, *The Professional Stranger: An Informal Introduction to Ethnography* (New York: Academic Press, 1980).

2. Branislaw Malinowski, *A Diary in the Strict Sense of the Term* (New York: Harcourt, Brace and World, 1967).

3. Barney Glaser and Anselm Strauss, *The Discovery of Grounded Theory* (Chicago: Aldine, 1967).
4. Edwin Ardener, "Belief and the Problem of Women," in Shirley Ardener (ed.), *Perceiving Women* (Toronto: J. M. Dent and Son, Ltd., 1977), p. 1.
5. *Ibid.*, pp. 1–2.
6. See my wider study, Lydia Kung, "Factory Work and Women in Taiwan: Changes in Self-Image and Status," *Signs* 2/1 (Autumn 1976):35–58.
7. For background on this area, see Emily Ahern, *The Cult of the Dead in a Chinese Village* (Stanford: Stanford University Press, 1973); Margery Wolf, *House of Lim: A Study of a Chinese Farm Family* (New York: Appleton Century Crofts, 1968) and *Women and the Family in Rural Taiwan* (Stanford: Stanford University Press, 1972).
8. Janet W. Salaff, *Working Daughters of Hong Kong: Filial Piety or Power in the Family?* (Cambridge: Cambridge University Press, 1981).
9. C. Wright Mills, *The Sociological Imagination* (New York: Oxford University Press, 1959), p. 143.

7. TAIWAN GARMENT WORKERS

1. *Establishment Survey on Employment, Hours, Earning and Labor Turnover in Secondary Industries in Taiwan Area*, Manpower Requirements Survey, No. 1 (July 1973).

8. TAIWAN ELECTRONICS WORKERS

1. In 1977, the proportion of all women aged 20 or older who were formally divorced was only 1.1 percent, while the proportion that were currently married was 73.3 percent. Ministry of Interior, *Taiwan Demographic Fact Book* (Taipei: Ministry of Interior, Republic of China, 1978), Table 9, p. 346. Given the stigma of divorce, many couples are undoubtedly informally separated and not represented by these statistics.
2. Margery Wolf, *The House of Lim: A Study of a Chinese Farm Family* (New York: Appleton Century Crofts, 1968); Árthur P. Wolf and Chieh-shan Huang, *Marriage and Adoption in China, 1845–1945* (Stanford: Stanford University Press, 1980).

9. WAGE EARNERS IN HONG KONG

1. Louise Tilly and Joan Scott, *Women, Work and the Family* (New York: Holt, Rinehart and Winston, 1978).
2. "Rainbow" and Wai-gun were selected from 28 women interviewed in depth from 1971 to 1976. The most extended period of fieldwork was carried out in 1973. Each of the women I interviewed interpreted differently the relative conflict of family needs and personal desires, depending on a number of structural variables. Daughters who matured in poor families, who were eldest children, and whose fathers were absent or did not earn a wage were more likely to place the needs of their families ahead of their own.
3. In addition to the studies by Kung and Arrigo in this volume, see Robert T. Snow, "Dependent Development and the New Industrial Worker: The Case of the Export Processing Zones in Philippines" (Ph.D. dissertation, Harvard University, 1977).

10. THE CHINESE BIOGRAPHICAL METHOD: A MORAL AND DIDACTIC TRADITION

1. Much later, Chiang Ch'ing, Mao's wife, followed this precedent when she gave her biographical material to Roxanne Witke.

2. Hua Kuo-feng's speech in memorial of Mao Tse-tung, *Peking Review* 39 (September 1979). However, even this speech cannot be taken as the definitive appraisal of Mao's role in history.

3. I heard many stories about Chiang Ch'ing's licentious life when I was in China in August and September 1978. The *People's Daily* and other official publications were full of her alleged misdemeanors.

4. Mary Sheridan, "Young Women Leaders in China," *Signs* 2/1 (Autumn 1976):59–88.

5. These stories still mark the consciousness of today's Hong Kong and Taiwan youth, including young and minimally educated women. This is strikingly evident from the lives of the women reported by Kung, Arrigo, and Salaff in this volume.

11. YENAN WOMEN IN REVOLUTION

1. Delia Davin, "Women in the Liberated Areas," in Marilyn B. Young (ed.), *Women in China*, Michigan Papers in Chinese Studies, No. 15 (Ann Arbor: Center for Chinese Studies, University of Michigan, 1973), pp. 73–91, especially p. 76, and "Women in the Countryside of China," in Margery Wolf and Roxanne Witke (eds.), *Women in Chinese Society* (Stanford: Stanford University Press, 1975), pp. 243–273.

2. For a description of the Yenan production drive, see Mark Selden, *The Yenan Way in Revolutionary China* (Cambridge: Harvard University Press, 1971).

3. Jack Chen, *The New Earth* (Carbondale: Southern Illinois University Press, 1973), pp. 138–139.

4. There are 36 pamphlet biographies of labor model lives in the Yenan collection at Hoover Institution, Stanford University; these three are the only lives of women models.

5. Mary Sheridan, "The Emulation of Heroes," *China Quarterly* 33 (January–March 1968):47–72, discusses models in the Cultural Revolution. Mary Sheridan, "Young Women Leaders in China," *Signs* 2/1 (Autumn, 1976):59–88, discusses leadership training and describes five women's lives.

6. First Grandfather would have been Ch'en Min's father's biological father. Note that all the relationships of Min's family thus reflect on the problems of adoption.

7. This was somewhat old for her class but not unusual in the period. Young people often began schooling late rather than remain illiterate. Mao Tse-tung entered primary school when he was 17.

8. These "little devils" were children uprooted or orphaned by the war. They were fostered and raised by the revolutionary army.

9. Brigadier General Wang Chen's renowned 359th Brigade, stationed in Nanniwan, led the army effort in the 1942–1944 border region production drive.

10. Like Old Lady Liu (next life history), Min was an outsider who brought her valuable knowledge of spinning to an area where women lacked the skill.

11. Brigadier General Wang Chen was a well-known army leader. The mention of his wife's gift to Min indicates support by the leadership for her work.

12. One *catty* of cotton sold for 1,000 *yüan*. She was prepared to save 150,000 *yüan* for the government. Her production and economizing plans were headlined in the *Liberation Daily* on December 21, 1943.

13. This refers to Mao's speech, "Let's Get Organized," in *Selected Works of Mao Tse-tung* (Peking: Foreign Languages Press, 1965), vol. 3, pp. 153–161.

14. This was during China's great inflation.

15. Peasant refugees entered the border region through the northwest corner, moving southward, and Liu lived near their entry point. The areas south of Suite, especially around Yenan, were underpopulated and badly needed additional people to assist with agriculture and other production for the anti-Japanese war effort. The border region government's assistance and welcome to refugees were therefore quite different from the treatment they received in regions of China controlled by the Kuomintang, which was, instead, hostile or at best negligent.

16. A folio is a folded page in a Chinese sewn-bound book.

17. In Kuomintang areas, poor women sold their breast milk, often at the expense of their own babies' nourishment. The author here is very careful to explain why Feng-lien could spare the milk, probably because the selling of milk and the consequent neglect of one's own children were forbidden in the Yenan area.

12. "ON THE EVE OF HER DEPARTURE"

1. By Ma Chi-hung and Wang Tsung-jen, *Jen-min Wen-hsüeh (People's Literature)* 8 (Peking, 1980):36–41. "Departure" and "going away" refer to her death and funeral.

2. Party members pay a percentage of their earnings to the party. Ting Chih-hui and her husband, Liu Teh-mou, about whom we know little, each must have earned about 250 *yüan* a month. She had subsidized accomodations, and a car, and also lived frugally. She was undoubtedly able to save a substantial sum, as could her husband. Here she is returning her savings to the party.

3. See B. Michael Frolic, *Mao's People: 16 Portraits of Life in Revolutionary China* (Cambridge: Harvard University Press, 1980), especially chapter 1, for a discussion of the experiences of cadres during the Cultural Revolution.

CONCLUSION

1. Norma Diamond documents the relative loss of status of skilled women's work in the PRC in "Collectivization, Kinship and the Status of Women in Rural China," *Bulletin of Concerned Asian Scholars* 7 (January-March, 1975):25–32.

2. For another cultural context, see Robert T. Snow, "Dependent Development and the New Industrial Worker: The Case of the Export Processing Zones in the Philippines" (Ph.D. dissertation, Harvard University, 1977). An historical comparison is found in Louise Tilly and Joan Scott, *Women, Work and the Family* (New York: Holt, Rinehart and Winston, 1978).

3. Judith M. Bardwick, *In Transition* (New York: Holt, Rinehart and Winston, 1979).

4. Norma Diamond believes that contemporary Taiwanese women are less likely to strive to break their shackles than their early twentieth century mainland Chinese forebears. "The Status of Women in Taiwan: One Step Forward, Two Steps Back," in Marilyn Young (ed.), *Women in China: Studies in Social Change and Feminism* (Ann Arbor: Center for Chinese Studies, University of Michigan, 1973), pp. 211–242.

5. Harry Braverman, *Labor and Monopoly Capitalism: The Degradation of Work in the Twentieth Century* (New York: Monthly Review Press, 1974).

BIOGRAPHICAL SKETCHES

LINDA GAIL ARRIGO lived in Taiwan for five years as a teen-ager and attended National Taiwan University. She studied anthropology, economics, and population at Stanford University and received her M.A. in 1975. The research for the life histories in this volume was funded by the Rockefeller and Ford Foundations' Research Program on Population and Economic Development. She is also known for her 1977–1979 human rights work in Taiwan.

JEROME CH'EN is professor of history at York University and author of two biographies, *Mao and the Chinese Revolution* (London: Oxford University Press, 1965) and *Yuan Shih-k'ai* (Stanford University Press, 1972). For nearly 20 years, he has been collecting information on the life histories of over 1,300 warlords and soldiers. This personal archive comprises one of the rare sources for his monograph, *The Military-Gentry Coalition* (Toronto: Joint Centre on Modern East Asia, University of Toronto, 1979). Biographies and memoirs of Chinese and Western intellectuals and travelers are a major source for his book, *China and the West—Society and Culture* (London: Hutchinson, 1979).

DEBORAH DAVIS-FRIEDMANN is assistant professor of sociology at Yale University. In the summer of 1979, she spent three months in China, interviewing labor union representatives and retired workers under the joint sponsorship of the U.S. National Academy of Sciences and the Chinese Academy of Social Sciences. More extended discussion of the elderly in contemporary China may be found in her book, *Long Lives* (Harvard University Press, 1983). She was a co-principal investigator in a comparative study of retirement in Eastern Europe and China sponsored by the U.S. National Institute of Aging.

ELIZABETH LOMINSKA JOHNSON received her Ph.D. in anthropology at Cornell University and is currently curator of collections at the Museum of Anthropology, University of British Columbia. In this capacity, she has prepared many exhibits with Chinese themes and has collected ethnographic materials in Hong Kong. Her research interests include Chinese culture, kinship, and women's roles in society. Her writings include "Women and Childbearing in Kwan Mun Hau Village," in Margery Wolf and Roxanne Witke (eds.), *Women in Chinese Society* (Stanford: Stanford University Press, 1975), and (with Graham E. Johnson)

257

Walking on Two Legs: Rural Development in South China (Ottawa: International Development Research Centre, 1976). The research for the life history in this book was supported by a grant to the village of Kwan Mun Hau by the University of Toronto/York University Joint Centre on Modern East Asia, for which she is very grateful.

LYDIA KUNG is interested in employer-worker relations and industrial organization in Chinese society. Further discussion of factory women in Taiwan may be found in her articles "Factory Work and Women in Taiwan: Changes in Self-Image and Status," *Signs* 2/1 (Autumn 1976):35–58, and "Perceptions of Work Among Factory Women," in Emily Ahern and Hill Gates, (eds.), *The Anthropology of Taiwanese Society* (Stanford: Stanford University Press, 1981).

ANDREA MCELDERRY is associate professor of history at the University of Louisville. She is concerned with Chinese banking and has written *Shanghai Old-Style Banks, 1800–1935* (Ann Arbor: Center for Chinese Studies, University of Michigan, 1976). Her interest in life histories grew from a desire to examine the personal connections between founders of banks. She is currently conducting research on modern Chinese banks and bankers and is also preparing an article on Hsiang Ching-yü, head of the Women's Section in the 1920s of the Chinese Communist Party. Oral history is one of her research tools, and she is organizing an archive of oral history interviews with people in the Louisville area who have traveled or worked in east Asia.

JANET W. SALAFF is professor of sociology at the University of Toronto. She is interested in family roles of Chinese women and she has completed a monograph containing the lives of 10 Hong Kong women, *Working Daughters of Hong Kong* (Cambridge: Cambridge University Press, 1981). She is currently researching family structures of married Chinese women in Singapore.

ANDREA SANKAR received her Ph.D. in anthropology from the University of Michigan and has been a postdoctoral fellow in medical anthropology at the University of California Medical Center, San Francisco. She is presently a research associate at the Institute of Gerontology, University of Michigan.

MARY SHERIDAN is a visiting professor at Beijing Agricultural University in China. She has been visiting Jingang Brigade near Chongqing for 10 years (1973–1983) and lived there for two years to study their vegetable farming system (1979–1981). This work has been published in two monographs by the Rural Development Commitee of Cornell University, *Peasant Innovation and Diffusion of Agricultural Technology in China* (1981) and *Vegetable Farming Systems in a Chinese Mountain Village* (1983).